PRAISE FOR *SPECTACLE*

**Winner of the 2016 NAACP Image Award
for Outstanding Literary Work**

**Named a Best Book of the Year by
NPR, the *Boston Globe*, *Library Journal*, the *San Francisco
Chronicle*, *The Root*, and the *Huffington Post Black Voices***

"A riveting account of one of the most startling episodes in the sorry history of race in America. Ms. Newkirk is a crisp storyteller as well as an experienced journalist whose investigative skills bring alive both her cast of characters and the age in which they lived."
—Fergus M. Bordewich, *Wall Street Journal*

"Here is a gripping and painstaking narrative that breaks new ground. Now, after a century, Benga has finally been heard."
—Harriet Washington, *New York Times Book Review*

"[Ota Benga's] story has been told before, but the journalist Pamela Newkirk fleshes it out with chilling human dimension and rich anthropological perspective in her engrossing new book, *Spectacle*."
—Sam Roberts, *New York Times*

"*Spectacle* by Pamela Newkirk is required reading. Based on years of research, Newkirk masterfully explores the circumstances that culminated in Benga's horrifying ordeal, and then goes a step further to unpack the layers of racism, wealth, and imperialism that made this racist spectacle possible."
—NPR

"This is an explosive, heartbreaking book. It unfolds with the grace of an E. L. Doctorow novel and spins forward with the urgency of a wild tabloid story."
—James McBride, National Book Award–winning author of *The Good Lord Bird*

"What became of Benga is best left discovered by readers of this revelatory book. Suffice to say that the shock of it will haunt you. Newkirk's dispassionate, powerfully understated writing lets her sorrowful account speak for itself. Just as important, the author doesn't draw any parallels to all the ghastly, contemptible acts committed against African Americans today. She doesn't need to. The story of Ota Benga alone shows in horrific detail how for so many, and for so long, black lives have mattered little." —John McMurtrie, *San Francisco Chronicle*

"Writing with precision and moral clarity, Newkirk indicts a civilization whose 'cruelty was cloaked in civility,' leaving us to examine its remnants." —*Boston Globe*

"*Spectacle* brings to the fore shameful events in American history of racial prejudice and cruelty in the name of science. Ota Benga was a young Congolese man of petite stature who, upon arrival to the United States from Central Africa, was displayed in a human zoo exhibit at the St. Louis World's Fair. Award-winning journalist Newkirk crafts a must-read social history." —*Chicago Tribune*

"Newkirk turns her sharp eyes to a dark historical footnote."
—*Essence*

"Award-winning journalist Pamela Newkirk skillfully pieces together this long-buried instance of racism and exploitation that shattered a young man's life." —*The Root*

"Five minutes with this book and you'll know that *Spectacle* is a well-penned work." —*Courier & Press*

"Uncovering this shameful chapter of US history, Newkirk challenges Verner's reputation as a hero who rescued Benga from cannibals and highlights those who helped Benga live the remaining years of his life with dignity." —*Booklist* (starred review)

"An inspired and moving work of intrepid scholarship."
—*Kirkus Reviews*

"Meticulously detailed. . . . Readers will be moved, especially when reading about the tragic turns Benga's life took in the years after he was released." —*Publishers Weekly*

"Newkirk gives us more than the tragic story of one Congolese man. She offers a look into the history of American eugenics and the concepts of racial anthropology that have served as the foundation for racial intolerance for generations." —*Library Journal*

"Newkirk's account of this shocking and shameful story is forceful." —*New Yorker*

"Pamela Newkirk has taken a careful, highly readable look at an episode that lays bare so much about our not-so-distant past. It's all here: the dreams of glory in African exploration; appalling racism; and the moving, tragic odyssey of a forgotten man who was the victim of both."
—Adam Hochschild, author of *King Leopold's Ghost*

"Haunting and heartbreaking. . . . More than a century later, historical documentation has been able to add dimension to Benga's memory for a more exhaustive view of his tragic time in America." —*Ebony*

"Newkirk's investigation is a nuanced account of Benga's relationship with Verner and Hornaday, a subtle look into what it meant for a colonized African to be free and how the pursuit of scientific knowledge played a role in racial subjection. Newkirk makes the convincing argument that Benga's biography isn't simply the story of one man, but is 'also the story of an era, of science, of elite men and institutions, and of racial ideologies that endure today.'" —*Jezebel*

"In this enthralling social history, Newkirk reveals the truth about Ota Benga, the people who exploited him, and the heroes who fought vainly to save him." —*MORE* magazine

"Painstakingly researched and heartbreaking. . . . Newkirk does an exemplary job of respecting the damaged dignity of her subject." —*In These Times*

"Newkirk gives the life of Ota Benga a proper eulogy. She crafts an intriguing tale around the many uncertainties of his biography, sometimes even stopping to analyze his state of mind. I greatly credit the author for parsing through volumes of inaccurate news reports in search of even the smallest grains of truth." —*The Bowery Boys*

"*Spectacle* is multilayered and often fascinating." —*News & Advance*

"This book reveals a little-known and shameful episode in American history, when an African man was used as a human zoo exhibit—a shocking story of racial prejudice, science, and tragedy in the early years of the twentieth century." —*Journal of Pan African Studies*

"In the new book *Spectacle*, Pamela Newkirk tells a tale that is more than astonishing." —JStor Daily

"Newkirk, an award-winning journalist, casts a light on history and race in America in the early 1900s with the story of Ota Benga, a Congolese 'pygmy' who was used as a traveling human zoo exhibit after he came to this country." —NBC BLK

SPECTACLE

ALSO BY PAMELA NEWKIRK

LETTERS FROM BLACK AMERICA
A LOVE NO LESS
WITHIN THE VEIL

SPECTACLE

THE ASTONISHING LIFE OF
OTA BENGA

PAMELA NEWKIRK

Amistad
An Imprint of HarperCollins*Publishers*

HarperCollins books may be purchased for educational, business, or sales promotional use. For information, please e-mail the Special Markets Department at SPsales@harpercollins.com.

A hardcover edition of this book was published in 2015 by Amistad, an imprint of HarperCollins Publishers.

FIRST AMISTAD PAPERBACK EDITION PUBLISHED 2016

Designed by Suet Yee Chong

Library of Congress Cataloging-in-Publication Data has been applied for.

ISBN: 978-0-06-220102-7 (pbk.)

20   OV/LSC   10 9 8 7 6 5 4

TO THE MEMORY OF
MBYE OTABENGA

PYGMY:

(1) Late fourteenth century, Pigmei, "member of a fabulous race of dwarfs," described by Homer and Herodotus and said to inhabit Egypt or Ethiopia and India, from the Latin *pygmaei* and Greek *pygmaios*, meaning "dwarfish," or "of the length of a pygme; a pygme tall." In seventeenth century referred to chimpanzees or orangutans and during mid-nineteenth century applied by Europeans to the equatorial African race.

(2) Chiefly derogatory, a very small person, animal, or thing.

—*From Online Etymology Dictionary*

CONTENTS

PART III: FREE

AUTHOR'S NOTE

While many aspects of the story that follows seem unfathomable, every scene, quotation, and observation is drawn from historical accounts preserved in letters, newspaper articles, diaries, anthropological field notes, and other historical documents. Any conjecture is clearly articulated as such and solely intended to prompt a plausible consideration of matters for which evidence is not available. At times Benga's unrecorded and unrecoverable words and thoughts can be inferred from familiar human actions, gestures, and comportment.

Throughout the text the word "pygmy," which some people consider a pejorative name for the small forest dwellers of Central Africa, is set off as here, unless used in a direct quotation, to suggest its loaded meaning.

This is wholly a work of nonfiction intended to chronicle the life and times of a man at the turn of the twentieth century, a period marked by Westerners' conquest of Africa and its people, and everywhere, it seemed, by an inversion of the meanings of good and evil, black and white. At the presumed summits of civilization, cruelty was cloaked in civility and a brooding darkness was hailed as light.

New York City

PREFACE

In 1906 a young man from the Congo known as Ota Benga became the subject of headlines around the world when he was exhibited in a cage with an orangutan at the Bronx Zoo Monkey House. Tens of thousands of New Yorkers flocked to the zoo to behold the so-called pygmy, who stood four feet eleven inches and weighed a little over one hundred pounds. That this occurred in a preeminent American city in the twentieth century would seem enough to cause astonishment. But there's far more to the story than meets the eye.

While on the surface this appears to be the saga of one man's degradation—of a shocking and shameful spectacle—on closer inspection it is also the story of an era, of science, of elite men and institutions, and of racial ideologies that endure today. Benga left no written account of his own, and others have filled the gap with conspiratorial silence, half-truths, and even flagrant deception. As a result, what has been officially recorded and recycled in hundreds of accounts around the globe is a flourishing, ever-expanding fiction. So this book is also a story of secrets, lies, denial, and overdue reclamation.

Through a forensic-type inquiry we can unearth missing chapters from Benga's extraordinary journey and in the process retrieve portions of our past from the waste bin of history. As we retrace Benga's footsteps from Central Africa through Europe and America, we find him in the shadow of a lettered elite. In its correspondence, journals, books, photographs, and other historical documents, he clings to the margins, doggedly asserting his humanity; insisting that his story—that our story—be truthfully told. If we lean in we may hear the muffled voice of a man long thought silenced, and see ever more clearly who we were as the century turned in America's imperial city.

PART I

CAGED

ONE

GARDENS OF WONDER

Saturday, September 8, 1906, was sunny and warm, and New York's parks beckoned city dwellers from their cramped apartments and crowded streets. For William Temple Hornaday the agreeable weather was another blessing in a week of good fortune. As director and chief curator of the New York Zoological Gardens, Hornaday had been excited for days over an unexpected acquisition and knew the balmy weather ensured optimum attendance. The exhibit was one that he hoped would enhance his already formidable reputation as the nation's foremost authority on zoology and naturalistic displays. As the park gate swung open, the bearded and mustachioed Hornaday, five feet seven inches tall, proudly greeted visitors at the entrance and cheerfully directed them to what he boasted was his best attraction yet.

Since opening in 1899 the New York Zoological Gardens, set on 261 acres in the burgeoning Bronx, had become a crown jewel of the newly constituted Greater New York City.

A year earlier, on a rainy New Year's Eve, 100,000 New Yorkers had welcomed the consolidation of Brooklyn, the Bronx, Queens, Staten Island, and Manhattan with an exuberant celebration in City Hall Park.

Andrew Haskell Green, the civic leader who for three decades had championed the unification, dubbed Greater New York the "Imperial City," saying that it was now second only to London in population. Manhattan already had one of the world's finest ports; the nation's greatest concentration of corporations, banks, and retailers; and a larger population than Boston, Baltimore, and Philadelphia combined. It was a hub of intellectual life, with Columbia and New York universities; the largest book publishing houses and nationally circulated magazines and newspapers; and Greenwich Village, a haven for artists, writers, and rebels. The consolidation merged ninety-six independent governmental units and a multitude of races, ethnicities, and cultures into one teeming city of 3.5 million people that was twice the size of Chicago, its closest rival in the United States.

The Bronx, with its large stretches of farmland, industrial plants, and country estates, was now one of five coequal boroughs, and in 1904 was linked to Manhattan by a gleaming new subway system that halved the time it had taken to commute by elevated steam railroad.

The creation of the New York Zoological Gardens heralded a spiritual and architectural renaissance during which New York imagined itself as more than a municipality—it was now a metropolis, a term coined by Herodotus to describe Athens in the fifth century B.C.

The park design, like that of other ambitious developments sprouting across the city, showed the influence of the neoclassic "White City" in the Chicago World's Fair of 1893. Under the direction of Chicago's Daniel Burnham, the nation's top architects had created a majestic model city of shimmering white beaux arts buildings, grand boulevards, luxuriant gardens, and imposing statuary evoking ancient Greece. Charles McKim of the prestigious New York–based McKim, Mead, and White was among the team members. He would take what he learned back to New York, and three years later Columbia University moved from its severe Gothic Revival campus at Forty-Ninth Street and Madison Avenue to a thirty-two-acre campus in upper Manhattan's Morningside Heights inspired by the agora of ancient Athens.

The soaring ambition of the zoological park's founders and patrons was no less apparent in the opulent design by another New York–based firm, Heins and La Farge, which also looked to ancient Greece for inspiration. George Lewis Heins and Christopher Grant La Farge had met as students at M.I.T., the first American university to adopt the neoclassic curriculum of the École des Beaux-Arts. La Farge, son of the famous artist John La Farge, was also a founding board member of the zoological society, and Heins was the designated New York State architect. With $125,000 from the city and another $250,000 in start-up capital from the likes of John D. Rockefeller, John Pierpont Morgan, and Andrew Carnegie, no expense was spared to create a neoclassic wonderland. Rafael Guastavino of Barcelona was commissioned to install his signature terra-cotta-tiled and domed vaulted ceilings, which graced some of the country's most elegant buildings. To ornament the facades, artists were brought in to create friezes using the zoo's live animals as models. A towering seventeenth-century fountain, adorned with four playful cherubs on unicorns held aloft by mermaids, would be purchased by William Rockefeller and shipped from Rome.

Engraved invitations to the November 8, 1899, inaugural ceremony were sent to three thousand of the city's and nation's most esteemed citizens. On a cold, blustery, overcast day, several dozen distinguished men of finance, education, government, and philanthropy huddled on a platform at Grand Central Terminal before boarding a special 2:15 P.M. train to the Fordham Road station in the Bronx. At 3 P.M. a procession of carriages arrived at the zoological park's northwest gate at Southern Boulevard and Pelham Avenue, where Hornaday, wearing a military-style cap with a gold-cord eagle, stood waiting, his assistants in gray uniforms and caps in a single file behind him.[1] Guests entered what, to

the founders' chagrin, became known as the Bronx Zoo along a glisten-
ing limestone path that cut through dense forest and over the Bronx
River below. A symmetrical pair of stately winding stairways carried
park-goers to what would be a palatial court. Five beaux arts pavilions,
to be situated around Baird Court—named for the late secretary of
the Smithsonian Institution and later renamed for the Astor family—
would not appear for another two years. The Primate House, the first
of the pavilions, would open to the public on December 21, 1901.

Still, there was already much to behold, including a sparkling
pool with bobbing sea lions and the Aquatic Bird House, an elegant beaux arts pavilion adorned with lifelike sculptured birds on
its facade. A breathtaking array of 843 animals—including caribou,
zebras, wolves, bears, a 175-pound python, and a 12-foot alligator—
were on display. Levi P. Morton, the former U.S. vice president and
governor of New York, as president of the New York Zoological Society officiated at the ceremony from a flag-draped platform outside
the Aquatic House.

Among the two thousand guests were some of the financiers and
industrialists who had ushered in America's Gilded Age: banker John
Pierpont Morgan; Central Pacific Railroad builder Collis P. Huntington; copper mining magnate William E. Dodge; coal and steel mo-
gul William C. Whitney. Seth Low, the former Brooklyn mayor and
Columbia University president who would soon become the second
mayor of Greater New York City, was also in the illustrious crowd, as
was Frank Baker, director of the National Zoological Park.[2] Morton
singled out for special recognition the eminent scientist Henry Fairfield Osborn, vice president of the New York Zoological Society and
chair of its executive committee, describing him as "the man who has
done more than any other for the establishment of this Zoological
Park."[3] Osborn, a Columbia University professor and head of paleontology at the American Museum of Natural History, had effectively
courted members of his affluent social circle, including his uncle

Pierre—banker J. P. Morgan—to raise money for the new park. He had also, as a founding member of the board of managers, taken a lead role in charting the zoological park's scope and location, and in hiring its first director. Few had worked as tirelessly for this auspicious occasion.

Savoring the moment, the eloquent and formal Osborn told guests that the park, unlike any in Europe, is "projected upon a scale larger than has ever been attempted before."

Peering outward, with a sweep of his arm to suggest a distant horizon, he attempted to convey the magnitude of the occasion. "Two hundred thousand years ago the great Ice Sheet cut its giant grooves through Bird Valley where we are standing, and through Beaver Valley yonder, on either side of the broad ridge of granite which the engineers are now leveling for the imposing buildings on Baird Court."

The zoological garden, he said, "will bring its wonders and beauties within the reach of thousands and millions of all classes who cannot travel or explore. The intelligent scientific design and administration of this park in the popular American spirit alone justifies its establishment and maintenance by the city as a new force in our educational system and as a delightful pleasure ground."[4]

Now, seven years later, the zoological gardens would make good on that promise. For days excitement had been building over the park's latest acquisition. Even before he was hired Hornaday had expressed a desire to create an exhibit on park grounds featuring Native Americans to illustrate the home life of the aborigines of North America. So it was timely when Samuel Phillips Verner came calling. Verner, who described himself as an African explorer and former missionary, had written to Hornaday on August 28 requesting a meeting to discuss the possibility of the zoo temporarily housing a chimpanzee and two reptiles he had brought back from Africa.

Hornaday did not know much about Verner, whom, coincidentally, an editor at *Century* magazine had recently written to inquire about "from a scientific point of view."[5] Hornaday could not find Verner's name in *American Men of Science*, a directory of the nation's leading scientists begun by the Carnegie Institution; or in *The Naturalist*, the journal of conservationists and natural history devotees.

But given Verner's wish to house—not sell—an animal worth $300, Hornaday assumed he was a man of means. While animals were not ordinarily accepted on deposit for less than a year, one as valuable as a chimpanzee brought to America by an African explorer merited Hornaday's consideration.

Two days later the two men met. The details of their meeting were not recorded in writing, but the mutually satisfactory outcome would soon be apparent to all.

"Rejoicing in the fact of the happy coincidence of the meeting of yesterday afternoon," Verner wrote, adding, "and asking you—by the way—not to believe what newspaper men write of me."[6]

By all appearances, Hornaday was far less interested in the details of Verner's reputation than in the African treasures, which exceeded his wildest expectations. Hornaday was happy to temporarily board Verner's chimpanzee, and he was ecstatic over an unexpected coup, which he breathlessly detailed in an article that would be published in the October 1906 issue of the *Zoological Society Bulletin*. But nothing in the bulletin could have prepared park-goers for what they would find on that sunny Saturday, September 8, 1906.

Hornaday could barely contain his excitement as the masses swarmed into the park that day. He directed one and all to the Primate House.

Waves of women in long skirts and bonnets and men in suits and derbies streamed along the path from Fordham Road, scaled the graceful winding stairways, and went past the pool of sea lions. They had come from mansions along Fifth and Madison Avenues, and from teeming ghettos on the Lower East Side and in the Tenderloin

District. They eagerly flocked to the left side of the court, to the elegant beaux arts pavilion flanked by columns with the words "Primate House" etched into the stone lintel above its ornate archway.[7] High above the doorway, carved into the triangular tympanum crowning the building, was an intricately depicted family of orangutans, foreshadowing what lay ahead.

They filed along the narrow, dark corridor, through the stench of humid feces and monkey musk. Undaunted, they marched over a carpet of discarded peanut shells, carefully scanning the monkeys, lemurs, chimpanzees, orangutans, and baboons, until they reached the far end, where they found, displayed in an iron cage, Ota Benga, his slight 103-pound, four-foot eleven-inch chocolate-colored frame sheathed in white trousers and a khaki coat. His small brown feet were bare.

"*Ist das ein Mensch?*"—Is it a man?—one woman asked in German.

"Something about it I don't like," said another.[8]

Could this caged creature be, many no doubt wondered, the incarnation of one of the characters in best-selling books like Charles Carroll's *The Negro a Beast,* published in 1900, or the "half child, half animal," described in Thomas Dixon's *The Clansman*, published the previous year, "whose speech knows no word of love, whose passions, once aroused, are as the fury of the tiger"?

Could he be the missing link, the species bridging man and ape that preoccupied leading scholars?

Some were probably made uneasy by eyes that radiated understanding. This small being with smooth brown skin and small solemn eyes sat erectly and neither swung from an apparatus nor made seemingly vile gestures. He was composed, if somewhat sad. In fact, except for his child-size stature and teeth meticulously filed to sharp points, he appeared no different from an ordinary "Negro." But if he was wholly human, would he be in a cage in a fetid monkey house?

As many as five hundred people at a time crowded around to

gawk at the diminutive Ota Benga while he preoccupied himself with
a pet parrot, deftly shot his bow and arrow, or wove a mat and hammock from the bundles of twine placed in the cage. Children giggled
and hooted with delight while adults laughed, many uneasily, at the
human spectacle.

TWO

THE BRONX ZOO
MONKEY HOUSE

SEKA: To laugh or laugh at; be amused, deride, make
sport or fun of, scoff at, taunt.

—From *Grammar and Dictionary of the Buluba-Lulua*
Language, William McCutchan Morrison

Since its opening three days before Christmas in 1901 the
Primate House, with more than one hundred animals
representing some forty species, had been a source of fascination. The death in 1902 of a chimpanzee and four orangutans
from *B. coli* had generated headlines, as did a fire in the cage of a
ring-tailed monkey, which prompted the *New York Tribune*'s inaccurate and sensationalized "Fire in Monkey House: Chimpanzee Helps
Put Out Blaze in His Cage."[1] The fire, set by a park visitor, had in
fact been extinguished by a zoo attendant. But neither of those incidents rivaled the man in the monkey house.

The cage Benga inhabited had been built at the southern end of

the Primate House to keep the monkeys warm and make the orangutan easier to observe. Benga's cage, like those of his housemates, was
connected to a room inside the building. And like the orangutan and
monkeys, he was at the mercy of the keepers, who decided when he
could enter the building and elude the crowds. Until then, he was un-
avoidably on display and, like his housemates, subjected to the disquieting hysteria and stares of a seemingly endless stream of spectators.

Benga became the object of pointing fingers, audible gasps, and
bellowing laughter. Alone and locked in a monkey house cage he
could, in the September Indian summer heat, smell the stench of
ape feces, urine, and musk laced with the foreign odors of hundreds
of spectators packed into the steamy, cramped quarters. Even if he
could not comprehend their language but could feel both the sting of
their scorn and the pang of their pity. In their wide eyes his humanity, like one's image in a fun house mirror, monstrously distorted.
He was cornered, and exposed to cackling hyenas under a glaring
spotlight.

We cannot know exactly what Benga felt, but research on the
psychological trauma associated with shame suggests that it is not
substantially different from the effects of physical torture. Studies also consistently show a strong correlation between event-related
shame and post-victimization symptoms including depression, post-
traumatic stress disorder, withdrawal, and phobias.[2] One researcher,
J. P. Gump, found that the most profound shame results from the destruction of your subjectivity when "what you need, what you desire,
and what you feel are of complete and utter insignificance."[3]

That would certainly apply to Benga as he endured the gawking
of spectators utterly indifferent to his feelings. They howled. Gasped.
Gaped. Pointed. Jeered.

Benga frequently walked to the door with eyes pleading for his
keepers to release him from public view.

"Shame is such a searing painful experience that its characteristic defense is turning away from the stimulus situation," another

researcher has said.[4] Andrew Morrison observes, "Shame induces a wish to become invisible, unseen, to sink into the ground or to disappear into the thick, soupy fog that we have just imagined."[5]

Occasionally Benga was mercifully permitted to roam the forest under the watchful eye of park rangers. However, once discovered, he was hungrily pursued by park-goers, and returned to his cage. He was a sensation.

"Bushman Shares a Cage with Bronx Park Apes" was the headline in Sunday's *New York Times*. The five-hundred-word article described Benga's captivity as a dark comedy, in which the tragic hero was, in the view of the Men of Science, an inferior creature. The article would cast the newspaper as a central character in Benga's unfolding trauma.

"The human being," the article said, "happened to be a Bushman, one of a race that scientists do not rate high in the human scale. But to the average non-scientific person in the crowd of sightseers there was something about the display that was unpleasant."[6]

However unsettling, the exhibit on the respectable grounds of a world-class zoological park had been sanctioned by Hornaday, one of the world's leading zoologists, and by Henry Fairfield Osborn, among his era's most eminent scientists.

As an undergraduate at Princeton University Osborn had spent three months at Cambridge University under the tutelage of the famous British zoologist Francis Balfour; and a summer at London's Royal College of Science with biologist Thomas Huxley, who became known as "Darwin's bulldog" for his fierce championship of the theory of evolution by natural selection. Osborn went on to earn a doctor of science degree from Princeton, where for twelve years he taught biology and comparative anatomy. Princeton, although it is located in New Jersey, fifty miles from New York City, was, in character and composition, a southern school.[7] Up through the time Osborn attended and later taught there, much of its faculty, administration, and male student body had been drawn from former slaveholding southern families. Moreover, unlike Harvard and the other Ivy League schools, which by then admitted African American students, Princeton would, during Osborn's lifetime, take pride in excluding them. In 1904, the university's president, Woodrow Wilson, an 1879 alumnus, said that while its policy did not explicitly ban blacks, "the whole temper and tradition of the place are such that no Negro has ever applied for admission and it seems very unlikely that the question will assume a practical form."[8]

Segregation was still a fact of life during Osborn's years there and did not end at the university gates; it prevailed across the city. African Americans were one-seventh of the population but were barred from white schools, churches, hotels, restaurants, and other public facilities. They also lived in highly segregated neighborhoods, and while they could attend the black grammar school, there was no town high school open to them. African Americans who wished to continue their education past grammar school would have to go to nearby Trenton, where the first black Princeton native graduated from high school in 1899. (The student was William D. Robeson Jr., whose younger brother Paul would become one of Princeton's most famous natives.) So if Osborn had not developed an acute sense of racial superiority in the upper echelon of Fairfield and New York, he certainly had by the time he left Princeton.

Like fellow zoo founders Roosevelt and Grant, Osborn was listed in New York's Social Register and belonged to the city's most exclusive social clubs, including the Century, Tuxedo, University, and Knickerbocker. But unlike them, he was not merely an amateur naturalist. Osborn was a bona fide Man of Science.

In 1891, at the age of thirty-four, he was simultaneously appointed as head of a new biology department at Columbia University and director of the paleontology department at the American Museum of Natural History.[9] By the time the zoological park opened, he was the nation's leading paleontologist and had been elected the first dean of the faculty of pure science at Columbia University; elected vertebrate paleontologist for both the U.S. Geological Survey and the Canadian Geological Survey; and had served as president of the august New York Academy of Science. He would go on to become a fellow of the American Academy of Arts and Sciences, receive honorary doctorates from Oxford and Cambridge, and achieve fame for naming *Tyrannosaurus rex*. For nearly twenty-five years, beginning in 1908, he would serve as president of the American Museum of Natural History.

Osborn's stature in the academy was matched by his prodigious wealth and towering social status. Not only was his mother descended from an influential *Mayflower* family, but his father was railroad magnate William Henry Osborn, cofounder and president of the Illinois Central Railroad. Osborn's uncle Pierre, the banker J. P. Morgan, was among the world's richest and most powerful men who in 1893 had saved the United States Treasury from bankruptcy.

As for Hornaday, his role lobbying for the National Zoological Park in Washington, D.C., and serving as its first superintendent, had already secured him nationwide prominence even before he was appointed to oversee the New York Zoological Gardens.

Now, thanks to Ota Benga, Hornaday's park appeared prominently in headlines that rivaled the sensational coverage of the murder, three months earlier, of Stanford White, architect to the rich and famous, by the jealous millionaire husband of an American sex goddess, Evelyn Nesbitt. What Benga's exhibition lacked in steamy sex, money, and celebrity, it made up for in novelty and surprise. For New Yorkers, it was a cheap afternoon thrill. For the twenty-five-cent admission fee and a five-cent ride on the subway, they could see what until now they had only read about: a genuine African "savage." On Sunday, the day most New Yorkers learned of the exhibit, admission was free.

The news value of the unlikely story was heightened by its coverage in the *New York Times*, a newspaper that in the ten years since its acquisition by Adolph Ochs had increasingly become known for straightforward journalism that steered clear of the gratuitous titil-lation found in rivals like the *New York Sun*. The *Times'* stature had been bolstered two years earlier by its relocation to the newly con-structed Times Tower, a sleek twenty-five-story Gothic skyscraper on Longacre Square—actually a triangle bordered by Forty-Second Street, Broadway, and Seventh Avenue. Later that year it was renamed Times Square, marking the paper's ascent. The *Times'* growing stat-ure and moderate editorial stance rendered all the more remarkable the story of Benga's Bronx Zoo debut in Sunday's edition.

For Benga, each second may have seemed an eternity, but for Hornaday, the debut was a resounding success. He assured a reporter that the exhibition had been authorized by the Zoological Society. Madison Grant, the society's secretary, had in fact been intimately involved in the negotiations to secure Benga. As an exhibit, Benga personified the society's mission, expressed by Osborn on the park's opening day: the zoological park was meant to educate the masses who could not travel and explore, and to serve as "a delightful plea-sure ground."[10]

Hornaday also insisted that the exhibit was in keeping with hu-man exhibitions in Europe, breezily suggesting the Continent's in-disputable status as the world's paragon of culture and civilization.[11] Hadn't Sara Baartman, a southern African woman, been exhibited, barely clad, throughout London and Paris as the "Hottentot Venus" until her death in 1815? The famous scientist Georges Cuvier, pro-fessor of comparative anatomy at the National Museum of Natural History in Paris and founding father of vertebrate paleontology, be-lieved Baartman's ample derriere was evidence that her people, the Khoikhoi, were oversexed. After her death he performed an autopsy and concluded that she and the so-called Hottentots were more akin to apes than to humans. He made a cast of Baartman's body and preserved her brain, genitals, and skeleton, ensuring that even in death, she'd draw a crowd. While Benga was being exhibited in a monkey house cage, Baartman's remains—her brain, genitals, and skeleton—were still on display in case number 33 at the Paris Musée de l'Homme.[12]

While today most people of all races would find such behavior both racist and morally contemptible, in the era's elite white circles Cuvier was generally considered an embodiment of scientific truth.

Long after Baartman's death human zoos celebrating Europeans' conquest of purportedly primitive people remained popular in Europe; these included zoos in Hamburg, Barcelona, and Milan. Carl Hagenbeck, a seller of wild animals, exhibited Samoan and Sami people to great success in 1874. So popular was his 1876 exhibit of Egyptian Nubians that it toured Berlin, Paris, and London.[13] A year later Geoffroy de Saint-Hilaire, director of the Jardin Zoologique d'Acclimation in Paris, organized exhibits of Nubians and Inuit seen by one million people; and in 1885, King Leopold II of Belgium exhibited several hundred of his newly conquered Congolese people in Brussels to appreciative crowds.[14]

Hornaday conceded that these had all been *human* zoos; none of the people had been exhibited in a monkey house cage. But he was an inveterate showman, and he saw the exhibition as in keeping with the mission of the zoological gardens. He hoped that he had not given his colored brethren reason to believe that Benga's placement in a monkey house suggested any close analogy of the African "savage" with apes.

"Benga," he wryly assured them, "is in the primate house because that's the most comfortable place we could find for him."[15]

THREE

CRIMES OF THE CONGO

As word of the sensational exhibition ricocheted across the city, Hornaday made plans to keep Benga on display until late fall, and possibly until spring. In anticipation of his extended residence in the monkey house, the enterprising zookeeper prepared an article for the cover of the October issue of the park's monthly *Zoological Society Bulletin*.

In his manuscript, Hornaday had used the title "Exhibition at the Zoological Garden," but he changed it to "An African Pygmy" for publication. The article was accompanied by a photograph of Benga, bare-chested and looking dismayed as he peered into the camera holding a monkey on his hip. Hornaday described Ota Benga, said to be twenty-three, as "a genuine African pigmy, belonging to the sub-race commonly miscalled 'the Dwarfs.' "[1]

In language intended to elevate the spectacle to one worthy of sober disquisition, he wrote: "Ota Benga is a well-developed little man, with a good head, bright eyes and a pleasing countenance. He is quite pleased with his temporary quarters in the Zoological Park, and the

Park people like him quite well. He has much manual skill, and is expert in the making of hammocks and mats. It is purposed to give him a good supply of materials upon which to exercise his ingenuity."[2]

He continued: "Ota Benga is black—though not what is known as 'coal black'—beardless, and very well formed. He knows about 100 English words, but it is not Mr. Verner's purpose to educate him beyond the necessities of his own sphere."

How long he would remain at the Zoological Park, Hornaday said, no one could say, but for now he would be there accompanied by Verner's chimpanzee that was also temporarily housed with the ape collection.

He said Verner had found Benga near the confluence of the Kasai and Sankuru Rivers, held captive by "cannibalistic savages" known as the Baschilele. "Mr. Verner," he wrote, "prompted solely by the instincts of humanity, ransomed Ota Benga and attempted to convey him back to his own country."[3]

Given the various conflicting accounts offered by Verner as to how he acquired Benga, the true story will probably never be known. However, all his versions underscore how the Belgian king Leopold II's conquest of the Congo had rendered Benga and his people vulnerable to slave traders and self-styled American explorers. In accounts in the *St. Louis Post-Dispatch*, and in one he wrote for *Harper's Weekly*, Verner claimed that he found Benga being held captive by the Baschilele tribe, who had killed his wife and children during a raid on their village.[4] He identified Benga as a member of either the Chirichiri or the Badi tribe. In those accounts Verner claimed he purchased Benga from the Baschilele for a pound of salt and a bolt of cloth. In the *Zoological Society Bulletin* Hornaday breezily recounted that version of events without a hint of judgment or surprise. He also recited Verner's claim that Benga was mercifully spared being devoured by the cannibalistic Baschilele tribe. Whether Verner actually believed that the Baschilele were cannibals, or simply sought to lend an air of grace to Benga's circumstances, is not known. However, there's no

mention of cannibalism in a letter Verner had written after he encountered Benga. Futhermore, a 1910 report by Great Britain's Royal
Geographical Society described the Baschilele as "the most friendly
among the tribes that we encountered during our journeys."[5] And
Ngokwey Ndolamb, while he was a doctoral candidate in anthropology at U.C.L.A., said cannibalism was not practiced by the Baschilele,
who associated it with sorcery.[6]

In another account, published in the *Columbus Dispatch* in South
Carolina, Verner said that he found Benga with several other members of his tribe a few miles from his settlement and that he arranged
with the chief to bring Benga to America.[7] In yet another account
Verner claimed that Benga had been captured by enemies of his tribe
who were in turn defeated by troops of the Belgian-ruled government,
who then held Benga.[8] In that retelling he claims that they released
Benga, who elected to travel with him on hearing that "I wanted to
employ Pygmies." There would be more adaptations to come.

Regardless of how he secured Benga, what is known is that
Verner had been commissioned by organizers of the St. Louis World's
Fair of 1904 to procure so-called pygmies. Just how he would do that
was never stipulated. However, given what's known about the period,
it would seem a simple enough feat. During Leopold II's savage reign
over the Congo between 1885 and 1908, ten million or more of Benga's people were systematically murdered, and more were tortured
and enslaved, while the country's resources were plundered. Leopold
enforced labor through routinely executed rape, mutilation, torture,
and murder to enrich himself by feeding the international demand
for rubber, copper, and other minerals.

If Benga was, as Verner contended in one account, a slave whose
wife and children had been killed during a raid on their village, it
is more likely that he would have been put to work on a chain gang
than that he would be cannibalized by the Baschilele. But however
Benga was obtained, and whatever his circumstances were in Leopold's Congo, he was now the temporary property of the Bronx Zoo

in New York and was being described like an exotic beast in the October issue of the *Zoological Society Bulletin.*

The atrocities of Leopold's regime were first exposed in 1890 by George Washington Williams, an African American Civil War veteran, minister, lawyer, journalist, and historian. Born in Bedford Springs, Pennsylvania, in 1849, Williams was already a prominent minister in Cincinnati when in 1879 he became the first African American elected to the Ohio state legislature.[9]

At the end of 1889, in meetings with President Benjamin Harrison and Senate Foreign Relations Committee chairman John Sherman, Williams disclosed his plan to travel to the Congo to investigate conditions.

Railroad scion Collis Huntington, an early patron of the Zoological Society, agreed to sponsor Williams's trip. By January 1890 Williams arrived in Brussels, where he met with Belgian officials who tried to persuade him to postpone his trip.

If Benga was in fact twenty-three while at the zoo, he would have been about eight years old when, in 1890, Williams arrived in the Congo on the British and African Steam Navigation Company's *Gaboon.* Over a period of six months Williams visited villages, mission stations, and government posts along the riverbanks. Stunned by what he observed, he wrote an *Open Letter to His Serene Majesty Leopold II, King of the Belgians and Sovereign of the Independent State of Congo.* The sixteen-page letter, written on July 18, 1890, detailed the brutal mistreatment of the Congolese, who he said were, in Leopold's name, subjected to murder, forced labor, rape, torture, and other atrocities.

"Your Majesty's Government has sequestered their land, burned their towns, stolen their property, enslaved their women and children, and committed other crimes too numerous to mention in detail," Williams wrote.[10]

Instead of the hospitals, schools, and other public services Leopold claimed to have generously bestowed on his subjects, Williams found debauchery, duplicity, and a state that had waged an unjust war against innocent people. "Your Majesty's Government is engaged in the slave-trade, wholesale and retail. It buys and sells and steals slaves," he said. "The labour force at the stations of your Majesty's Government in the Upper River is composed of slaves of all ages and both sexes." [11]

He said slaves were freely offered to him in broad daylight. Belgian officers, he said, shot African villagers for sport, for intimidation, or to capture their women to exploit as concubines.

His eyewitness accounts stood in stark contrast to characterizations of Leopold as a benevolent ruler—most notably by the famous British explorer and journalist Henry Morton Stanley.

Among Williams's findings was that Stanley and his assistants had plied village chiefs with gin or had used trickery and force to get them to sign over their land to Leopold II. He said the alleged 450 treaties were secured with only Stanley's servant as a witness. Moreover, he said, Stanley's name "produces a shudder among this simple folk when mentioned; they remember his broken promises, his copious profanity, his hot temper, his heavy blows, his severe and rigorous measures, by which they were mulcted of their lands." [12]

He concluded: "Against the deceit, fraud, robberies, arson, murder, slave-raiding, and general policy of cruelty of your Majesty's Government to the natives, stands their record of unexampled patience, long-suffering and forgiving spirit, which put the boasted civilization and professed religion of your Majesty's Government to the blush."

Williams called on the international community "whose majestic laws you have scorned and trampled upon" to form a commission to investigate the charges in the name of humanity, commerce, constitutional government, and Christian civilization. He also appealed to antislavery societies, philanthropists, leaders, statesmen, "and the great mass of people everywhere" to "hasten the close of the tragedy your Majesty's unlimited Monarchy is enacting in the Congo."

The letter was widely circulated throughout Europe and the United States. In a letter to the U.S. secretary of state, James G. Blaine, Williams memorably coined the term "crimes against humanity" to describe Leopold's bloodcurdling rule over the Congo.

In 1908 international outrage finally resulted in the dissolution of Leopold's rule there. However, it would come two years too late for Ota Benga, who was now at the mercy of a Bronx zookeeper who cheerily referred to him as "the little African savage" and insisted that Benga "has one of the best rooms in the primate house." [13]

FOUR

HORNADAY'S FOLLY

William Temple Hornaday was no stranger to the plight of the Congo. In 1887 he had launched a searing critique of the "devil's work" being done in the Congo by the international community "in the name of commerce and civilization." His book *Free Rum on the Congo: And What It Is Doing There* pressed for the suppression of the gun, liquor, and slave trade and condemned the "deliberate, systematic debauchment of fifty millions of ignorant savages by the agencies of our sadly imperfect civilization."[1] Hornaday particularly condemned the spread of alcohol in Africa.

"We have seen many great wrongs inflicted upon helpless people in the name of commerce, but none excepting slavery equal to the flooding of Africa with a tidal wave of cheap and deadly rum."[2]

Hornaday argued that it was better to allow Africans to "live in and thrive in the blissful ignorance of savagery" than to ruin them with civilization. "Were I a king of naked savages on the Congo on the Zambesi, I would resist the Caucasian to the death," he wrote, saying it would be better to die of bullets than brandy.[3]

Then, in words that a century hence would ring with irony, he wrote: "One hundred years from now posterity will look back with horror upon the period of African slavery, and be lost in amazement while trying to divine how intelligent human beings could be as heartless and cruel. . . . [W]hen they read of this, I say, they will stand aghast and cry, 'Why did not the Christian world rise up as one man to stop this fiendish traffic? Where was the curse of God?' "[4]

That very sentiment could well have occurred to Benga as he endured his pitiable fate 6,350 miles from home in a squalid monkey house. But nearly two decades after publishing *Free Rum on the Congo*, Hornaday appeared more interested in staging a spectacle than in saving souls.

Coverage of Benga's exhibition in the Sunday *New York Times,* coupled with balmy weather and word of mouth, ensured even bigger crowds that day. Hornaday capitalized on the publicity by moving Benga from the chimpanzee cage to an even larger crescent-shaped structure at the southwestern end of the Primate House. This cage was now littered with bones to suggest cannibalism. Added too was a sign outside the cage that read:

THE AFRICAN PYGMY, OTA BENGA.
Age, 23 years. Height, 4 feet 11 inches.
Weight 103 pounds. Brought from the Kasai River,
Congo Free State, South Central Africa,
By Dr. Samuel P. Verner.
Exhibited each afternoon during September.

For the *Times* reporter, the sign posted by park officials was incontrovertible evidence that Benga did not just happen to be in the primate cage, but was in fact intentionally placed there as a zoological exhibit.

"Any suspicion that the exhibition was the result of error was contradicted by yesterday's developments," reported the *Times*.[5]

Thousands flocked to the park, their trip facilitated by the rapid transit system's one-year-old 180th Street stop, which conveniently shortened the walk from the train station.

While the Primate House would, on a typical autumn Sunday, be heavily attended, news of a caged Bushman brought record crowds. Nearly a quarter of a million people would visit the zoo that month, almost twice as many as had come the previous September.[6] Practically everyone who entered the park headed directly to the Primate House to see Verner's "pygmy." Those who had arrived early were disappointed to learn that they would have to wait until the 2 P.M. matinee.

Shortly before 2 P.M., Benga appeared in an arena-like cage, equipped with a bow and arrow, a new target made of clay, and a pet parrot. A short time later, he was joined in the cage by Dohong, an orangutan.

Three hundred to five hundred spectators at a time crowded around to gape at the pair. Those who had been present the day before noted that Benga's feet, which had been bare, were now covered by canvas shoes. The two captives were sometimes locked in each other's arms; at other times, Dohong was placidly perched on Benga's slight shoulder, or the two frolicked with Benga flinging Dohong like a ball. The crowds reveled in these antics. For Benga, Dohong provided a needed distraction, and also companionship and affection, all of which he had been denied.

The *Times* reporter noted the similarities between Benga and Dohong, saying that Benga was not much taller than the orangutan, and their heads were alike. "Both grin in the same way when pleased," he added, casually suggesting a closer kinship between Benga and the ape than other humans shared.[7]

A bewildered Benga occasionally sat silently on a stool, staring—at times glaring—through the bars as his tormentors hysterically howled their approval. Benga occasionally mimicked the menacing mob, as he did when a knicker-clad boy goaded him to shoot his bow and arrow, commanding, "Shoot, shoot."

"Shoot, shoot," Benga mocked back.[8] The crowd roared. In fact, Benga found that, like the monkeys, he was a source of amusement whether he sat motionless, erupted in anger, or sought to allay his anxiety by playing with Dohong or shooting his bow and arrow.

But not everyone was amused by Benga's misfortune. The Reverend Dr. Robert Stuart MacArthur, the influential pastor of Manhattan's Calvary Baptist Church on West Fifty-Seventh Street, stood among the heckling, howling herd that Monday, and he was outraged.

"The person responsible for this exhibition degrades himself as much as he does the African," MacArthur said. "Instead of making a beast of this little fellow we should be putting him in school for the development of such powers as God gave him."[9]

MacArthur said he would contact the city's black clergy to organize a protest against the exhibit. "Our Christian missionary societies must take this matter up at once."

In MacArthur, Benga had found a formidable ally. Born in 1841 and reared by Scottish immigrants in Quebec, Canada, the red-haired, silver-tongued MacArthur was, at age sixteen, already dubbed "the boy preacher." By the time he graduated from the University of Rochester in 1867 he had become an American citizen and decided on a life in the church. At Rochester Theological Seminary his oratorical prowess and prolific writing earned him the first-prize gold medal at his May 12, 1870, commencement. Three days later, at age twenty-nine, and newly ordained, he was in the pulpit as Calvary Baptist Church's fifth pastor. During his stewardship the congregation mushroomed from 238 to 5,000 and in 1883 moved from modest quarters on Twenty-Third Street to an imposing early–English Gothic building with a 229-foot spire and a 1,500-seat sanctuary on West Fifty-Seventh Street near Sixth Avenue. Within a few years luxury apartment buildings sprang up around it, as did Carnegie Hall across the street. In 1896 MacArthur, by then a national figure with one of the United States' largest Baptist congregations, was awarded an honorary doctorate by

Columbian University, later renamed George Washington University, in Washington, D.C.

MacArthur's progressive church ministered to the city's burgeoning immigrant population but also attracted scores of professionals and prominent families, including the Colgates.[10] As one of the nation's most renowned clergymen, MacArthur was widely published; his sermons were reprinted in books and periodicals. He became a confidant to President William McKinley, who denounced lynching in his 1897 inaugural address but did little to formally address it or the worsening disenfranchisement of blacks during his presidency.[11] Calvary had outposts across the city and missionaries around the globe, and MacArthur became a forceful and beloved advocate for the disenfranchised, including the city's beleaguered African Americans, many of whom lived in the nearby San Juan Hill and Tenderloin areas between the mid-Thirties and Fifty-Eighth Street on Manhattan's West Side.

Three decades after the Civil War, in the face of widespread racial discrimination, MacArthur reminded whites that "the race question applied to the North as well as the South." Provocative and impassioned, he prodded them: "Are white men afraid of the supremacy of black men? Do they dare not give black men an equal chance in this country? Is this not the land of the free? Is this not supposed to be the home of the brave? What right have we to put upon the black man any race disabilities which we refuse to accept for ourselves? Let there be one rule for all. Men are to be judged not by color but by character."[12]

MacArthur demurred when in 1900, during a meeting with President McKinley and McKinley's vice president, Theodore Roosevelt, he was offered an ambassadorship to any European country of his choosing. MacArthur cited his unfinished ministry. A year later, McKinley was assassinated.[13]

MacArthur would continue his bold and compassionate ministry, and on September 9, 1906, it was directed at Ota Benga. His indignation elicited headlines in New York's newspapers that captured the excitement of the unfolding drama.

"Man and Monkey Show Disapproved by Clergy" was the *Times'* Monday-morning headline. Other New York papers played catch-up with headlines like the *Globe*'s "Lively Row over a Pigmy," and the *Evening Post*'s "A Pygmy Among the Primates."

But for all of his influence, MacArthur was taking on more than a feisty zookeeper. He was challenging an esteemed institution whose cofounders included a president of the United States; an eminent scientist; and the high-society lawyer Madison Grant, the Zoological Society's secretary. Moreover, Hornaday was himself the nation's foremost zoologist and a close acquaintance of President Theodore Roosevelt, with whom he shared a love of taxidermy and wildlife conservation.

In 1885, three years after Hornaday had joined the Smithsonian Institution as the chief taxidermist, his *Two Years in the Jungle* became one of the century's most widely read travel books.[14]

Hornaday's work calling attention to the imminent extinction of the bison won him acclaim across the country and in March 1888 inspired a personal visit by Theodore Roosevelt during his tenure in Washington as U.S. Civil Service commissioner. The twenty-eight-year-old Roosevelt and thirty-four-year-old Hornaday formed a lifelong friendship based on their love of the West, hunting, horses, and adventure. Hornaday later said that in the first hour of their first meeting Roosevelt shared with him a "serious secret, and we dealt in secrets forever after."[15]

When in 1896 the New York Zoological Society looked to hire its first director and chief curator, Hornaday, then age forty-one, was the obvious choice. He was offered a two-year contract at an annual salary of $5,000—the equivalent of roughly $128,000 today—to help create and run the new zoological park.[16]

From the Bronx Hornaday led the national campaign for the establishment of federally protected bison ranges, and a year before

Benga's exhibition he cofounded, with Theodore Roosevelt, who was by then president of the United States, the American Bison Society.

So it was with impeccable credentials and influential friends that Hornaday presided over the world's largest and most modern metropolitan zoo, whose founders were quick to note that it was four times bigger than any in Europe. The renowned zoologist could now claim credit for the zoological park's latest sensation: the exhibition of Benga, an African "pygmy," in the monkey house.

FIVE

BENGA'S BRIGADE

On Monday morning the city's black clergy, urged by MacArthur, gathered for an emergency meeting at the Mount Olivet Baptist Church. Under the bold leadership of the Reverend Dr. Matthew William Gilbert, Mount Olivet, with a congregation of 1,800, was one of the nation's largest black Baptist churches and a beacon of protest and pride for black New York. In 1907 the magazine *Colored American* called it "the mecca to which Baptists from all parts of the country make pilgrimages."[1]

Mount Olivet, like the other black churches, hotels, and medical and legal establishments lining West Fifty-Third Street between Sixth and Seventh Avenues, was a study in African Americans' achievement. By 1906 whites had fled the fashionable strip of elegant brownstones following the addition of a noisy elevated train station. The new occupants made the most of it. In 1900 Charles T. Walker, Mount Olivet's illustrious pastor from 1889 to 1904, established the city's first black YMCA, affectionately called "the colored Y." The strip was also home to the Maceo and Marshal hotels, Lymas

Williams's National Waiters Restaurant, and the Society of the Sons of New York. Founded in 1882, the Society of the Sons was one of the era's most prestigious black social organizations.

Under Gilbert, Mount Olivet remained a vibrant hub of African American uplift even as real estate developer Phillip Payton began running newspaper ads luring "colored tenants" to Harlem by promising "a class of apartments never before rented to our people."[2] Gilbert had national reach as corresponding secretary of the National Baptist Missionary and Education Convention, and from Mount Olivet flaunted his black pride like a uniform.[3] Earlier that year he had shouted down author Thomas Dixon for saying that blacks were "half devil and half child" and should be removed from American soil. Gilbert retorted that blacks in America *were* home, and would not peacefully assent to being colonized in Liberia, Haiti, or elsewhere. "He is right; we would fight," he affirmed, adding that perhaps Dixon, a Baptist minister and a descendant of German immigrants, should go back to Germany.

"Or," Gilbert added in a booming voice, "we will agree to go back if they pay us for the services we have rendered to this country during the many years we were slaves up to now."[4]

With Gilbert's blessing, an ad hoc group of clergymen formed a committee and appointed as chair Reverend James H. Gordon, superintendent of Howard Colored Orphan Asylum in Brooklyn's Weeksville section. Gordon, a native of Virginia who had been a pastor of Baptist churches in Nicetown, Pennsylvania, and more recently on Manhattan's West Fifty-Ninth Street, had been hailed by the *Brooklyn Eagle* as "one of the most eloquent Negroes in the country."[5] He was also chair of the New York Baptist Convention, a chapter of the national organization of African American Baptists.

That afternoon the group visited MacArthur at his nearby Fifty-Seventh Street home. He advised them to witness the abomination at the zoo that he had seen the previous day.

The committee of clergymen boarded a train to the zoological park. Gilbert was out of town, but among those traveling with Gordon was Reverend George Sims, who since 1893 had been pastor of Union Baptist Church on West Sixty-Third Street. A year earlier, Sims had moved his flourishing congregation from a three-hundred-capacity edifice on Sixty-Eighth Street and West End Avenue to an elegant brick and limestone building at 204–206 West Sixty-Third Street that seated a thousand.[6] Also on hand were Reverend S. W. Timms of Holy Trinity Baptist Church in Brooklyn, and Reverend Dr. William Henry Slater, who since 1900 had been pastor of Shiloh Baptist Church in New Rochelle.

As the clergymen entered the rank Monkey House, they were surprised to find that Benga was not on display. However, they soon found him ambling outside his room in the company of Dohong. Their attempts to communicate with him failed. However, Benga's sadness was palpable and the sign outside his cage stoked their outrage.

"We are frank enough to say we do not like this exhibition of one of our own race with the monkeys," Gordon fumed.[7] "Our race, we think, is depressed enough, without exhibiting one of us with apes. We think we are worthy of being considered human beings, with souls."

The clergymen, like other African Americans, were already on edge. In Manhattan racial tensions that six years earlier had erupted into a murderous rampage by mobs of whites through the black-populated Tenderloin district were subsiding, but many people were still uneasy. The murder in 1903 of Greater New York's champion Andrew Haskell Green by a black furnace tender again fueled racial tension. Green, considered the "father of Greater New York," had once served as president of the New York Zoological Society and had been a close friend of Osborn's family. Green's murder by an African American may have exacerbated Osborn's already low opinion of blacks, which found expression in his writing.

In 1906 the newly formed Committee for the Industrial

Improvement of the Condition of the Negro in New York—a fore-runner of the National Urban League—sent letters to southern newspapers urging blacks to stay put. Black New Yorkers were still routinely discriminated against and subjected to segregated public accommodations, including theaters, restaurants, and hotels. But legal discrimination in New York paled compared with that in the South, where two-thirds of African Americans still lived. There, the lynching of African Americans persisted; sixty-five lynchings were reported in 1906 alone. A month before Benga's exhibition in the zoo, a front-page article in the *Times* reported the brutal lynching of five blacks by a mob of two thousand in Salisbury, North Carolina, who stormed the jail where the men awaited trial.

A week later came news that members of the all-black Twenty-Fifth Infantry Regiment were accused of killing a white bartender and wounding an officer in a melee in Brownsville, Texas, the previous day. Twelve of the men were imprisoned without formal charges and without a trial, despite the fact that all had been accounted for in their barracks.

New York's Gilchrist Stewart was dispatched by Booker T. Washington to represent the men. However, despite the evidence that the men were accounted for in their barracks, and also despite evidence that the shells found at the scene had been planted, 167 of the men would be dishonorably discharged and accused of perpetrating a "conspiracy of silence" by denying their involvement. Despite pleas from black leaders, including Booker T. Washington, Roosevelt would sign the order denying the men—who had been deprived of legal counsel or a hearing—back pay, pensions, and eligibility to serve in the future. Roosevelt, considered a racial moderate for his time, unapologetically defamed the innocent men, saying, "Some of the men were bloody butchers; they ought to be hung."

Years later many would remember this as a low point of Roosevelt's presidency. In 1932 Julia Foraker—the wife of U.S. senator Joseph Foraker, who at the time had rebuked Roosevelt—recounted it in her memoir: "Everybody alive and awake a quarter of a century ago remembers the Brownsville scandal." The dishonorable discharge of the men remains the sole instance of mass punishment without a trial in U.S. military history. While the men's lives were unalterably derailed, the order was nonetheless reversed in 1972 by President Richard Nixon following a new investigation and a bill introduced by Representative Augustus Hawkins of Ohio.

In 1906 the Brownsville affair was among a series of high-profile slights of African Americans. That summer, amid unyielding violence and despair, the Niagara Movement, a civil rights group, held its second meeting at Storer College in Harpers Ferry, West Virginia. W. E. B. Du Bois and Lewis Douglass, son of the late Frederick Douglass, were among the fifty men and women in attendance. In an "Address to the Country," the group vowed to press for equal rights and claim for themselves all the rights of free-born American citizens.

Benga's exhibition three weeks later would mark a new low in race relations and would set the status of blacks in the United States and abroad in high relief.

As he pondered Benga's fate, Gordon was convinced that he was capable of development, a word liberally used by elite Americans, black and white alike, to draw a line between purportedly civilized and uncivilized people. Indeed, he believed Benga was bright. "We think we can do better for him than make an exhibition of him—an exhibition as it seems to us to corroborate the theory of evolution—the Darwinian theory."[8] Many in the academy applied Darwin's evolutionary theory—and the notion of survival of the fittest—to race, insisting that it, rather than historical events, explained the plight of blacks and the supposed racial superiority of whites.

But Hornaday said that while he did in fact support Darwin's theory, "I am giving the exhibition purely as an ethnological exhibit."[9] He said it would allow visitors to see how things were done in

Africa. Unrepentant, he declared that the show would go on just as the sign said, "each afternoon during September" or until he was ordered to stop it by the Zoological Society's executive committee headed by Henry Fairfield Osborn.[10]

Given Hornaday's daily 11 A.M. telephone conversations with the society's secretary, Madison Grant, who in turn spoke each day to Osborn, it was clear that no such order had been issued. Furthermore, Hornaday—who years earlier had hired a clipping service to collect his frequent appearances in newspapers—was apparently enjoying his celebrity. He boasted to reporters that the only reason for Monday's reprieve was the low turnout of paying customers that day. The zoo was free five days a week, but on holidays, Mondays, and Thursdays admission was twenty-five cents for adults and fifteen cents for children.

Reached by telephone, Samuel Verner, the man who had deposited Benga at the zoo and then left, insisted that neither he nor the park profited from the exhibit.

"The public," he insisted, "is the only beneficiary."[11]

Verner also claimed that Benga, despite appearing shaken and being locked in a cage at the mercy of his handlers, was there of his own volition. "He is absolutely free," Verner illogically claimed.

Then, contradicting that assertion, he said, "The only restriction that is put upon him is to prevent him from getting away from the keepers. That is done for his own safety."[12]

Despite the cage and the sign indicating Benga's daily exhibition, Verner groped for ways to rationalize the arrangement. "If Ota Benga is in a cage," he reasoned, "he is only there to look after the animals. If there is a notice on the cage, it is only put there to avoid answering the many questions that are asked about him."

Furthermore, Verner improbably maintained that, contrary to what appeared to be an attempt to apply Darwin's theory to race, the exhibit was actually intended to illustrate the wide gap between "pygmies" and apes: "The zoological and the psychological gap between the pygmies and the apes constitute a cataclysm."

Verner also took pains to explain why he had placed Benga in the zoo to begin with, his reasons revealing a striking lack of compassion or empathy for Benga. Verner said that he had applied to the Salvation Army and the police for temporary lodging, and that the former had suggested placing him with a colored family. Verner dismissed the idea "inasmuch as the little African savage would not have understood them anymore than he would a white person."

Moreover, Verner reasoned that Benga required a caretaker capable of handling someone who was "not fully responsible for his acts," blithely suggesting that the young African captive was incapable of rational thought or civilized behavior. Verner said it was Hornaday who suggested placing him in the zoo, where visitors could see "how they did things in Africa."[13] However preposterous his reasoning, the remarkable events leading up to Benga's exhibition appear accurate, given Hornaday's earlier expressed desire to exhibit Native Americans at the zoo.

Verner said he regretted that feelings were hurt but in an apparent nod to Christian faith assured the reporter that care would be taken not to exhibit Benga on Sundays.

Gordon was incredulous.

"The trouble seems to be that Dr. Verner did not apply to the proper persons," he said.[14]

Gordon said he would be more than happy to take Benga.

The committee left the park vowing to take the matter up the next day with Mayor George Brinton McClellan Jr. Meanwhile Hornaday went back to conducting the affairs of the zoo. One order of business was writing a memorandum to the keepers of the primate and lion houses to inform them that owing to illness, the Monkey House would have to forgo a morning janitor. The Monkey House, then, would be even more malodorous than usual.

Meanwhile, editors at the *Times* prepared an editorial to signal that they had tired of the affair.

"Send Him Back to the Woods" was the headline on Tuesday.[15]

Echoing the sentiments of the esteemed Men of Science, the editors were confounded by the protests.

"We do not quite understand all the emotion which others are expressing in the matter," they said. "Ota Benga, according to our information, is a normal specimen of his race or tribe, with a brain as much developed as are those of its other members. Whether they are held to be illustrations of arrested development, and really closer to the anthropoid apes than the other African savages, or whether they are viewed as the degenerate descendants of ordinary negroes, they are of equal interest to the student of ethnology, and can be studied with profit." [16]

Divesting Benga of human emotion, and ignoring accounts of his apparent distress reported in the *Times'* own pages, the editorial said it was absurd to imagine Benga's suffering or humiliation. "Pygmies," the editors held, "are very low in the human scale, and the suggestion that Benga should be in a school instead of a cage ignores the high probability that school would be a place of torture to him. . . . The idea that men are all much alike except as they have had or lacked opportunities for getting an education of books is now far out of date." [17]

This, after all, had been the view espoused by generations of leading scientists. Louis Agassiz, the Harvard professor who at the time of his death in 1873 was arguably America's most venerated scientist, had for more than two decades insisted that blacks were a separate species, a "degraded and degenerate race." [18] More recently Daniel Garrison Brinton, a professor of linguistics and archaeology at the University of Pennsylvania, in his address as outgoing president of the American Association for the Advancement of Science, rebutted claims that education and opportunity accounted for varying levels of achievement along racial lines.

"The black, the brown, and the red races differ anatomically so much from the white, especially in their splanchnic organs, that even with equal cerebral capacity they never could rival its results by equal efforts," he said.[19]

In a handwritten note to Hornaday, Osborn expressed his delight at the *New York Times* editorial, saying it expressed his view exactly. However, he cautioned that Benga should be quietly withdrawn from the cage "or else make it very apparent that he is acting the part of a keeper."[20] This marked the beginning of an intentionally deceptive narrative that would persist in the Zoological Society's future accounts of the episode.

Meanwhile the clergymen planned to visit City Hall to meet with Mayor McClellan, Greater New York's third mayor, who a year earlier had beaten back a challenge to his reelection by the *New York Journal*'s publisher William Randolph Hearst. They hoped to find an ally in this popular, courtly forty-year-old who, as the city's chief executive, also happened to be an ex officio member of the Zoological Society.

SIX

FIGHTING CITY HALL

TUESDAY MORNING, SEPTEMBER 10, 1906

City Hall glistened like a fairy-tale castle in the warm morning light. The white marble building, completed in 1812, had been inspired by an eighteenth-century French palace and was meant to signify the city's budding prosperity and prestige. Above the column-flanked doorway, five arched wide-eyed windows witnessed the clergymen's arrival. From atop the cupola, the statue of Justice balanced a pair of steelyards across her broad shoulders and fixed the visitors in her dignified gaze.

The ministers were poised for battle as they bounded up the stairs and approached the grand entrance leading to an open portico. Ornate tiles unfolded behind the front door beneath a majestic rotunda flanked by a double floating staircase. They followed the stairs to a second-floor landing where ten Corinthian-style columns supported a coffered dome and a central circular window received the morning light. The enveloping opulence signaled power as a bugler signals dawn. But the clergymen were on a mission and would not be seduced. In their meeting with McClellan they would be respectful but firm. Benga's exhibition, they would tell the mayor, was a moral outrage. It must be halted at once.

The ministers had come armed with a letter of introduction from MacArthur.

During the meeting at his home, he had probably briefed them on the ways of the mayor, whose youthful charm and affability belied his political cunning.

He was the son and namesake of the famous Civil War general, who had unsuccessfully challenged Lincoln for the presidency and later became governor of New Jersey and an officer of the Illinois Railroad. The younger McClellan held undergraduate and graduate degrees from Princeton University and in 1892, at the age of twenty-six, had been elected to New York City's board of aldermen. A few years later, he had briefly served as acting mayor before being elected to Congress, where he served on the powerful Ways and Means Committee.

McClellan had resigned from his fifth term in Congress in 1903, after defeating New York City's one-term mayor Seth Low, a former president of Columbia University and mayor of Brooklyn.

Probably wearing their crisp Sunday finery, the ministers entered the reception area and politely requested a meeting with the mayor. They waited quietly and snapped to attention when Frank O'Brien, the mayor's secretary, appeared. The mayor, he said, was too busy to meet them. Gordon responded by handing him the letter of introduction from MacArthur. O'Brien left and then returned, holding a letter addressed to Gordon.

It read: "His honor suggests that you bring your complaint to the attention of the officers of the society."[1]

The ministers were stunned. "If Mayor McClellan won't see us it certainly won't do him any good," Gordon fumed. "Certainly the mayor, the executive head of the city, may put a stop to an indecent exhibition, to a showing in public of one of our race so as to show the Negro as a Darwinian relative of the chimpanzee."[2]

Gordon insisted that the mayor had the authority to act, but after being snubbed asked to whom they should direct their protest. They were told to see Madison Grant, the Zoological Society's secretary, in his office at 11 Wall Street.

And with that, they were unceremoniously dismissed.

The mayor and his secretary had probably read about the planned visit in that morning's newspaper. It is also possible that McClellan communicated with members of the Zoological Society by telephone. His father, after all, had been a close associate of Osborn's father. In any event McClellan was nonconfrontational by nature, and both he and O'Brien were former newspaper reporters and keenly aware of the voracious appetite of the press. Not even a morsel would be thrown its way. For the duration of the controversy McClellan did not enter the public fray; nor did he mention the episode in any of his official or personal correspondence filed in the archives.

The offended ministers headed to the Wall Street office of Madison Grant. It is unlikely that the men then knew of Grant's extreme racial views, which a decade later would be distilled and published in his book *The Passing of the Great Race*.

But perhaps they did know that twelve years earlier it was the debonair Grant who had asked Theodore Roosevelt to form a committee devoted to the establishment of a zoological park. Impressed with the twenty-nine-year-old Grant's vision and vigor, Roosevelt obliged by appointing him chairman. Over dinner Roosevelt advised Grant that if he was ever going to turn his dream of a zoological park into a reality, the election of William Strong as mayor in 1894 provided the best opportunity.

That year Grant wrote an article for *Century Magazine* in which he examined the imperiled fate of the buffalo and advanced the idea of a state-of-the-art zoological park.[3] The city had operated the popular nine-acre Central Park Menagerie since 1861, but by the 1880s it was overcrowded and foul-smelling, eliciting support among Fifth Avenue's affluent residents for a new location. But Grant had far more ambitious goals. Grant believed a world-class zoo would be educational, provide a breeding program for buffalo, and promote wildlife conservation. In 1895 he went to Albany to lobby state lawmakers, including his good friend Assembly Speaker Hamilton Fish. By April an "Act to Incorporate the New York Zoological Society and to Provide for the Establishment of a Zoological Garden" was passed and signed into law.[4]

But Grant's leading role as a cofounder of the zoo would be overshadowed by his influential book *The Passing of the Great Race*, which advocated cleansing America of "inferior races" through birth control, antimiscegenation and racial segregation laws, and mass sterilization. He argued that Negroes were so inferior to Nordic whites that they were a separate species and infamously warned: "Whether we like to admit it or not, the result of the mixture of two races, in the long run, gives us a race reverting to the more ancient, generalized and lower type. The cross between a white man and an Indian is an Indian; the cross between a white man and a negro is a negro; the cross between a white man and a Hindu is a Hindu; and the cross between any of the three European races and a Jew is a Jew."[5]

Grant said that over the past century Americans' altruistic ideals and sentimentalism had made the nation "an asylum for the oppressed." He described his own plan as a "practical, merciful, and inevitable" solution for ridding society of undesirable groups.

Prior to publication Grant shared the manuscript with Osborn, who offered suggestions and would collaborate with Grant on a subsequent edition. In a preface to the fourth edition, Osborn wrote:

> [I]n no other human stock which has come to this country is there displayed the unanimity of heart, mind and action which is now being displayed by the descendants of the blue-eyed, fair-haired peoples of the north of Europe. If I were asked: What is the

greatest danger which threatens the American republic to-day? I would certainly reply: The gradual dying out among our people of those hereditary traits through which the principles of our religious, political and social foundations were laid down and their insidious replacement by traits of less noble character."[6]

Theodore Roosevelt, by then president of the United States, was quoted on the jacket, calling the work a "capital book—in purpose, in vision, in grasp of the facts our people must need to realize."[7] William J. Sollas, a renowned Oxford anthropologist, in a letter to Grant, said he envied "the pleasure you must have had in building up your rich store of facts into a compact body of doctrine." Even the progressive *Nation* magazine applauded Grant's "distinct qualities of originality, conviction and courage," and the *New York Herald* called the book a "profound study of world history." These endorsements from leading voices in the American mainstream, if not the progressive stream, underscored how ingrained racist and anti-Semitic thinking was in the national psyche. Nearly alone in the academic wilderness was Franz Boas, the German-born Columbia University anthropologist, who insisted that race is a product of culture, not of biology.

In his review of Grant's book in the *New Republic* Boas said that the views Grant expressed were "dangerous," all the more so because of the sterling reputation of Grant and Osborn and their worthy contributions to the New York Zoological Gardens and the American Museum of Natural History. Boas held that race could not explain intelligence or personality traits, and he dismissed Grant's work as "dogmatic assumptions which cannot endure criticism." He also dismissed as outdated the idea of positioning races along an evolutionary chart. "In place of a simple line of evolution there appears a multiplicity of converging and diverging lines which it is difficult to bring under one system of control," he argued. "Instead of uniformity, the striking feature seems to be diversity."

But Boas, despite his Ph.D. in physics and geography, was

drowned out by a chorus of American and European scientists who ranked the world's races on a ladder of civilization, with Europeans at the top and Africans at the bottom. Boas's aberrant thinking would cost him funding and for nearly two decades exile his voice to the margins. Grant and his adherents could blame Boas's critique on his Jewish ancestry. Boas would of course ultimately exert greater influence on the developing field of anthropology, but Grant's and Osborn's view would hold sway up through the first two decades of the new century. Osborn would be elected a fellow and vice president of the American Association for the Advancement of Science and president of the New York Academy of Sciences, and become a stalwart member of the Eugenics Society, which was founded by the Zoological Society board member Charles Davenport. The Harvard-educated Davenport was on the faculty at the University of Chicago and considered a leading biologist when he established the Station for Experimental Evolution at Cold Spring Harbor, Long Island, in 1904. There he attempted to apply Mendelian genetic theory to human biology and classify racial groups on the basis of biologically prescribed characteristics.

That the proponents of these views could determine attitudes and laws in the United States and abroad would not bode well for African Americans, Jews, and others deemed inherently inferior. Meanwhile racialist theories were planted in the fertile soil of American science and the hardy vines of even the extreme eugenicists extended to Theodore Roosevelt's White House and beyond. In 1906, Willet Hayes, assistant secretary of agriculture, established a "Hereditary Commission" to advise the government on ways to "better the race" and stem the "vicious elements in the cross-bred American civilization." In 1910 the Eugenics Records Office was officially founded in Cold Spring, New York, with financing by the widow of the railroad baron E. H. Harriman.

This records office was later funded by the Rockefeller family and the Carnegie Foundation and would play a key role in the passage

of a series of laws in 1924, including the Immigration Restriction
Act, to stem the tide of immigrants from eastern and southern Europe and Asia; the Virginia Racial Integrity Act, which banned
marriage between whites and nonwhites; and Virginia's Eugenical
Sterilization Act, which permitted the sterilization of asylum inmates who were epileptic, severely disabled, "mentally retarded," or
"feeble-minded."

The Passing of the Great Race would go through four printings
in the United States and be translated into German. It was read by
Hitler and later cited during the Nuremberg trials. Hitler quoted
Grant copiously in his speeches and was said to have written Grant
a letter saying that "the book is my Bible."[8] And while Osborn,
Grant, and *The Passing of the Great Race* would become historical
footnotes, Hitler, long inspired by the eugenics movement, would
oversee the passage of sterilization, anti-immigration, and marriage
laws aimed against Jews that resembled some passed in the United
States. His ultimate plan for racial hygiene would, soon afterward,
stun the world.

Not surprisingly, the ministers, who were neither fair-haired
nor blue-eyed, were politely snubbed by Grant. He told them that
Benga would be at the zoo for only a short time and that Verner
would then take him to Europe. Grant also said, maintaining the
narrative concocted by Osborn, that Benga was at the zoo to help
care for the animals.

But the ministers were rankled and outraged by Benga's continued exhibition, just as most whites would surely be by a similar display of a European. They left Grant and headed to the nearby Nassau
Street office of Wilford H. Smith, a friend, confidant, and personal
lawyer of Booker T. Washington. Two years earlier Smith had become the first black lawyer to successfully argue a case before the
U.S. Supreme Court. Before that he had been the first to argue before
the Alabama supreme court. Beginning in 1902, with Washington's
covert sponsorship, he filed a series of lawsuits challenging the dis-

enfranchisement of blacks under Alabama's new constitution. As a result of Smith's efforts, a man had been released from prison because qualified blacks had been excluded from his jury. Smith was hailed across the country as a civil rights champion.

What, the black New York clergymen now asked, could Smith do to secure the release from the zoo of Ota Benga? Smith agreed to review the matter.

Gordon, joined by Sims, headed back to the Bronx Zoo to check on his protégé. They arrived at around 3 P.M. to find Benga, with a guinea pig, in a cage surrounded by several hundred spectators. "The crowd seemed to annoy the dwarf," reported the *Times*. Noting the free admission that day, the article said, "Many persons went to the park on purpose to see him."[9] Gordon announced that an "indignation meeting" would soon be held and that MacArthur would be among the speakers. If other white clergymen joined the protest, none appeared in the newspaper accounts of the period.

On Wednesday Smith summoned the clergymen back to his office to inform them that he had consulted the corporation counsel, the city's attorney, and would appeal to the court for Benga's release. It is also likely that Smith discussed the matter with Booker T. Washington, given their close, though covert, communication.

John Henry E. Milholland, a wealthy white New York businessman who founded the Constitution League to protest disenfranchisement of blacks in the South, sent Smith a telegram pledging to help finance Benga's case. He had contributed substantial funding to numerous civil rights causes, including an investigation of the Brownsville, Texas, melee. Earlier that year Milholland organized a meeting at New York's Cooper Union that drew three thousand people, including W. E. B. Du Bois and Mary Church Terrell, to galvanize support for black suffrage and federal anti-disenfranchisement legislation. Far to the left of the white mainstream, he called for unified protests, lawsuits, and lobbying.[10] That year he also addressed Booker T. Washington's National Business League, taking scientists to task for their claims of black inferiority and noting that through-out history oppressors have denigrated those they oppress.

"Cultured Greece classed all who were not Hellenic barbarians. The Gentile world was abhorred by the Hebrews of old as unspeakably vile," he said. "Wrapt in the serene security of its imaginary superiority, the ruling race has delighted to degrade all others." [11]

The combination of Smith's stature, Milholland's financial backing, and the threat of a lawsuit undoubtedly captured the attention of the Zoological Society's officials.

Back at the zoo Hornaday took Osborn's advice and quietly removed the sign outside Benga's cage. Spectators, however, continued to flock to the monkey house, hoping to steal a glimpse of the "pygmy." And Hornaday, ever the showman, continued to field requests for photographs and interviews from around the country and Europe.

"Dear Sir," read a letter from the *Sketch* published by the *Illustrated London News*. "I am interested to see that you are showing a Bushman in a cage with some apes. Could you lend me a photograph showing man and monkeys together for reproduction in *The Sketch*." [12]

And in a note attached to a photograph of Ota Benga sent to Franklin Fishler of the American Press Association, Hornaday wrote: "We send you herewith a photograph of the African Pigmy, and a copy of a statement prepared by me regarding him. In describing him, please be sure to refer to this institution as the 'New York Zoological Park,' and not as the 'Bronx Zoo.' " [13]

Similar requests poured in from newspapers and magazines across the country and in France and England. On Thursday the *Times* published a letter written by Dr. M. S. Gabriel, who said he had seen Benga at the zoo and found the objections to the exhibit "absurd." He said that while the ministers protested Benga's presence in a cage, it was, on the contrary, "a vast room, a sort of balcony in the open air," which allowed visitors to observe the African guest "while breathing the fresh air." [14]

Furthermore, he said Benga's childlike ways and broken English were pleasing, "and the visitors find him the best of good fellows." [15] It's a pity, he said, that Hornaday did not give lectures related to such exhibits. "This would emphasize the scientific character of the service, enhance immeasurably the usefulness of the Zoological Park to our public in general, and help our clergymen to familiarize themselves with the scientific point of view so absolutely foreign to many of them." [16]

Hornaday saved the clippings and proudly shared them with Osborn.

"The enclosed clippings are excellent," Osborn replied. "Benga is certainly making his way successfully as a sensation." [17]

SEVEN

BENGA SPEAKS

I n public Hornaday appeared as upbeat and in control as ever on Thursday, September 12, as he fielded press inquiries and held court for the public. But behind the scenes, the zookeeper was anxious. The *New York Times*, which until now had appeared indifferent to Benga's exhibition, suddenly began to question its wisdom, perhaps in response to the growing protests from prominent critics like Milholland, MacArthur, and Wilford Smith. The popular exhibition was suddenly becoming a scandal, and the notoriety coupled with the nascent legal battle was beginning to fray Hornaday's nerves.

Worse yet, Benga himself, who had until now appeared resigned to his fate, had become combative. Hornaday vented his frustration to Osborn, noting Benga's restlessness, the protests, the threatened lawsuit, and an article that appeared in that morning's *Times* claiming Benga had been in a cage the previous day.

"He did not set foot in the cage during the entire day," Hornaday protested. "The label of information about him had been taken down, and as an exhibit he has fallen into innocuous desuetude."[1]

Hornaday complained that Benga had become "a white elephant," confiding that "he is so hard to manage."[2] However, he said, after a long conversation he and Grant had agreed that despite the uproar, they would do nothing to suggest, even vaguely, that they had bowed to the colored ministers' demands.

"I would rather keep him here for the whole month than to be brow-beaten by a Committee of negro ministers who are only anxious for newspaper notoriety," Hornaday fumed, appealing to Osborn: "I hope you will sustain us in it."[3]

But he would need Verner to bring his unruly charge under control. That day, as keepers attempted to lead Benga to the monkey house, he rebelled by wrestling and kicking the attendants and threatening to bite his way free. Here, research on shame-related events can once again prove instructive. There is substantial evidence that under such circumstances shame often precedes anger "and shame and anger independently [predict] posttraumatic stress disorder."[4]

Startled by the mounting insurrection, Hornaday sought instruction from Verner, who had been staying in Manhattan at the Hotel Belleclaire, on West Seventy-Seventh Street off Broadway, a few blocks from the American Museum of Natural History. In recent days, Verner had been conspicuously quiet.

"Boy here became quite unmanageable," Hornaday scribbled in a note to Verner, addressed to the Belleclaire. "Will not obey keepers and resists control. Think it unwise for us to punish him for several reasons. Call me or phone. W. T. Hornaday."[5]

However, his note to Verner sent to the Belleclaire arrived too late, for a day later, Verner wrote from Brevard, North Carolina, casually telling Hornaday to forward future mail to him there.

"Drop me a line occasionally to let me know how matters are," he chirped, the weight of Benga's care obviously lifted from his shoulders.[6]

Verner enclosed a handwritten note in Tshiluba for Benga, with instructions for Hornaday to read it to him phonetically, which he would do several days later.

On Friday Benga somehow ended up in the reindeer pen and was chased up a tree. He had to be retrieved by a park ranger, who led him back to his cage. The next morning Hornaday, still unable to reach Verner, sent a desperate wire to Verner's father in Columbia, South Carolina: "Please wire address of your son, Samuel P. Verner. Desire to telegraph him today. Answer prepaid."[7]

But Samuel Phillips Verner had his own troubles. Fresh from an eighteen-month journey through the Congo, he had sailed to New York with visions of claiming his place alongside the era's eminent scientists. He had first gone to the Congo in 1895 as a missionary, but now hoped to be recognized as a full-fledged scientist and explorer. In many ways, he seemed a man for the era. Endowed with sandy hair and probing blue eyes, he believed he was destined by science to occupy the top rung of civilization's evolutionary ladder. The same men who had described Africans as "pithecoid" or "ape-like" and as "midway between the Oran-utang and the European white" believed that people with Verner's physical attributes were biologically superior to all others.[8]

And while Verner held no advanced degrees and was not among the Men of Science invited to a meeting in Washington in 1903 to organize a national anthropology society, he was nonetheless listed in 1905 as a founding member of the American Anthropological Association.[9]

He had also written articles on "pygmies" for leading popular publications including the *Atlantic Monthly* and the *Spectator* in London; and his book *Pioneering in Central Africa*, chronicling his exploits in the Congo, had been issued by the Presbyterian Committee of Publication in 1903. Hornaday would refer to him in published material as Dr. Verner, an indication of the esteem he

believed was Verner's due, presumably because of his African treasures exhibited at the zoo.

On his arrival in New York Verner planned to sell his specimens
and possibly land a position as a scientist—the occupation he noted on
the ship's passenger list on his voyage back to the United States—or as
a lecturer, with Benga included among the "very interesting things"
he was bringing from Africa.[10] He was also brimming with ideas
for articles, which he immediately began offering to newspapers and
magazines. But nothing had gone as planned.

He arrived in New York, strapped for cash, on July 30 and within
days was being hounded by a sheriff who had a warrant for his arrest—he had written a bad check on August 2, three days after he arrived. He now owed the Guardian Trust Company $260.30 plus $2.50
in interest, the equivalent of about $6,600 today.

En route from the Congo Verner had already sold a chimpanzee
in Sierra Leone for thirty-five pounds, and in July he had written to
a shipping agent from a hotel in Liverpool, England, seeking passage
for himself and an African "Pygmy," along with fifty cases of specimens including orchids, and two chimpanzees. The problem was that
he did not have the money to pay for the voyage.

"I have come from Central Africa unexpectedly and have cabled
for more funds, but do not know whether I shall hear in time and I
am very anxious to go at once," he wrote.[11]

Verner said his cargo was ample security and he was certain he'd
be able to make the check good on his arrival in New York. An official at Cunard graciously obliged.

However, one of the chimpanzees he hoped to sell had contracted
tuberculosis and Verner was still desperately negotiating with the
Zoological Society to sell the other. While he came close to securing
a position at the American Museum of Natural History, the effort ultimately failed, and the sheriff had impounded the cases of specimens
he had stored at the museum.

And then there were irksome rumors. According to some people, he had gone insane; others said that he was broke and had abandoned his wife and two children. While there is no indication that the rumors were ever published, they obviously haunted Verner, who in letters repeatedly asked his correspondents not to believe what was written of him.

Verner had recently confided his troubles to Hermon Bumpus, the head of the American Museum of Natural History, assuring Bumpus that he was born and bred a gentleman "however unfortunate have been the results of some hard times I have had to endure." [12] While recent troubles had "cut me to the quick," he said he was blameless, adding, "But I know how to take better medicine." [13] Verner was still hoping that Bumpus would add him to his lecture schedule.

In the meantime Verner vigorously courted editors who might publish articles about his African adventures. On August 13 *Century* magazine acknowledged receipt of his query. Its editor had already written privately to Hornaday, to inquire about Verner. On August 14 Walter Hines Page, a partner in the Doubleday publishing house and editor of *World's Work* magazine, accepted an article on opportunities in Africa. A day later the *Atlantic Monthly* wrote to decline a proposed article entitled "Adventures Among the Pygmies." An editor from *Collier's* wrote to say that a map and part of the article Verner had written were "unintelligible." [14]

In dire need of cash and with a sheriff on his tail, Verner was desperate to leave New York but first needed to unload Ota Benga, who would, among other things, require an additional fare and food.

Hornaday had initially jumped at the chance to temporarily board Ota Benga, but what had seemed a blessing now seemed a curse. Benga was hardly the compliant scientific exhibit he had envisioned. Verner, fearing arrest, could not unburden him and rode out the crisis a safe distance away in Brevard, North Carolina.

By Sunday, September 16, a week after his debut, Benga was no longer in the cage, but roamed the park under the watchful eye of park rangers. Still he was not free. That day a record forty thousand people visited the zoo, nearly all to see Ota Benga. Wherever Benga went, hordes followed in hot pursuit, "howling, jeering and yelling," reported the *Times*.[15] The rowdy crowd pursued Benga, and when he was cornered, some people poked him in the ribs or tripped him, while others merely laughed at the sight of a frightened "pygmy." In self-defense, Benga struck several visitors, and it took three men to get him back to the monkey house.

Hornaday had long shared Osborn's and Grant's contempt for the lower-class zoo-goers, whom he privately described as "low-lived beasts who appreciate nothing and love filth and disorder."[16] Now, the unruly mobs overwhelmed the park rangers. Benga had excited their raw emotions and Hornaday had tired of the chaos. He wrote to Verner on Monday, September 17, to report that Benga had again resisted authority.

"I regret to say that Ota Benga has become quite unmanageable," he wrote.[17] "He has been so fully exploited in the newspapers, and so much in the public eye, it is quite inadvisable for us to punish him; for should we do so, we would immediately be accused of cruelty, coercion, etc., etc. I am sure you will appreciate this point."

Immune from punishment, Hornaday complained, "the boy does quite as he pleases, and it is utterly impossible to control him."[18]

Unable to fathom Benga's resistance to his captivity with monkeys and apes, Hornaday expressed dismay that Benga threatened to bite the keepers whenever they tried to bring him back to the monkey house "and would undoubtedly do so if they should persist."

Given the insurrection, Hornaday was prepared to relinquish the reins. "I see no way out of the dilemma but for him to be taken away."[19]

Meanwhile Benga's daily adventures in the wilds of the New York Zoological Gardens had become a newspaper publisher's dream. Neither journalists nor the public could get enough of Benga, whose adventures in the picturesque zoological park were a daily source of headlines. "Zoo Has a Pygmy Too Many," reported Monday's *New York Sun*. From the depths of his debasement, Benga was a star.

That day, a keeper managed to catch Benga after he was once again chased through the park by a jeering mob. He reportedly asked how Benga liked America. "Me no like America," Benga forlornly replied.[20]

EIGHT

BACKLASH

B y Monday morning, Hornaday had had enough. After a full week of escalating controversy compounded by an increasingly rebellious Benga, he was ready to release his defiant captive.

"Ring up the Brooklyn Howard Colored Orphanage Association," he bellowed. "Tell them they can get busy tinkering with his intellect."[1]

Hornaday's frustration had already been captured in an article in that morning's *New York Sun*, in which he complained that Verner had said he intended to leave Benga only temporarily, assuring Hornaday that Benga would be a big drawing card for the zoo. But now Hornaday cited the ever-present unruly crowds and Verner's delayed return to retrieve "this untamed ebony bunch of bother."[2]

"He promised to come back and get this pygmy creature and take him away back to Congo or Timbuktu—the further away the better," Hornaday said. "And he hasn't come. And we don't know where to find him. And we are just about ready to take to the psychopathic ward."[3]

He also faced mounting criticism, with William Randolph Hearst's *New York Journal* that morning condemning the exhibition as "bad taste." "These men [of the Zoological Gardens]—with good intentions probably, but without thought and intelligence have been exhibiting in a cage of monkeys, a small human dwarf from Africa."[4] The editorial said that the exhibit held up to scorn the African race, which deserved sympathy and kindness from whites, given the brutality it had endured. The editorial concluded by calling the exhibit "disgusting" and a "shameful disgrace to every man in any way connected with it."[5]

The editorial took direct aim at Hornaday and his colleagues at the Zoological Society, but indirectly rebuked all who raucously reveled in the human spectacle. Those included thousands of New Yorkers, and editors at the *New York Times*, the *New York Sun*, and the *New York World*. The *World* was owned by Joseph Pulitzer, Hearst's former mentor, now his rival, whose staff he had raided by offering higher salaries. Fresh from a defeat in New York City's 1905 mayoralty election, Hearst was a now a candidate for New York State's governorship, from the political left. His chain of newspapers championed labor unions, municipal ownership of utilities, and a progressive tax that imposes higher rates on the rich; earlier, these papers had supported the Cuban rebels against Spain. Hearst, born into privilege, was a courtly contrarian who had been booted from Harvard and hosted civic events in New York, where he also distributed food, clothing, and coal to the city's destitute. Whether owing to politics or moral outrage, Benga was the latest beneficiary of Hearst's largesse.

Hornaday fired off a letter to Verner expressing his frustration along with his serious consideration of Gordon's scheme to place Benga in the Howard Colored Orphan Asylum in Brooklyn. Its director had been so insistent, said Hornaday, that he was tempted to put the idea to the test. As for Verner's suggestion to send Benga to South Carolina, Hornaday feared that he had no one available to successfully manage Benga, noting, "He has struck a number of visitors and has risen [Cain] generally."[6]

By all appearances, Benga's attacks were provoked. That day Benga was again chased through the park by feral visitors. "Always the crowd; in the monkey house, through the lion house, under the trees, by the wolf den—always hunting, hunting this African person," Hornaday said.[7]

Benga temporarily sought refuge in Hornaday's office, where the director, attempting to calm him, phonetically read him the letter Verner had written three days earlier:

> Ota Benga
> Moiyo! Meme kula katataka. Meme Kinkebba Mukashe Kwa
> wewe Meme gusa wewe shikima pola me Balunda bwebwe.
> Moiyo!
> Fwela

Hornaday had no way to decipher this odd letter, in which Verner apparently asks Benga not to discuss a woman from his village. He also says he expects to return soon and counsels Benga to remain calm.[8]

Hornaday had initially said he would wait to hear from Verner before contacting the orphanage, but the afternoon skirmishes prompted him to take immediate action. He wrote in a postscript to his own letter, "The boy must either leave here immediately or be confined. . . . Without you, he is a very unruly savage."

Hornaday picked up the phone to call Gordon, by then designated by the National Baptist Ministers' Convention to arrange for Benga's release. Gordon was not at his home in Brooklyn, but his wife, Mary, when informed of Hornaday's willingness to release Benga to their care, immediately boarded a train to fetch him. However, while she was en route to the zoological gardens, Gordon and Hornaday reached each other by phone and discussed the terms of the release. Hornaday said he would agree to release Benga only if Gordon signed an agreement vowing to return him to Verner whenever Verner wished. That was, after all, the agreement he had made when he took possession of Benga. Gordon flatly refused.

"It's all off," Gordon said.[9]

He added, "I'm sure the committee wouldn't agree to let the little African savage go back into the custody of a person who allowed him to be caged with monkeys for public exhibition. No, sir. I wouldn't sign any such agreement as that."[10]

"He wants the pigmy for good," Hornaday complained, explaining the failed negotiations. "Says he will not sign an agreement to give him back to Dr. Verner when the latter wants him. To that I wouldn't agree."[11]

Hornaday took umbrage over Gordon's characterization of Verner as unfit to care for Benga. "I have known Dr. Verner for a long time and know him to be an eminently respectable and good man," he said of the man he had briefly met two weeks earlier. Gordon offered to meet him at the zoo to discuss the matter further, a proposition Hornaday refused.

"Therefore, the pigmy stands in status quo and our only hope for relief from the embarrassing situation that his unruliness brings upon us is by your coming after him to take him away," Hornaday complained to Verner. "The newspapers have made so much of his presence here and everything that he does that it is not wise to take on risks of further sensations. I am sure you will appreciate this part of the attention. We have tried quite hard to control the lad and make him a possibility here; but we must give it up."

While Benga was in the office, Mary Gordon appeared at the gate but was denied entry into the park. It's likely that Hornaday instructed attendants to ward her off, given the breakdown in negotiations.

She later told her husband that a man at the gate told her that Benga had been "driven to desperation" by disorderly crowds in the park on Sunday and Monday.

The ministers regrouped at Mount Olivet to plot their next course of action. They said they hoped to hold a meeting with Hornaday and Benga, but Hornaday dismissed their plan as futile. Reporting on the failed negotiation between the ministers and Hornaday, the *Times* noted that "the fight for the custody of the African savage received new impetus again." [12] The *Times* also reported that Benga was once again chased through the park, as he had been the previous day. But that item was tempered by news that Benga played a mouth organ with vigor "and the crowd had a treat such as Benga hasn't furnished heretofore." [13] The article said that later in the day he bounced a rubber ball. "Holding the mouth organ with his left hand, he bounced the rubber ball with his right."

The clergy, however, probably took solace in the critical editorials in Hearst's *New York Journal* and the Philadelphia-based *North American*, an influential newspaper published by Thomas Wanamaker, the politically progressive son of the mercantile and department store tycoon John Wanamaker. The *North American* was the nation's oldest newspaper and under Wanamaker regularly featured commentary from the political left, including the lawyer of socialist Emma Goldman. Under the headline "Civilization," the *North American* noted the irony of purportedly civilized Anglo-Saxons exhibiting an African man for their amusement.

"For ages man has acted in just this way," it said. "We entice the backward race into our well-secured back yard and tease it with straws or knives or laws. We become a nation of sociologists, look at the curious object's teeth, feel his muscle, prick his skin. We try to make him swallow a constitution and wonder whether he can sit up straight when it gets lodged at a painful angle in his abdominal region." [14]

As the crisis deepened, the public increasingly weighed in

regarding Benga's plight. That day another letter was written to Hornaday—a letter that would, more than any other, underscore the bizarre nature of Benga's predicament as something of value in the global market. Josephine Vandes, of Saint-Raphaël, France, had read about Benga in the *Journal* in Paris.

"I have seen that in New York a man African is exhibited with some monkeys in the Garden Zoologique de Bronx," Vandes wrote to Hornaday. "If you would sell him to me not too dear for I am not rich. If he is in good condition write me his age and the care he ought to have and if we are able to understand ourselves. I would then send some one to see him and discuss the price of purchase." [15]

Ten days later, Hornaday would forward the letter to Verner to gauge his interest: "I refer to you this enclosed letter (but without being sure that it will interest you) and I will inform Mademoiselle Josephine Vandes." [16]

There is no record of Verner's response.

Benga, a global sensation, was also invited to attend a show at the opulent Hippodrome, a one-year-old, 5,300-seat theater on Sixth Avenue named for the famous Greek stadium and billed as the world's largest theater.

On Tuesday, September 18, Hornaday politely declined the invitation. He was afraid that Benga had already received too much attention. He likewise declined an offer from a self-described "colored manicurist" to groom Benga's nails.

Benga had also become a poet's muse. On Wednesday, September 19, the *Times* published a poem by M. E. Buhler that captured the frenzy and frivolity of the episode:

> From his native land of darkness,
> To the country of the free,
> In the interest of science
> And of broad humanity,

Brought wee little Ota Benga,
Dwarfed, benighted, without guile,
Scarcely more than ape or monkey,
Yet a man the while!

So, to tutor and enlighten—
Fit him for a nobler sphere—
Show him ways of truth and knowledge
Teach the freedom we have here

In this land of foremost progress—
In this Wisdom's ripest age
We have placed him in high honor,

In a monkey's cage!
'Mid companions we provide him,
Apes, gorillas, chimpanzees
He's content! Wherefore decry them

When he seems at ease?
So he chatters and he jabbers
In his jargon, asking naught
But for "Money—money—money!"[17]

However, the next day the *Times* wavered regarding its position on Benga's plight. In an editorial worthy of Hamlet, it questioned whether Verner had a right to determine Benga's fate.

"Ota Benga is not a child or a slave," the editorial said of the penniless and debased foreign captive who spoke limited English and who was, against his wishes, living in a monkey house.[18]

"He is, of course, a human being, of a sort, with enough intelligence, apparently, to have a more or less effectual word as to his own disposition," the editorial said. While it did not indicate just how he would do that without money, language skills, or even, as far as anyone knew, a way to return home, the painstakingly measured exposition expressed doubt that Benga would be better off in an orphanage, or in a family unfamiliar with ethnology, than in the care of Hornaday. However, it added, "It is not pleasant to think of Ota Benga as an object of jeering curiosity that suggests only too successfully [to] the crowd that he is an animal."[19]

However, the editorial predicted that this sort of "public interest" would soon subside, "and it may be that this pigmy could develop all his possibilities where he is. This view of the matter, however, is scientific rather than humane, and the colored Baptists could raise several objections to it that might be, or pass as, valid if judiciously presented in court."[20]

The carefully modulated editorial distilled the dilemma Benga's captivity posed for many among New York's white elite. Given the negative view of Africans promoted by the era's leading scientists, including the Zoological Society's own Osborn, Benga's captivity did not offend the sensibilities of those convinced that he belonged to a human subspecies, if he was human at all. Even so, given the controversy, even those who were in accord with the exhibition, as the editors of the *Times* had initially appeared to be, were made uneasy.

That day the *New York Age,* the feisty and influential African American newspaper, became one of the first to characterize Benga as an "inmate" and an unwilling captive. It was published by Timothy Thomas Fortune, the civil rights activist and orator, who was one of the most prominent African American journalists of the era. The *Age* had a front-page story under a prominent headline:

OTA BENGA TO BE RESCUED

AND EDUCATED BY PREACHERS

African Pygmy Was Exhibited in Monkey Cage at the Zoo

On Benga's tenth day in captivity, a tall African American zoo attendant was assigned to him, probably as an indication that zoo officials were by now sensitive to the racially fraught scandal and were seeking to quell tension. The attendant waved away spectators as he led Benga into the woods.

Meanwhile, "public interest"—the euphemism employed by the *Times'* editors to describe the pursuit of Benga by violent mobs—continued to flourish. That Friday a crowd invaded the park and pursued Benga as he ambled through the woods. Benga ran toward the monkey house, then abruptly stopped to fire an arrow, striking a red-haired pursuer who called for vengeance.

As Benga aimed to fire another arrow, he was thwarted by a keeper and locked in the monkey house. Sometime that day Hornaday received more unwelcome news. Verner sent a wire at 8:30 A.M. saying that he would be further delayed by a flood.

"Coming as soon as possible," he said, asking Hornaday to execute instructions authorizing him to wire money from the purchase of the chimpanzee to the Guardian Trust Company to settle the debt that had resulted in a warrant for Verner's arrest. "Keep two hundred for me. Pay rest to Trust Company," Verner instructed.

Hornaday sent a wire informing Verner that he would wire money without delay, but urgently added: "How about pigmy?"

Verner's character, heretofore an afterthought, was now a consuming concern for an increasingly distressed Hornaday. Who was this odd person who would deliver an African and a monkey to the Bronx Zoo and nonchalantly leave town without notice? It was clear he had financial troubles, but when would he retrieve his problem "pygmy"?

As the crisis deepened, Hornaday, like a child who had consumed too much ice cream and is suddenly stricken, was pitifully, if belatedly, contrite.

"Situation about boy is unendurable," he wired to Verner. "Do hurry."[21]

NINE

NATURE'S FURY

On Tuesday, September 18, a major storm was barreling toward North Carolina, where Verner awaited news from the Bronx about Benga. As tension mounted in the zoological gardens, a treacherous typhoon and tsunami in Hong Kong killed ten thousand people. That was the latest of several natural disasters during the year, beginning with two earthquakes: one on April 16 in Chile that killed twenty thousand people, and another two days later in San Francisco that killed four thousand and destroyed much of the city.

Now, as if one with Benga, ninety-mile-per-hour gusts hurtled across the South. Two hundred people were stranded in Wrightsville Beach, North Carolina; buildings were damaged in Charleston; a crew on board a schooner was stranded for two days without food. By the time the storm ended, seven people had been killed and $2 million in damages—roughly $51 million in today's dollars—had been reported in the Carolinas.

On Wednesday, September 19, another storm appeared as a tropical depression in the Caribbean Sea. Verner said Brevard was water-bound owing to a "tremendous rise" in the French Broad River. He said the entire valley was a lake and he had no way to get to the railway located six miles away.

"I am of course anxious for news about Ota Benga," Verner said in a letter to Hornaday.[1]

"I did not wish to have the appearance of running with him from criticism," he said. Hornaday probably bristled at Verner's curious suggestion that Benga "appears to be entirely happy and content."[2]

However, Verner advised Hornaday: "If he should become too nervous, a dose of some sedative might be good, as I frequently found in the estatic frenzies which sometimes occur among the natives in Africa; tho I never had to use any for him."[3]

Whether or not this advice was heeded cannot be determined, as Hornaday does not discuss the matter in his correspondence and no records of Benga's medication or meals have been recovered.

Verner enclosed another letter for Benga:

Mbye, Moiyo! Fwela Kutuma moiyo abungi. Yandi Kusala mu-dima kwa musoko wa yandi kwa komona suba kwa wewe Mutalka mikusi yandi kula kiva kubikila wewe, ne Kula Kwa mosoko wa yandi. Wewe kushikima pola malengila. Moiyo.—
Mulaunda yebi. Fwela

"*Mbye, Moiyo!*"—Greetings, Mbye—is one of the first indications that Ota Benga is not the African captive's full name. During his voyage to the United States, the name that appeared on the ship's passenger record is Mbye Otabenga. In letters directed to Benga, Verner often addressed him as Mbye, but he did not appear to use the appellation when referring to Benga to others. In any event, Benga's age, his tribal affiliation, and the circumstances of their meeting would continually change in public accounts offered by Verner.

In the letter Verner told Benga that he was looking for a woman

and asked if Benga could help him find her. He said that there was no
way to come for him now but that he would come in a few days. He
again counseled Benga to remain calm.[4]

Verner urged Hornaday not to be alarmed by any "restlessness"
on Benga's part. "I shall come for him as soon as I can," he said, in-
structing Hornaday to send a check for $275 to pay his debt to the
Guardian Trust Company with the purchase of his chimpanzee by
the zoo.

On Thursday another storm raged along the Gulf Coast and
across the South, claiming at least 134 lives. More than 300,000 bales
of cotton were destroyed in Mississippi; Lake Pontchartrain over-
flowed, flooding New Orleans. Vessels were sunk or swept ashore;
railroads and wharves were torn asunder; and roofs, like windswept
hats, were ripped from buildings. Verner blamed the storm for "stopping the mail carrier, breaking the railway, and doing all sorts of
damage."

"Of course you are doing your best for Ota Benga," Verner wrote
to Hornday. "Do not be unduly disturbed by any restlessness on his
part."

While Hornaday prayed for the storm to pass, and Benga's captivity and the Brownsville affair inflamed the passions of blacks across
the nation, another type of tempest was brewing in Atlanta, Georgia.
A series of articles alleging that black men had attacked white women
put the city on edge. The stories came in the midst of a vitriolic gu-
bernatorial campaign in which black men were targeted by a white
electorate ill at ease with Atlanta's flourishing African American
middle class.

Atlanta, with its thriving black businesses and the nation's highest
concentration of educated blacks, was also home to leading black institutions of higher learning, among them Morehouse, Spelman, and
Morris Brown colleges and Atlanta University, where that summer
Franz Boas—against a rising tide of racial terror, disenfranchisement,
and despair—delivered a heartening commencement address. At the

invitation of the scholar and activist W. E. B. Du Bois, he reminded African Americans of their glorious African past.

Boas evoked a continent of thriving civilizations—replete with artistic and architectural achievements, military prowess, and innovation.

"While much of the history of early invention is shrouded in darkness, it seems likely that at a time when the European was still satisfied with rude stone tools, the African had invented or adopted the act of smelting iron," Boas proclaimed.[5] "To those who stoutly maintain a material inferiority of the Negro race and who would dampen your ardor by their claims, you may confidently reply that the burden of proof rests with them, that the past history of your race does not sustain their statement, but rather gives you encouragement."

But it was a daunting future that concerned many blacks. All summer Hoke Smith, a lawyer and former owner of the *Atlanta-Journal*, ran on a platform of black political disenfranchisement, appealing to white fear. He equated black enfranchisement with sexual attacks on white women and declared, "We are the superior race and do not intend to be ruled by our semi-barbaric inferiors."[6] His leading opponent was Clark Howell, publisher of the *Atlanta Constitution*, who insisted that his opponent was ill equipped to control the menacing black male. Each man used his own platform to ramp up votes and newspaper sales. That August, Smith emerged the winner in a landslide. Although the race had come to an end, Atlanta's newspapers continued to run hysterical headlines accusing black men of raping and molesting white women. Eventually, Atlantans awakened to front-page headlines decrying yet another black-on-white assault. "Half-Clad Negro Tries to Break into House" was splashed across the front page of the *Atlanta Journal*, and throughout the day city papers ran extras announcing additional assaults.

As with New York's newspaper coverage of Benga's exhibition, Atlanta's newspapers would play a lead role in their city's sensation. But Atlanta's newspapers would go even further: they were not merely hecklers. They would actually spur the action on the streets.

"Two Assaults," read one eight-column headline in the *Atlanta Evening News* that Saturday.

"Third Assault," read a later edition.

"Extra! Third Assault on White Woman by a Negro Brute," newsboys shouted in downtown Atlanta's Five Points district. "Extra! Bold Negro Kisses White Girl's Hand!"

All afternoon bands of furious white men, some waving copies of the newspapers, gathered in the wilting heat on Decatur Street. By nightfall the restless crowd had swelled to more than five thousand white males of all ages. Hours of venomous chatter finally erupted into riots as men raced through the streets clubbing, shooting, and stabbing black passersby, and ransacking and destroying black-owned shops.

During four days of rioting, more than twenty-five blacks and two whites were killed, kindling fear and dread among the nation's African Americans. More than one thousand African Americans fled the city, including the editor of the *Voice of the Negro*, who was threatened because he had told the *New York World* that the riots were caused by "sensational newspapers and unscrupulous politicians." Months later, many African Americans were enraged that forty blacks had been imprisoned and charged in the shooting death of an officer while only twenty whites were jailed and merely charged with rioting, despite the deaths of two dozen African Americans.[7]

Meanwhile, international interest in Benga intensified, with requests for illustrations and interviews pouring into the Zoological Society from across the country and Europe. Hornaday continued to milk the publicity. In a letter to London's *Sketch* on September 27 he said, "I have much pleasure in sending you, by this mail, a photograph of our pigmy, in accordance with your request of September 15th. Ota Benga is really a very interesting little man, and is undoubtedly a genuine pigmy."[8]

Hornaday asked the editor not to believe accounts reported in the American press, claiming that they had been manufactured by the "colored" ministers.

"He was seen in a cage only three times and each time entered of his own accord and for his own purposes," Hornaday deceptively maintained. "Once he was actually seen in the cage with the Orangutan, playing with the creature, because of his friendliness for the animal. This is absolutely all there is of truth in the great hot-weather sensation."[9]

This new version of events, of course, contradicted previous accounts by Hornaday, who at the outset had boasted of the exhibit, alerted the media, posted a sign, littered the cage with bones, set hours, and written an article in the *Zoological Society Bulletin*. His newly fabricated narrative also defied the thousands of eyewitnesses, and the dozens of newspaper articles that the exhibition had inspired.

An editorial in the *New York Times* blamed Benga for the brouhaha at the park. The editors reasoned that since Benga, with the aid of black Baptist ministers, was released from a monkey house cage he, and not raucous park-goers, had become a public nuisance.

The *Times* humorously recalled the run-in with Benga's red-haired attacker, and offered a prophecy: "The red-headed man [...] will no doubt have a shining place in the legend, his flaming finial growing in time into a halo against which the whole drama, transfigured and sublimated, will float like a sun-kindled mirage in the desert."[10] The editors predicted that the man would hold a place "in what may turn out to be a particularly interesting mythology."[11]

The *Chicago Tribune* joined the lighthearted banter over Benga's predicament under the headline: "Tiny Savage Sees New York; Sneers."[12] Three thousand miles away, the *Los Angeles Times* covered the sensation on Sunday, September 23, under the headline: "Genuine Pigymy Is Ota Banga: Can Talk with Orangoutang in New York."

The *Indianapolis Sun* reported that Ota Benga, "the South African pigmy," was "more man than beast."[13] The following Monday the *Times* ran an article in which John F. Vane-Tempest, who described himself as an African explorer, contested the zoo's classification of Benga as a pygmy. Under the headline "What Is Ota Benga?" Vane-

Tempest said that on the basis of his experience, Benga was actually a southern African Hottentot. He claimed to have conducted a conversation with Benga "in the tongue of the Hottentots." He also alleged that Benga told him: "He liked the white man's country, where he was treated as a King, had a cozy room, a splendid room in a palace full of monkeys, and enjoyed all the comforts of home except a few wives."[14] The preposterous account was, nonetheless, presented as a straightforward news story. Vane-Tempest may well have been the same man identified eight years later as a real estate broker arrested in an embezzlement case, also reported by the New York Times.

In the midst of a frenzied free-for-all in which articles, editorials, and letters ranged from curious to outlandish, Mount Olivet's Reverend Matthew Gilbert wrote to the New York Times from the South to say that Benga's captivity had ignited African Americans' outrage across the country. "Only prejudice against the negro race made such a thing possible in this country," Gilbert said. "I have had occasion to travel abroad, and I am confident that such a thing would not have been tolerated a day in any other civilized country."[15]

He enclosed a sober statement from a committee of the Ministers' Union of Charlotte, North Carolina, that he said had been unanimously adopted. It read: "We regard the actors or authorities in this most reprehensible conduct as offering an unpardonable insult to humanity, and especially to the religion of our Lord Jesus Christ."[16]

But others were not so sure. The Minneapolis Journal published a photograph of Benga holding a monkey, and preposterously claimed, "He is about as near an approach to the missing link as any human species yet found."[17] Despite the protests, this newspaper reported that Benga was still living in the monkey house "and really enjoyed associating with the simians from his home jungles."[18]

TEN

DELIVERANCE

On Monday morning, September 24, Benga quietly watched keepers hose down the monkey cage in preparation for the park opening. As the park gates were set to swing open, Benga, either for his own amusement, or out of desire for a bath, or, more likely, as an act of rebellion, set off a panic by beginning to disrobe.

A handler prevented the unwelcome display, but Benga returned within minutes brandishing a carving knife, and it would take three men to subdue and disarm him. The handlers then confined him to his cage for the rest of the morning.[1]

And so began another day at the Bronx Zoo as Hornaday awaited the return of Samuel Verner. It had been two and a half weeks since Benga burst into public view and he continued to captivate the public; letters and humorous articles were published every day. In Hornaday's view, as he wrote to Miss D. E. Villah Gray, a colored manicurist, who offered to groom Benga's nails: "The pigmy has already achieved so much notoriety. It is best to keep him somewhat in the background."

Benga's latest rebellion, in which he brandished a knife, prompted the *Times* to report that he had "let some of the savage nature of the African forest come out."[2]

On September 26, with protests mounting, the city controller's office sent an official to investigate a report that the zookeepers were accepting payments to permit visitors to enter Benga's sleeping quarters. The unnamed inspector visited Benga, whom he found clad in a khaki suit and a soft gray cap. He remarked on Benga's "boyish appearance" and described him as an African native who park visitors believed was "some sort of a wild man who can understand monkey talk."[3] He concluded: "Without attempting to discuss the intellectual accomplishments or demerits of the gentleman, it may be stated that to the unscientific mind this native of Darkest Africa does not materially differ in outward appearance at least from some of the natives of darkest New York." He also was skeptical about claims that Benga's intellect was stunted and that he could understand the chattering monkeys. He said that he would be more convinced of Benga's arrested development if Benga did not speak some English, and that if Benga could understand the monkeys "he kept the secret well to himself."[4]

The tide continued to turn against Hornaday and the Zoological Society, with heated objections to Benga's captivity being printed even in the pages of the *Times*, which had previously appeared either indifferent to or supportive of the exhibition. But as protests mounted, the *Times*' position began to waver.

On Friday, September 28, the *Times* published a letter from Reginald Jevons, who characterized Benga's captivity as "ruthless disregard for a stranger's comfort, however low that stranger may be in the scale of humanity." Calling Benga "an unfortunate being among us," Jevons added that "as the public treat him, his life cannot be but a misery."

He concluded: "Such a spectacle is far from our National ideals, and should not be tolerated."[5]

Even southerners leaped at the opportunity to mock New Yorkers for the unseemly display.

Louisiana's *Lafayette Advertiser* described it as "A Northern Outrage." Characterizing Benga's plight as an offense against "the brother in black," the *Advertiser* noted that this time the "diabolical deed" was being committed in New York. "Yes, in the sacred city of New York where almost daily mobs find exciting sport in chasing negroes through the streets without much being said about it."[6]

One could only imagine the uproar had a human being been displayed in a cage with an ape in the South, the article went on. "[Theodore] Roosevelt, whose heart is beating strongly for the colored man as the congressional elections approach, would have ordered the federal district attorney to prosecute and imprison for violation of the laws against peonage every person implicated in the outrage." But with Benga a star attraction in the monkey cage "there was no thundering from Oyster Bay against the outrage and no orders to prosecute anybody." (Oyster Bay was Roosevelt's Long Island residence.)

As controversy swirled around Hornaday, there was at least one sign that his reputation would survive the scandal. That week the New York Academy of Sciences invited him to serve on a subcommittee bringing together exhibits "as would be representative of the advance of zoological work in recent years."[7]

Finally on the afternoon of Friday, September 28, Benga, escorted by the long-overdue Verner, bade farewell to the zoo. Benga asked to say good-bye to the attendants, to whom he gave his arrows, reserving the bow for the chief keeper.

Hornaday breathed a sigh of relief as Verner quietly left the park with the person who had first been exhibited in a cage twenty days earlier. The exhibition had contributed to a doubling of park attendance compared with the preceding year. Some 220,800 people had visited the park in September and nearly all, if not all of them, had seen Benga.[8]

Benga's departure would be as calm and contained as his debut was frenetic and flamboyant. Hornaday apparently did not wish to invite the fanfare that had accompanied the debut. No reporters were alerted to witness Benga's farewell.

Benga, wearing the same khaki uniform with gold buttons as the attendants, would be quietly lifted from the bowels of debasement in the Bronx Zoo monkey house to the height of African American achievement in Brooklyn's Weeksville section. There, he would enter the city's largest and most affluent African American community, complete with schools, churches, businesses, doctors, lawyers, and teachers steeped in Victorian ideals, to live in a finely appointed orphanage. Gordon was ecstatic.

"He looks like a rather dwarfed colored boy of unusual amiability and curiosity," Gordon said.[9] "Now our plan is this: We are going to treat him as a visitor. We have given him a room to himself, where he can smoke if he chooses."

Concerns had been raised by relatives about the welfare of the children residing at the orphanage once Benga—who had routinely been described in the press as a savage cannibal—arrived. "Why he'll eat my Matilda alive," one anguished mother told Gordon.[10]

Gordon assured anxious relatives that Benga would not board with the children, and that he would dine with the cooks in the kitchen. Gordon said Benga had already learned a surprising number of English words and would soon be able to express himself.

"This," he asserted, "will be the beginning of his education."[11]

PART II

CAPTURED

ELEVEN

SAMUEL PHILLIPS VERNER

The humiliating episode in the Bronx was only the latest trauma in Benga's life since his encounter with the peculiar man who had taken him from his homeland and left him at the zoo. Just who was this man who had dropped a bomb on the city and lurked in the shadows as it exploded?

By all accounts Samuel Phillips Verner had been a very bright boy. He was born in 1873 into an aristocratic slaveholding family on the Conneross Plantation in Oconee County, South Carolina. The state was the only one in the union where the majority of the legislators had been slaveholders, and it had been the first to secede following Abraham Lincoln's election.

Verner came of age at the time of a stormy backlash against black political and economic gains made during Reconstruction. In the decade following emancipation South Carolina's well-organized black majority elected eight of its own candidates to the House of Representatives. Blacks had also assumed positions as students, faculty members, and trustees at South Carolina College, which would

later become the University of South Carolina. But President Rutherford B. Hayes's removal of federal troops from the South in 1877
would return South Carolina's government to the Democrats and
white-minority rule.

By the age of three Verner—known to his family and friends
as Phillips—had already attended white supremacy rallies with his
father, a member of a South Carolina legislature rabidly devoted to
black disenfranchisement. The end of a leisurely life cushioned by
slavery was a cruel reality for many whites, who struck back as the
Ku Klux Klan. That blacks had long been the majority in South
Carolina intensified whites' fears and stiffened their resolve. From
the floor of the U.S. Senate, Benjamin Tillman, the former governor
and a friend of the Verner family, brazenly boasted that whites in
his state had suppressed the black vote. "We stuffed ballot boxes, we
bulldozed niggers and we shot em," he said, adding: "And we are not
ashamed." [1]

The return to power of Democrats in South Carolina meant the
imposition of poll taxes, literacy tests, and other measures that for decades restricted voting and jury duty to whites.

At an early age, the scholarly Verner felt deeply his responsibility to rechart his family's destiny. His heritage was one of accomplishment: not only was his father a lawyer and six-term legislator
and later comptroller general of South Carolina, but his maternal
grandfather was president of the University of North Carolina and
his uncle Samuel Phillips was president of Stillman Theological
Seminary and would later become U.S. solicitor general. In addition
to U.S. senator Benjamin Tillman, family friends included Atlanta's
newly elected governor, Hoke Smith; and Alabama's U.S. senator
John Tyler Morgan—men who shared his family's white supremacist ideals.

The firstborn of nine, Verner effortlessly climbed his way to the
top of his class at South Carolina College. By then the school, given

the diligent application of Jim Crow throughout the state, was once again exclusively white. Gone was Richard T. Greener, Harvard's first African American graduate, who in 1873 became South Carolina College's first black professor and librarian. Gone too were the African American members of the school's board of trustees. The school had not yet regained its pre–Civil War eminence as a training ground for the state's elite and had largely become an industrial school.

In 1892, at age nineteen, Verner graduated at the top of his class. As a member of the southern gentry, he was intent on assuming his rightful place in the hierarchy of men. But his celebration was short-lived. Verner would end the school year with the first of many mental collapses. Since childhood he had been befriended by phantoms. One of his earliest childhood companions was Tweedledee, perhaps inspired by the character in *Through the Looking-Glass*. Now Verner was convinced that he was a Hapsburg emperor. With his path to fame and fortune blocked by fits of delusion, he spent nearly a year working in the carpentry shop of J. P. Morgan's Southern Railway in Columbia, South Carolina.

The setback did not quell Verner's ambition. By 1894, Verner, with the help of his uncle, was well enough to land a teaching position at the Tuscaloosa Institute in Tuscaloosa, Alabama. The small school was founded in 1875 by Presbyterian pastor Charles Stillman and authorized by the General Assembly of the Presbyterian Church to train the black clergy. By then Verner's uncle had succeeded Stillman as superintendent, and William Sheppard, one of its graduates, had achieved fame as the "Black Livingstone" for the Presbyterian mission he had cofounded in the Congo. In 1895, a year after Verner's arrival, the school would change its name in Stillman's honor.

Verner had read *Robinson Crusoe* as a child, and while he was working for the railroad he read the travel books of David Livingstone and Henry Morton Stanley. Like many other Americans, Verner was dazzled by Stanley's daring African adventures in 1871 and his search for the missing explorer David Livingstone. On finding him, Stanley claimed to have said, "Dr. Livingstone, I presume?" a line that famously came to epitomize his poise and wit.

Verner wanted to go to Africa himself to achieve fame and fortune. During his two years at Stillman, he had made an impression on the founder's widow, Annie Stillman. She wrote to Verner's mother to report on her son's "unusual endowments." Around him she "trembled as in the presence of a force whose outcome I could not calculate."[2]

By then the Presbyterians' Board of World Missions was in dire need of white missionaries in the Congo. Samuel Lapsley, the Congo mission's white cofounder, had died of malaria in 1892, and his black cofounder William Sheppard had been propelled into a leadership role. But Sheppard's race proved a challenge, given the need to conduct business with Belgian officials and traders. The mission board was anxious for a white presence. For a time, it seemed that the problem had been solved. Shortly after Lapsley's death George D. Adamson and his wife arrived of the Luebo mission, and they were soon joined by Reverend Arthur Rowbotham of Scotland and Reverend DeWitt Clinton Snyder, from Brooklyn, along with their wives. But by September 1894 illness forced Rowbotham to return home, and five months later, Adamson's wife died, causing him to leave as well. On May 27, 1896, Snyder's wife died, prompting him to leave also.

The mission was once again without a white presence and Dr. Samuel Chester, executive secretary of the Board of World Missions, issued an urgent call for white recruits. He said it was "absolutely necessary" to have one white man "and very desirable that we have at least two" given relations with the state.

In an appeal posted in *The Missionary*, the board's news organ, Chester noted that more "colored men . . . are offering than we are able to send, but at present no white man is offering for the African work."[3]

But twenty-one-year-old Verner was eager to answer the call. Fortunately for him, family connections and the mission's urgent need for white recruits enabled him to bypass the usual three-year course of seminary study following his four years of college, provided that he passed the examinations. After a few weeks of study Verner was tested on three years of seminary training that included Latin, Greek, Hebrew, mental and moral philosophy, rhetoric, natural science, theology, church history, church government, and the sacraments. He managed to pass all except Hebrew, but once again, owing to the urgent need for his services, that requirement was waived and he was licensed under the provision for extraordinary cases.

On September 25, 1895, young Verner was ordained a Presbyterian minister and assigned by the Committee on Foreign Missions of the General Assembly of the Presbyterian Church to serve in the Congo. Less than three weeks later he applied for a passport, giving his occupation as "clergyman."

As he set out for Africa the young clergyman began to expose his ruthless ambition. He had already considered the role Africa should play in a Caucasian ascendancy. "Africa must be made a stronghold of Caucasian power, of Christianity, of European and American civilization rather than a cess-pool of Asiatic vice and corruption," he would later write, describing his thinking during his first voyage to Africa.[4]

He left New York Harbor on the liner *New York* in 1895, accompanied by Joseph E. Phipps, a native of the Caribbean island St. Christopher (St. Kitts) who had emigrated to Scranton, Pennsylvania. Phipps's grandfather had been born in the Congo and his parents in St. Kitts, where Phipps had worked as a rum distiller. According to an article in the Presbyterian newspaper *The Evangelist*, Phipps went to Scranton "as a 'Museum freak,' exhibiting himself as a dancer upon broken glass and fire."[5] He ended up in the city's Rescue Mission, where he was converted; eventually he attended the Moody Bible Institute in Chicago before being ordained by the Presbytery and appointed to the Congo mission. Like Verner, Phipps was appointed to a foreign mission without the requisite four years of college and three years of seminary study. According to *The Evangelist*, despite his "earnest spirit and knowledge of the Scripture" and the "loveliness of his disposition," Phipps "was utterly innocent of Latin, Greek and Hebrew."[6] Unlike Verner, he had not even graduated from college.

Still, the Presbyterian board dispatched Verner to Scranton, Pennsylvania, to meet his new colleague and attend Phipps's ordination before the two set sail for the Congo. While Verner's passport application dated October 1895 identified him as a clergyman, the ship's passenger list identified Reverend S. P. Verner as a missionary.

The two arrived in Southhampton, England, on October 31, 1895, and by January 1896 they had made stops in London for orientation and to be outfitted with appropriate clothing. They then went to Antwerp, where they boarded the *Roquelle*, a British cargo ship that Verner described as overcrowded with missionaries, traders, army officers, and Ashanti chieftains. Verner noted with surprise that Africans dined with their white shipmates.

The ship stopped in Madeira, Sierra Leone, Liberia, Gold Coast, Cameroon, and Boda before arriving in Matadi, a stone-lined village and entryway into the Congo basin 180 miles from the open sea. Along the way, Phipps became seasick, prompting Verner to complain that he had become a "booby-nurse to my negro companion. O, the helplessness of that race is simply appalling."[7]

Verner remained in Matadi for six months, boarding with Swedish missionaries and observing operations of state and church officials. While others, including British consul Roger Casement, described Matadi during that period as a humid, mosquito-infested site of mass starvation and open graves, Verner saw salient possibilities for white imperialism.

"The land which all the nations of history could not conquer at last has thrown open its doors, given up the keys of its treasure house, and over the crumbling dust of the heroes who died that it might live, the invincible Caucasian is marching on,' " he wrote.[8]

In February he made a brief trip to Luanda, the capital of Angola, to explore the prospect of establishing a sanatorium, perhaps out of his fear of another mental collapse or possibly to treat the prevalent tropical illnesses that had befallen many white explorers.

Before leaving Matadi Verner recorded his observations in a fourteen-page typed letter to the Mission Committee, in which he critiqued the Presbyterian operation. Noting that "the negro is inferior to the Anglo-Saxon," he found the mission deficient owing to the presence of black missionaries, who he said were not respected by the Congo state authorities. He complained that they could not be left alone and "require to be taken care of." [9]

Later, recalling his African journey, he wrote: "The expanding genius of the Caucasian race is the marvel of modern times." [10] However, he believed African Americans were well suited to work in the African continent because of their resistance to the sun and malaria and their "phlegmatic temperament" and "simplicity and earnest sincerity." [11] However, Verner advised that the salary of a colored missionary should be less "being commensurate with his capacity" and that his responsibilities be clearly delineated and his appointment be made probationary. In other words, Verner believed that black missionaries should have the same second-class status that they had in the American South.

In an article later published in *The Missionary*, he assured readers that the work at home and in the field would be under the supervision of "capable and sympathetic white men until success is fully assured." [12] A staunch defender of his South Carolina heritage, Verner was an avowed and unapologetic racist who later described himself as "the son of slave owners . . . educated in the cradle of secession." [13]

En route to Luebo, Verner traveled another 1,200 miles inland on the developing Congo Railway to the end of the line. He then trekked on foot for several weeks, stopping in Stanley Pool and studying brickmaking before catching a steamer up the Kasai River. In August 1896 Verner arrived at the Presbyterian Church's Luebo Mission.

Set against a hilly backdrop, the mission was by then a cultivated paradise of manicured lawns; flower-lined walls; bountiful mango, guava, banana, and citrus trees; and palm-thatched homes. The idyllic tropical setting was occasionally marred by a parade of emaciated Africans, chained together by their necks, caught in the widespread slave trade to work for the state. But where Verner expected to find invincible Caucasians, he instead found an all-black mission led by the tall and swashbuckling William Sheppard.

TWELVE

LUEBO MISSION

porting a pith helmet and gleaming white linen, the tall, muscular thirty-year-old William Sheppard was a vision of rugged masculinity and Victorian refinement. He bore few traces of his humble West Virginia roots. At Luebo, in the heart of Africa, he and his wife, Lucy, resided in a gracious five-room house with a low veranda and large white pillars. There he had presided over the rise of the mission from uncultivated territory to a landscaped compound with a church, school, and missionaries' homes. In Sheppard's amiable black presence Verner's disorientation gave way to the charm of southern hospitality as he feasted on Lucy Sheppard's chicken and biscuits and fell under the couple's spell.

"One could almost imagine himself, save for a few details, in old Virginia again," Verner wrote, waxing nostalgic, in a later account. "My welcome was all that heart could desire."[1]

A combination of good fortune and steely determination had enabled Sheppard to clear the hurdles set before an ambitious black boy coming of age in the Jim Crow South.

His road to the helm of the Presbyterian mission had been rocky and steep. Still, as the son of a barber and a mother who tended women at an upscale spa, he was exposed to opportunities rarely afforded young southern blacks. By the age of fifteen he had held a number of jobs to pay his way in night school at Hampton Institute, the industrial school for blacks in Hampton, Virginia. There Booker T. Washington was one of his teachers.

Sheppard graduated from Hampton in 1883, and then from Tuscaloosa Theological in 1886. For two years, now an ordained minister, he served as a pastor of Zion Presbyterian Church in Atlanta, and throughout those two years he requested a missionary post in Africa. However, he was eventually told that Presbyterian officials believed a single black man in the African interior would require white supervision. In 1890, at age twenty-four, after brief stints as a pastor in Tuscaloosa and Atlanta, he was finally commissioned to serve as a missionary in the Congo. By then the U.S. Presbyterian Foreign Mission had found him a willing white partner.

Their task was to build a post where no other mission had been. Other missions had been established in the lower Kasai region, but they set their sights on a remote section in the upper Kasai. At the time the region had few businesses and not much of a foreign presence. Once settled they were to build a school, church, and homes from which to spread Christianity through the Congo.

They arrived in Africa in May 1890, just two months before George Washington Williams would write his damning letter to King Leopold. It would take another ten months before they arrived in picturesque Luebo, a sparsely populated town of palm trees, luxuriant rubber forests, and rolling hills and valleys where cheering crowds welcomed them from the shore.

It was a striking contrast to the scenes of death, disease, and cruelty that had marked their way there: emaciated Congolese crewmen being brutally whipped; villagers who greeted them as if they were alien invaders, fearing that they would rape their women and steal their men for labor. On their way to Luebo they had seen villages burned by the state's Force Publique and starving laborers bound together by chains around their necks.

In Luebo they were warmly embraced by the Kete, a community of farmers and hunters. Over the next few weeks the two men explored the Kwango and Kasai Rivers and acquainted themselves with local people and customs. Among the Kete they found lawyers and judges, but also discerned a reverence for the Kuba, a tall, proud, aristocratic people attired in elaborately decorated kilts.

The Kuba were wealthy traders of ivory, gold, and rubber and their royal kingdom remained hidden from foreign explorers. For nine years attempted expeditions into the kingdom failed as explorers were confounded by a maze of secret paths.

Sheppard and Samuel Lapsley planned to uncover the kingdom together, but during a business trip in 1892 Lapsley unexpectedly succumbed to malaria, leaving Sheppard alone in charge of the mission. A day later, a devastated Sheppard soldiered on and discovered the celebrated Kuba kingdom.

In an episode that resembled a fairy tale, Sheppard was hailed as a member of the Kuba royalty and as the reincarnation of a long-dead king, Bope Mekabe. Among the Kuba—in the land of the Bushongo—he discovered an aristocratic community of skilled weavers, embroiderers, wood-carvers, and other artisans whose technology and culture had for centuries rivaled Europe's and whose artworks would later be displayed in the world's elite museums. Sheppard's discovery brought him induction into the British Royal Academy, international fame, and an audience with the queen.

However, although he was revered by the Kuba, Sheppard was snubbed by the Belgian officials and traders who controlled the import of food and supplies to the country's interior. As the newest recruit Verner was assigned to manage the mission's business affairs. Verner was in charge of the mail, transportation, the ordering of goods, and interactions with state officials and trading companies. He was, in essence, a white face on a mostly black mission that struggled to maintain a biracial team. Verner, however, fancied himself as a leader who had taken Lapsley's place.[2]

Verner successfully secured food, clothing, and other supplies from the Belgian traders and reorganized the delivery of mail and goods by relocating the mail station. He credited Phipps, his black fellow missionary, with building a new transport station, saying that "he performed his business duties and correspondence with surprising intelligence and accuracy."[3]

By November 1896 Verner had begun to consider other possibilities outside the mission. He reached out to the Smithsonian and offered it his services collecting artifacts. "If I live, I hope to return to America in three years," he noted in an odd letter to a Smithsonian official. "I do not wish to load myself with what would be of little value to you; and if you can indicate what you think I might get that would be specially acceptable, . . . I would be able to proceed more intelligently."[4]

He also contributed a number of peculiarly un-missionary-like articles to *The Missionary* under the byline "Rev. S. P. Verner." In one, he offered the observation that African women, like Italian women, are very attractive when young "and abominably ugly" when old.[5]

He shared his impressions of a woman named Queta, "who ran ten miles to meet me," describing her as heavyset with a kindly face, industrious, and cleanly in appearance, and adding that she "knows the virtues of hospitality also."

Three decades after the Civil War and the abolition of slavery, Verner continued to see potential in Africans as "the great coming laboring class of the world," with Caucasians as the "directing powers."

Apparently oblivious to history or the winds of change, following the Civil War and emancipation of enslaved African Americans he asserted: "I believe this is his destiny, and that he should be specially prepared for it."

Verner had no patience for the "sickly sentimentality" that inspired many missions to train African natives. The major work should be to evangelize. "You can no more intrinsically elevate the African with a calico dress than an American with a broadcloth suit."

By the spring of 1897 the restless Verner was bored by mundane tasks and frustrated by "the abominable and senseless 'system,' " which, he complained, required him to spend more time arranging for the transport and purchase of needed supplies than preaching. "If I don't break up this so-called system, I'll try to get up and run a Mission on my own," he wrote in a letter to his mother on his twenty-second birthday.[6]

It was fate when a commercial agent informed Verner of a village king's need for a white mediator. Eager to attain—like Sheppard—his own glory, Verner set out for the village, which he identified as Ndombe, some sixty miles southwest and five days away. He did not go alone; he had an entourage of about eighty people. Among the ragtag crew of Luebo villagers were Kondola and Kassongo, two young boys living at the mission who had apparently been orphaned during the war with the Belgian troops. The group also included Congolese men who carried Verner's hammock and other supplies and trading goods.

They traveled by canoes across the Lulua River and waded through streams before they arrived at Ndombe, actually a cluster of bucolic villages situated on the Lubi River near Wissmann Falls on the upper Kasai River. Verner described it as "the finest town I had yet seen and a marvel of cleanliness and order." Verner and his entourage were greeted by a man also called Ndombe, whom he described as six feet five inches tall, with broad shoulders, a regal bearing, skin of a bright copper color, and "Herculean" limbs. "Every movement and feature proclaimed him a king among men," Verner claimed.

Ndombe allegedly presided over numerous tribes, including the Bikenge branch of the Bakuba nation, along with people of Baluba, Biombo, Lele, Pende, and Mfula origin. The tribes in the Kasai basin were counted among the country's most skilled ironworkers, traders, agriculturalists, and thinkers. Explorers also frequently noted their striking physical appearance. Like other Congolese rulers, Ndombe may have been under increasing pressure to provide ivory, rubber, copper, and other resources to King Leopold's troops. Verner claimed that Ndombe wanted him to serve as an intermediary and appeal on his behalf to Leopold and President McKinley. What he promised Verner in return is not known.

It was during his stay in Ndombe that Verner caught his first glimpse of the diminutive men and women who lived in the forest on the edge of the village but were considered Ndombe's subjects. They came to town to trade the meat that they had hunted in exchange for produce and other necessities. Curious, Verner eventually followed one man to his campsite.

He entered a forest clearing just at the edge of the village and discovered a settlement dotted with beehive-shaped huts and bangi plants where he found "none other than the Pygmies of Herodotus, the fabled dwarfs of Ethiopia in reality and truth."[7]

For months Verner studied his discovery like a book, and later he wrote articles describing a community of cunning hunters and fishermen who worshipped nature and lived simply and peacefully. He uncharacteristically concluded that they displayed "in a greater or less degree, all the mental faculties which are characteristic of other men. The love of parents for their children is quite marked. The affectionate playfulness toward their dogs attracted my attention. The institution of marriage is recognized among them, and although polygamy prevails, there is the disapproval of laxity in these matters which one finds among the higher races."[8]

He also noted that the children were precocious and that the rational powers of the people he called Batwa were "beyond dispute."[9]

Determined to stay in Ndombe, Verner appealed to Belgian officials for authorization to open a mission station, something that he had neither discussed with church officials nor sought their approval for.

Back in Luebo, a letter from Dr. R. C. Rees, chair of the Foreign Mission Committee based in Nashville, awaited him. Rees diplomatically stated that while officials rejoiced in his "zeal" they were "pained at the spirit of insubordination." [10] He was ordered to "conform to the Manual" outlining missionaries' code of conduct, which he had blatantly disregarded by setting out to Ndombe. "Your counsel has weight with us, and we look forward to a most blessed ministry from you, for Africa and her sable children, but we are pained when our counsel to you is so lightly esteemed." [11]

Verner's actions also provoked a terse letter from his father, who declined his request for a $1,000 loan to set up his own shop. His father called his language "intemperate" and his plans to abandon his missionary post "madness." "Let me beg of you to take your situation more calmly and philosophically," he pleaded.[12]

Verner would remain in the Congo for another nine months as he nurtured his dream of a mission in Ndombe. He continued to appeal to American diplomatic envoys to endorse his plan to Belgian officials. Verner also claimed that he was in receipt of a contribution from the Church of the Strangers in New York to establish the mission. Indeed, D. Asa Blackburn, pastor of the church—which was first established at New York University—wrote to Verner on October 21, 1897, to ask if he had received the $25 contribution. He also asked Verner to report on what he had done with the $25 and what he would do with the $50 Blackburn planned to send. "I am interested in everything pertaining to Africa," he noted. He also asked: "What is a good slave worth in your country? I would not mind having two or three myself." [13]

It would take Verner's claim of an accident to allay the mounting tension between him and the church. On December 15, 1897, Verner alleged, he was exploring the woods surrounding Ndombe when he fell into a pit with a poisoned stake used to trap animals. He claimed that the stake made a two-inch tear in his right thigh, and that a village woman saved his life by advising his young Congolese companion to suck the poison from his wound. However, the account is questionable and could have indicated another mental collapse. In any event, the incident, whatever it was, would sideline Verner for two weeks. During this time he had a radical change of heart about the helplessness of the African race. He now praised black people for "the most faithful and remarkable fight against disease I have ever read of in the annals of African history."[14]

By the summer of 1898 his hopes for a state-sanctioned mission in Ndombe were dashed when he received official word that permission was denied and that he should immediately leave the village, owing to an outbreak of battles between the government and the nearby Lulua people. Three years earlier a rebellion by the Lulua had resulted in the death of four European officers and rising unrest. By 1897 the state reported that the rebels had been defeated, but fighting erupted again in 1898 and a brutal reign of terror was imposed on the region.

That summer William Morrison, a white missionary from Virginia who had been assigned to the Luebo Mission, went to investigate reports of regional unrest. He witnessed looting soldiers and villagers fleeing to the forest. Days later Ndombe's Baluba population was ordered to move to the state post at Luluabourg to work. Morrison threatened to publicly expose the plan, which was then abandoned. Verner reported witnessing a visit to Ndombe by some fifty Congolese soldiers who had come demanding rubber and ivory for the state. Verner said he tried to convince Ndombe that taxation was necessary, but claimed he also appealed to the troops to conduct their business peaceably. Once they left, Verner said, an estimated five thousand of Ndombe's armed men, fearing future retribution, fled the village. There were similar reports across the Congo as whole villages vanished as a result, according to Morel, of "slaughter, mutilation; emigration; sickness, largely aggravated by cruel and systematic oppression; poverty and even starvation."[15]

In one region alone, Roger Casement found the population reduced by 60 to 70 percent during the course of Leopold's rule.[16] In the Momboyo region six thousand people were reported killed or mutilated in six months. As tons of rubber and ivory were routinely shipped to the New World, similar reports of exterminated populations came from across the Congo.

By July 1898 the Zappo-Zap, a ruthless tribe of slave traders unleashed by the state to collect taxes, descended on the Bena Pianga country near Sheppard's Ibanj mission. Villagers' homes were pillaged and burned. On hearing of the raid, Morrison insisted that Sheppard investigate.

"Great terror prevailed throughout the whole region," reported Sheppard, who claimed that thousands fled to the forest as those left behind were shot and villages burned. It was the investigation by Sheppard and the revelation of mass mutilations and murders that stoked international outrage. During his investigation Sheppard was led to a stockade where he counted eighty-one human hands and bodies piled in a heap, the flesh carved off and some of it eaten. With his newly acquired Kodak camera, he recorded the atrocities in a series of gory images that would shock the Western world.

His eyewitness account, recorded on film, was corroborated by Lachlan Vass, a white missionary dispatched by Morrison to confirm Sheppard's report. Vass counted forty-seven corpses and said that "the whole country is pillaged and not a village left standing." [17]

That same year Lukengu, king of the Bakuba people, reported that state soldiers had fired on his village, located five days away from Luebo. While the villagers tried to fend off the attack with bows and arrows, fourteen of them were shot and killed. [18]

Before Verner departed, a besieged Ndombe dictated a message to him for President McKinley and Leopold, pleading for peace. Verner said Ndombe also sent President McKinley a robe and an ivory trumpet as gifts. Years later, during a search for the items, a Smithsonian official said they were not included in the collection acquired from

Verner and did not appear to be in the public collections of McKinley's memorabilia.[19] Among the items Verner sold to the Smithsonian is a "Bakuba chief robe," but it is not known if this was the same one Ndombe sent to President McKinley.

Disappointed and dejected, Verner reluctantly returned to Luebo, where a letter from Samuel Chester at mission headquarters awaited him.

"You are hereby ordered to return here as soon as you can make the necessary arrangements," Chester said. The recall was attributed to the "numerouos intimations in your letters and in those of the other missionaries, and from some statements in a letter received from your mother."[20] On the basis of news of his imperiled health, officials believed it would be wrong to keep him in the field any longer. "This letter is written with full appreciation of the fact that we may not be able to, and probably will not be able to send anyone to take your place by the time you have to leave."[21]

The same letter noted that the missions were crying out for more help. But despite the urgent need for recruits, Verner's controversial services, which had been marked by greed, insubordination, and apparent fits of madness, were no longer desired. DeWitt Clinton Snyder, a former missionary in Luebo, concluded that as a missionary Verner had been "a decided failure."[22]

That summer Verner began making plans to return home. But he would not leave unrewarded or alone. He packed as many pieces of art and artifacts—more than two hundred items—along with two monkeys; a wildcat; parrots; and Kondola and Kassongo, the two orphaned boys. The mutinous missionary would leave behind at least two children—a daughter and a son—whom he had fathered sometime between 1895 and 1898 with a Congolese woman residing at the orphanage in Luebo. Her age and her status at the orphanage could not be determined.[23]

THIRTEEN

KONDOLA, KASSONGO, AND VERNER'S AFRICAN TREASURES

The Leopoldville Belgian steamer carrying Verner, Kassongo, and Kondola arrived in Antwerp sometime in early 1899. There, Verner delivered to Leopold II Ndombe's appeal, in which the besieged Congolese king pleaded with his conqueror "to help the black people, to teach them, to keep the peace with them, and to be their friends." [1] While he was there, Verner again requested a concession in Ndombe, by then a site of bustling trade and industry.

Released from missionary service, Verner was no longer reticent about his commercial interest in the region, later writing, "I had discovered what was undoubtedly an enormously valuable territory, rich in rubber, in ivory and in mineral and metal." [2]

In Antwerp Verner gave Belgian officials a letter he had obtained from C. K. Davis of the U.S. Senate's Committee on Foreign Relations, supporting his request for a concession. "He is a personal friend of Senator Tillman, of South Carolina, who vouches for his high character and zeal in religious work," the letter stated.[3] However, Belgian officials granted Verner only the guardianship of Kassongo and Kondola, not the concession. Verner took note as the youngsters marveled at Antwerp's great buildings and "all the roar and rattle of the complex noises of metropolitan life greeting the ear."[4] The boys, "late from the dark recesses of inner Ethiopia," he wrote, "stood entranced."

Verner implausibly claimed that Kassongo asked, "Master, why do the white men leave all this to come to our land?"

Sometime in February, on a cold and blustery morning, the *Southwark*, carrying Verner, Kassongo, and Kondola, pulled into New York Harbor. In New York, Verner left the boys in the hallway of a lodging facility near Manhattan's Madison Square while he visited a former classmate living in the city. "The janitress promised to keep them in the hall until [the proprietor] came," Verner claimed. When he returned at 9 P.M. he discovered that the landlord had thrown Kassongo and Kondola out into the cold, dark night.

Through a cracked-open door, he claims, a man he believed to be the landlord shouted, "I put 'em out—I don't want any niggers here!"[5]

Verner set out in a desperate search for the boys. "The night was deepening, it was bitter cold and the wind howled over the snowy streets," he recalled of the hours he spent scouring the neighborhood for the boys. Verner described once again being plagued by "a raging tempest" and a "rocked and harrowed brain" as he scanned street after street.[6] He finally found them huddled together in front of a grocery store "before a window where they saw familiar bananas"—an unlikely sighting in the dead of night, but Verner would also later preposterously claim that he had introduced the watermelon to Africa.

Sometime during his visit Verner placed the surviving monkey and wildcat in the Central Park Zoo, which, while squalid and overcrowded, was the city's only menagerie. The New York Zoological

Gardens would open nine months later. Verner also took the opportunity to offer the boys to the Smithsonian.

In a letter to the Smithsonian's secretary, S. P. Langley, he said he was coming to Washington to offer to the institution items from his collection: one thousand cubic feet in volume and including more than two hundred masks, figurines, and other artifacts of the Baluba, Bakuba, Biombo, Teke, and Luluwa.

"I have also in this country two boys of the Batetela tribe of the Bantu race whom I should like the Institution to make models of," he wrote. "They could be used to illustrate photographically some of the arts and industries of their people."[7] It does not appear that the offer was ever accepted. No models or records of Batetela photographs or casts have been located in the Smithsonian's archives. Langley may have replied in person during his meeting with Verner.

The museum did, however, agree to pay Verner $200 for artifacts that included bowls, bows, masks, musical instruments, cloth, ceremonial robes, dolls, figurines, headdresses, stools, arrows, and jewelry and other adornments.[8] Langley also agreed to warehouse the remaining artifacts until Verner found a way to dispose of them.

In Washington Verner, ever eager to court journalists, discussed his expedition with a *Washington Post* reporter. The *Post* identified him as a missionary and scientist and noted his valuable ethnological collection deposited at the National Museum. While he was described as a missionary, Verner made it clear that his interests had shifted from the holy to the secular. He promoted business opportunities in the Congo Free State, prompting the reporter to observe, "He does not have the air of a missionary"; rather, he had that of a "shrewd but congenial gentlemen."[9]

In addition to his African treasures, the article also highlighted the "two pickannnies" he had brought back with him.

"Perhaps," said the *Post*, "they are entitled to some more dignified title than pickaninny," given that Kondola was the son of a famous chieftain. The article noted matter-of-factly that Kassongo, "the darker skinned boy," had a bullet hole in one of his ears, "the result of contact with a squad of Belgian soldiers." The two had a "very good" English vocabulary and insatiable curiosity. They were also well behaved "considering where they came from" and had "rather thick lips."

Kondola, the *Post* said, "[has] regular features, a good figure, and, to the casual observer, is the more intelligent of the two."

This observation about his intelligence was apparently attributable to his lighter complexion and "regular" features, since both boys were described as inquisitive and well spoken.

The two were described as happy, "as little negroes proverbially are," as they chattered merrily in their "strange" tongue. In the capital the two boys resided with a local African American on Eleventh Street. Verner stayed with relatives, probably his uncle Phillips, and visited Senator Tillman, "there being a warm friendship between them," the *Post* reported.

Verner, who in his later writing described Africans as exotic and even debased, told the *Washington Post* that they shared many traditions and much folklore with Americans of African descent.

From Washington Verner planned to take the boys to Tuscaloosa, Alabama, to enroll them in Stillman. On March 8 the three boarded a 5 P.M. train at the Sixth Avenue depot for their trip south. At one point Verner said he placed them in the Thornnwell Orphanage in South Carolina while he delivered a lecture. Once he arrived in Columbia, South Carolina, he placed them in the home of his butler, whose house he called "a sort of Mecca" for the city's African Americans.[10] He eventually took them to Stillman, where the boys quickly assumed a life as Americans and worked to pay their way through school.

"The progress of the lads has been extraordinary," Verner reported.[11] "They can now read and write; they know elementary geography and arithmetic quite well."

He said they were capable of writing letters and were devout

Christians. "They are faithful workman on the farm, and can use the ordinary mechanical tools fairly well." Verner said he hoped to get a concession of land for them from King Leopold so "that they may return to elevate their people."

With them settled, Verner followed what by now was a familiar pattern: he checked into a Baltimore sanatorium. Once again he was taunted by phantoms, one of whom he addressed as "Your Majesty." This time he remained hospitalized for more than six months. The 1900 census lists him as a patient at Sheppard and Enoch Pratt Hospital, a psychiatric hospital in Towson, a Baltimore suburb. He is also listed that year as living with his parents and wife in South Carolina, where he apparently moved after his discharge. Living with his parents would enable him to recover and seek gainful employment.

By the fall of 1900 Verner returned to work with a vengeance, writing a flurry of articles. Many followed a familiar theme: African savagery and cannibalism. Among them was one on Kassongo and Kondola entitled "An Educational Experiment with Cannibals," published in *World's Work*. It begins: "For African savages of the iron age to be studying for a university education in America is a unique illustration of the complete revolution in the relative conditions of men which the last few years have been working over the world." [12]

Describing them as members of the Batetela, a people who he contended knew less of European civilization "than any people on earth," and giving their full names as Kassongo Lusuna and Kondola Mukusa, he said that in the midst of a rebellion against the Belgian authorities, the boys became his charges. He claimed Kassongo was about fourteen and Kondola ten, calling them "parentless, homeless waifs from the great tide of surging humanity in the recesses of remote Ethiopia," and adding, "Thus they became entirely dependent upon me, and have been my wards now for five years."

Since Verner himself had arrived in the Kasai region in August 1896, he could not three years later have been the boys' guardian for five years, even if he had met them and claimed them as his charges on his arrival.

Verner alleged that Kassongo, the elder of the boys, had been captured by soldiers to carry ammunition and food. Kassongo, he claimed, "admits cannibalism; but he says it was practiced because the Arabs used to capture his people and feed them to the Manuema when meat was scarce, and that his countrymen were determined to avenge themselves in kind." However, in his chapter on the boys in *Pioneering in Central Africa*, he does not mention cannibalism and tells an entirely different story of how they ended up at the orphanage. In *Pioneering*, he claims that Kondola and Kassongo were among ten boys brought to the Luebo mission by Monsieur Paul le Marinel. He said they had become legal charges of the state and had to work to pay for their care. In this version of events, he claimed Kassongo had left his home voluntarily to accompany the soldiers, carrying food and weapons. He said Kassongo's father was a well-to-do landowner, "a man of consequence and influence."[13] Kondola, he said, was a child of the Bakussu division of the Batetela.

"The hope for heathen and barbarous races lies in their children; and the marvelous progress made by these African youth in accommodating themselves to the changed conditions, in assimilating Christian ideas, and in adopting the Western civilization, was the most helpful fact I observed during my life in Africa," he said.[14]

In the article in *World's Work*, by contrast, Kassongo became the nephew of the Batetela king and heir to the throne, while Verner called Kondola a "plebian, the son of a fisherman."

Then, appearing to model himself on Sheppard, whose discovery of the Kuba had earned him membership in the Royal Academy and worldwide fame, Verner said the Batetela were widely recognized throughout Central Africa for their intelligence, bravery, and industry. He said Kassongo and Kondola were among many boys who accompanied their elders to government posts. He did not divulge the nature of their work at these posts nor their widely reported utility as sites of state-enforced labor.

Instead, he alleged, "These people were such confirmed cannibals that it has been repeatedly asserted that they eat their own dead, and had boneyards instead of cemeteries."

Kassongo and Kondola, he noted "were of as savage a people as could be found on the globe."

He said that when they came into his care they would "lie, fight, steal, and gamble whenever the occasion offered." If true, that would mean Kassongo, at the tender age of ten, was already gambling. But now, presumably owing to Verner's guardianship, "they are of a better moral character than the average Negro in the Southern states of America."

As for his civilizing methodology, he offered this: "I used both moral suasion and the rod. I found soon after I made their acquaintance that the little savages really had a clear conception of moral distinctions, and their habits were the result of environment and not of originally defective moral constitution." It may be the first time Verner divulged that he had physically disciplined his young charges.

Their "natural wildness" and "utter lack of any inherited tendencies toward civilization" made them worthy subjects for study, he opined. Both learned to read and write in their native tongue "which I reduced to alphabetic characters," he said, adding, however, that he did not teach them any foreign language.

Verner allowed that he owed his life to the purportedly uncivilized Kassongo, who he claimed ran five miles to a native town to seek help when he fell into the ten-foot-deep pit and a poisoned stake tore through his thigh. Kassongo then is alleged to have valiantly sucked the poison from his leg. How Kassongo was not himself poisoned remains a mystery, or an indication that the story was, like so many others Verner told, fabricated. Verner recalled, as one of the most touching displays of "nobler ideas in these late cannibals' minds," the boys' treatment of Bunda, his infirmed cook. As Bunda lay dying of sleeping sickness, the boys fed and nursed him. "And when the poor lad died they helped to bear him to his lonely grave." The boys, he recalled, quietly walked to the steamer "tears streaming down their black faces." Verner seemed oblivious to the horror of burdening children with the task of caring for and then burying their countryman.

The article on his allegedly cannibal charges was accompanied by photographs of Kondola and Kassongo with Verner in the Congo, and more recent portraits of the two young men, wearing western suits, ostensibly evidence of Verner's civilizing mission.

In another article, published in the *Charlotte Observor*, Verner reported on a speech he alleges Kassongo gave at Stillman. He claims Kassongo challenged the idea that Africans were savages, quoting him as saying, "Some of these men have been talking to me about savage and civilized man. They say my people savage, but they civilized man." According to Verner, Kassongo went on to question the behavior of his African American classmates: "I see some men here they don't sweep their rooms clean in the morning. Is that civilized man? They come down to breakfast without wash their face. Is that civilized man?"

Verner said he had quoted Kassongo "as nearly as I can give his word," but cautioned that it must not be assumed the slovenly behavior described was permitted at Stillman.

Verner officially resigned from the mission that was beset that year by a massacre in a village near Luebo. Among the dozen or more killed was the Bushongo king Lukengu. Verner would later attribute his death to his resistance to civilization.

In 1900 Verner married Harriet Bradshaw, a schoolteacher from a prosperous Gainesville, Alabama, family.[15] A graduate of Peabody Normal College of the University of Nashville—now the Peabody School within Vanderbilt University—she had headed the mathematics department at Alabama Normal College in Livingston while

Verner was at Stillman. In a letter to a Smithsonian official Verner said the sale of the African artifacts had enabled him to start a family. But the condition of that sale was still a source of contention. Verner had written to the Smithsonian in November 1899 to say that he had "named and described the articles" and was preparing monographs on certain industries they illustrated: rubber collecting, textile manufacture, copper mining and manufacturing, and pottery. On the basis of that assurance, Verner was sent $200, but the articles described cannot be located among the accession records. Instead, there are scanty notes that were apparently dictated to Walter Hough, the curator. Years later Smithsonian officials said that Verner had not honored the agreement.[16]

During the summer of 1901 the Verners had their first child and Verner returned to Stillman, where he worked as superintendent of the industrial division.

Meanwhile Kassongo and Kondola were both working in Birmingham, Kondola in an iron foundry and Kossongo at a stable. On September 19, 1902, Booker T. Washington was scheduled to speak at the city's Shiloh Baptist Church, an impressive brick edifice on the Southside, completed a year before.

The speech would be a highlight of the twenty-second annual meeting of the National Baptist Convention, with some two thousand delegates representing sixteen thousand churches and more than two million black American Baptists. Washington was the nation's foremost African American figure, and his appearance ensured big crowds at a convention that had already drawn thousands from across the country. Kassongo was thrilled by the opportunity to hear the great leader, but something told Kondola not to go.

Hours before the scheduled event hundreds of people began flocking to the church. By the time it began there was standing room only, with the four aisles and the stairways filled over capacity. Pastor T. W. Walker attempted to calm the restless crowd packed into the hot church. He had already ordered the ushers to prevent any more people from entering, and police officers were stationed at the front door and in the gallery.

Finally Washington arrived. "No race similarly surrounded in history has made progress equal to ours," he proclaimed.

"As you go to your homes," he implored, "I trust that you will use every iota of your influence to get our young people to learn trades, to cease idling on the corners of streets."

He beseeched those gathered to take heart from the progress that had been made: "The race may be hindered and delayed in its progress, but if it has high ideals it can never be defeated."

One can only imagine Kassongo's elation as Washington urged the audience to go forward "with a firmer step and with a more determined heart, forward until there can be no question about our ability and success as a race."

At the end of Washington's speech, a delegate behind him—a minister—rose to congratulate him. A member of the choir sat down in the vacated seat. When the minister returned to his now occupied seat, an argument ensued, prompting a woman to yell, "Fight!" Some in the crowded church misheard this as "Fire!" and many people rushed to the church's six exits. As the choir began to sing, and Pastor Walker appealed for calm, there was pandemonium, and then a stampede. Even as ushers yelled that there was no fire, the panic-stricken throng rushed to the exits and more than one hundred people—men, women, and children—were trampled to death. Several hundred more were injured.

Among those fatally trampled were many of the delegates who had come from far and wide to attend the convention: Reverend G. W. Sledge of Gunnison, Mississippi; Reverend L. R. Price of New Orleans; Reverend Z. H. Johnson of Weir City, Kansas; Reverend James Kelly of Birmingham. The long alphabetical list of names in the next morning's paper chillingly showed the randomness of death. The largest number of the casualties were from Birmingham, including Sallie and Harriett Stokes; Reverend James Kelly; Robert Smith, and

Dr. A. L. Hill. Along with the named deceased were some who could not immediately be identified.

Days later the names of more casualties would be released. Among these was the teenaged Kassongo. As his American guardian authorized by the Belgian state, Verner sought to clear himself of any role in the tragedy. He promptly secured a letter written by Birmingham's mayor, W. M. Drennen, to U.S. secretary of state John Hay absolving anyone of responsibility. "From all evidence of the case," the letter read, "it appears no one, either the said Kassongo or his guardian Dr. Samuel Phillips Verner, or anyone else was responsible, it being purely accidental." [17]

FOURTEEN

THE HUNT

Sometime during the fall of 1903 Verner caught wind of plans for an exhibit of exotic races at an upcoming world's fair. It would be held in St. Louis beginning in May of the following year. Its organizers hoped to fascinate fairgoers with the wonders of science and produce an impressive display of human progress on a scale never before attempted.

Verner immediately reached out to William John McGee. As the head of the Smithsonian's Bureau of American Ethnology and president of the newly formed American Anthropological Association, McGee was arguably the nation's leading anthropologist. He was also president of the National Geographic Society and was now, as head of the fair's ethnology department, charged with the task of mapping human development "from the dark prime to the highest enlightenment, from savagery to civic organization, from egoism to altruism."

In late September Verner, in a handwritten letter, said he was offering his services in "securing some African Pygmies and other

Anthropological specimen" for the exposition. He said he had just learned of this opportunity and was writing before he could reach his office to send references. However, he noted his role, four years earlier, in bringing a large collection of ethnological material to the Smithsonian—"the largest ethnological collection every brought to this country from Central Africa, as well as the boys of the Batetela cannibal tribe." [1]

Since then, he added, he had written extensively on scientific matters in Africa, "especially concerning the Pygmies, among whom I lived for two years." In addition to his articles on "pygmies" published in the *Spectator* in London and the *Atlantic Monthly*, another on "The Yellow Men of Africa," the copper-hued people with aquiline noses he claimed to have discovered in Central Africa, had been accepted for publication in *American Anthropologist,* the publication of the American Anthropological Association.

Verner told McGee that since the death of a Dr. Challier, he could now claim "with modesty" to be the best-known authority on African affairs, with the possible exception of Sir Harry Johnston, "whose work, however, has not been so strictly scientific."

Verner proposed a budget not exceeding $1,000 to complete the mission in five months. In addition to "Pygmies," he would also bring "many interesting ethnological specimens" and, if desired, some of the "*red* Africans (indigenes, not half-bred at all)."

He also told McGee he'd be happy to forward additional information. He asked McGee to reply by telegram to him in care of the Hotel Carroll in Vicksburg, Mississippi, or to the Stillman Institute, where he still worked as head of the industrial department.

McGee replied that he would consider the matter. McGee had initially hoped to secure Akko "Pygmies" from deeper in the African interior, believing them to be less affected by other cultures, but he was nonetheless intrigued by Verner's proposal. At the same time he was skeptical about Verner's very low budget: $1,000 could not possibly cover two trips to the Congo, one to send the large delegation and the other to return it along with dozens of artifacts. Also, could Verner be trusted to execute such a high-level mission?

A week later, Verner wrote again, attempting to allay any reservations McGee had. This time he told McGee about his personal friendship with King Leopold and the many courtesies the king had accorded him, including free use of the state steamer. In fact, Verner maintained, he had only recently received a letter from Leopold assuring him that he would have no problem executing the diplomatic mission. Furthermore, he noted that his book *Pioneering in Central Africa*, would be published within a few weeks and that he would send McGee a copy.

On receiving the second letter McGee immediately replied and frankly revealed his apprehension. Verner's estimates included neither expenses for government contracts, "which I understand would necessitate $100 each if brought from Belgian territory," nor costs for bringing neighboring tribesmen and interpreters, let alone for the return trip of the delegation.

While the terms of cooperation were, in general, "gratifying," McGee was not any more certain about Verner's suitability for the task than he had been in his previous correspondence. However, he agreed to meet Verner in person either in St. Louis or, later in the month, in Washington, D.C. McGee offered to reimburse Verner for the cost of transportation.

Verner leaped at the chance to meet in St. Louis on October 18. Before leaving, he wrote again to say he had been busy with his book and his estimates were only preliminary. He claimed that he was the only white man who had ever resided at the court of Ndombe, the king of the Batwa, a term for "pygmies." In a postscript he noted that Ndombe lived near English and Portuguese territory and that there were "Pygmies" in each territory: "We can have a choice of governments to deal with."

To accomplish the mission, Verner proposed securing from the navy a gunboat or warship, which would "greatly lighten enferences and and be preferable for many other reasons."[2] Apparently this menacing and bizarre proposition did not deter McGee. On the contrary it may have convinced him of the lengths to which Verner would go to execute the mission.

Three days after their meeting, McGee officially wrote a letter offering Verner leadership and control of the expedition. He stipulated that Verner must secure the voluntary attendance of twelve "Pygmies" and about six neighboring tribesmen and, once the Exposition had closed, return them safely to their homes. Verner was also to obtain all permissions and the support of "His Majesty, King Leopold of Belgium" and Leopold's colonial officials in Africa and conclude his mission in time to install the group on the fairgrounds by May 1, 1904.

Of a budget of $8,500, $500 was for Verner's compensation and $5,500 was to be disbursed prior to the group's arrival, with $1,000 of that in cash or transportation orders, $1,000 in a letter of credit, and $1,500 in vouchers to ship material to the Exposition. An additional $1,500 was set aside for unforeseen contingencies. If Verner was able to place the Africans on the fairgrounds for less than $5,500, he could retain half of the savings. The remaining $3,000, to return the delegation, would be allocated in St. Louis.

In a deal finalized on October 22, 1903, Verner, "by authority of the Louisiana Purchase Exposition Company," was commissioned a "special agent" to conduct an expedition into the African interior to obtain anthropological material and offer "certain natives the opportunity of attending the Exposition in person."[3] In his revised proposal submitted on October 30, Verner agreed to bring back a dozen "Pygmies," four "red people," and two "black people." In his revised proposal, Verner wrote: "All the above twelve to be Pygmies (Batwa or Tueki)." He also promised: "One fine type of the Real Africans, preferably Ndombe of the Bikenga. Three more of these Red people, preferably of Ndombe's choosing. Two natives, each of a distinct ethnic types of any of the above."

The exacting list called for the retrieval from the Congo of "one pygmy patriarch or chief. One adult woman, preferably his wife. Two infants, of women in the expedition," and "four more pygmies, preferably adult but young, but including a priestess and a priest, or medicine doctors, preferably old." [4]

In addition he promised to bring back as many examples of their home life, religion, and culture as he could, including a full set of religious emblems and ceremonial objects, and a blacksmith shop. He would also obtain photographs of villages and individuals engaged in various activities and ethnographic information covering a broad range of subjects.

Verner also agreed to return with examples of the best and worst primitive homes along with building material, presumably to enable the Africans to build homes on the fairgrounds. Also on his list were sets of sleeping mats, pottery, "wood fire making apparatus," knives, spears, traps, bows, and darts, along with observations on nomenclature, fertility, and folklore.

Unspoken was just how one went about procuring people. But whereas slavery had been abolished in Missouri in 1865, four decades later it still flourished in Leopold's Congo, where Verner had proposed bringing a navy warship or gunboat to "greatly lighten enferences." Exposition officials were apparently willing to look the other way as Verner embarked on his mission.

Verner was handed official letters of recommendation signed by McGee as president of the American Anthropological Association and acting president of the National Geographic Society. In another letter, addressed to His Excellency King Leopold, McGee said Verner's role was essential for the fair's success, and appealed to the king for his support. In a letter of introduction on the National Geographic Society letterhead, McGee noted that Verner was connected with the National Anthropological Association "and other organizations of scientific character." [5] Verner had also received a letter to U.S.

diplomatic and consular officers from David Francis, president of
the Louisiana Purchase Exposition. In the letter Francis introduced
Verner as a special agent and asked the recipients to extend courtesies befitting their duties. For good measure, Verner additionally
obtained a letter from U.S. secretary of state John Hay, addressed to
Leopold, which indicated that Verner was authorized to perform the
special mission.

In late November 1903, Special Agent Verner set sail from New
York Harbor. He was accompanied by Alonzo Edmiston, an African American native of Petersburgh, Tennessee. Born in a one-room
cabin and motherless by age twelve, Edmiston had worked his way
through Tuscaloosa Theological Seminary and was pursuing studies
in medicine. Verner's invitation, however, was "too great an opportunity to pass up."[6] Like other students at Stillman he had long marveled at the legendary exploits of William Sheppard. There's some
indication that they were accompanied by a second African American man. On the ship from Antwerp to Africa, Verner requested
a first-class cabin for himself and two second-class rooms for two
African American men.

In early December, just as Roger Casement was returning to London to file his report, Verner and Edmiston were in London for orientation and to be outfitted with tropical equipment. From London
Verner wrote to report that Ambassador Choate seemed "particularly
pleased" with their enterprise and U.S. foreign minister Townsend
was "all that one could wish."[7] He added, "If only King Ndombe
and his Lilliputinns are as amenable as our other friends we ought
to accomplish the most notable feat of science hitherto in the twentieth century."[8] In London Verner also visited the Military Equipment
Company, a military supply store on Savile Row, to order cartridges
for his Winchester and Colt revolvers, among other items. A store employee wrote on Christmas Eve, asking Verner to provide samples of
the items to be ordered.[9] For no apparent reason, Verner assured the

employee that he had letters of introduction from His Excellency and Townsend, perhaps due to questions raised about the large order of military supplies.

Verner planned to sail to Antwerp with Belgium's governor-general to secure permission from Leopold's emissaries to execute the mission and use the government's steamer in the Congo.

From Brussels he reported that both the secretary to the king and the Belgian secretary of state, Chevalier Cuvelier, "who is, next to the King, the most influential of all the men with whom I shall have to deal," had assured him of their cooperation and the use of the state steamer.[10] He was to meet the governor-general in the Congo the following Monday, and was about to have an audience with the king. In Brussels, he received a letter from the U.S. Consular Service in Tenerife noting the available steamers, presumably for his return trip. "Anything you desire me to arrange for you will be pleased to do so," wrote the official, who said Verner might be interested in taking back local inhabitants, the Guanches, for the fair.[11]

From Antwerp Verner wrote to assure McGee that all that could be done for the mission's success would be undertaken "at any personal risk and labor however great."[12] King Leopold was "so much interested" that he was attending the fair "in *persona propria*."[13] Verner said that full permission had been officially given for all of their plans, "and now for the Pygmies."[14]

Verner and Edmiston sailed to the Congo. At least eighty cases of supplies—including rifles and ammunition—that Verner had ordered from the military supply store were shipped separately.[15]

In Matadi they purchased provisions—coffee, biscuits, tissue, and the like—for the long journey to the upper Kasai. In a letter from Boma, Verner wrote to "His Excellency, The Goveror-General" to solicit his support for this diplomatic mission. He wished to find a maximum of twenty-four "Pygmies" and stressed that the exhibition was not for money, "but for scientific investigation."[16]

The next day, in a letter to McGee, Verner spelled out three possible contingencies: the consent of the Batwa, but not of the Tueki; the possible consent of both; the refusal of both. Verner said he was sure the Tueki would not consent at once, but he had always counted on the cooperation of the Batwa. "As to the first, I think if the Batwa consent, I ought to catch the first steamer with them."

By mid-February it appeared that Verner and Edmiston had a dispute. In a letter to McGee, Verner reported that everything was going well "less the disapprobation of a missionary who did not like things scientific could count for something."[17] Might Edmiston have been uneasy, even horrified, by Verner's assignment to hunt "pygmies"? It's unlikely that Vermer had divulged the details of his mission in advance of their trip.

Edmiston had a nobler mission in mind. Not long after they arrived in the Congo, he parted company with Verner and continued on to Luebo to visit Reverend L. A. Vampert. "So delighted was I at the opportunity of seeing him again that I walked forty miles in one day alone through the jungle," he wrote. He likened Luebo to "what an oasis in a great desert must be to a weary traveler." There he would meet his future bride, Althea Brown. A year later Edmiston was assigned by the Presbyterian Foreign Mission to work in the Congo, where he remained for thirty-eight years.

Meanwhile, Verner continued on his hunt for "pygmies." "We approach the crucial issue of the pygmies ascent with every other factor so far eliminated," he reported.[18]

It remained only to arrange for water transportation to the final destination, and he had already been assured of that. Verner's assignment stipulated that the Congolese should willingly accompany him to St. Louis. He assured McGee that their willingness was more likely now that he was able to take "a more considerable equipment than I at first contemplated," an apparent reference to the military supplies he had purchased in London.[19]

Verner reiterated that he had, in a previous letter to McGee, "covered the ground of what I thought wise in the event of a non-assent of the pygmies"; however, that letter has not been located.

McGee replied: "As you are now placed, you are a law unto yourself and I have implicit confidence in the competence of the court."[20]

The letter implicitly sanctioned whatever was necessary for Verner to do to carry out his mission.

A week later Verner wrote to a local official to express his delight that he had been given "every attention and courtesy" from the state, and repeated that he had been granted permission from officials in Antwerp to "take with me some of the indigenes." He said he would make two stops: first in Bassongo, the site of a district state post; and then in Kasai near Ndombe, where he had first encountered the forest dwellers during his missionary days.

"I may have the pleasure of presenting some of the pygmies to your Excellency at Boma before many months," he wrote. The next day he informed McGee of his discovery of at least five other settlements "thus increasing the investigations and of securing some of the pygmies."[21]

Verner told McGee that he visited the state post at Bassongo to await transportation to Wissmann Falls. It was there that he reported his first triumph.

"The first pygmy has been secured!" he exclaimed on March 20, 1904, the day Ota Benga's life would irrevocably change.[22]

FIFTEEN

VERNER'S PREY

Verner told McGee that Ota Benga was obtained from a village where he had been held captive, at a remote site in the forest "twelve days march from any white settlement." There was no mention of cannibalism. And while it is possible that Verner went alone into a remote location in search of his prey, Bassongo was the site of a well-known slave market and government post where human trafficking was pervasive. Still two hundred miles and ten days from Wissmann Falls in the upper Kasai, Verner told McGee, he had "thought it well to secure him at once, even if we get all we wish for from Ndombe." [1]

Later, retelling the tale of Benga's capture in a *Harper's Weekly* article, Verner said that while waiting for a ship at the confluence of the Sankuru and Kasai Rivers, opposite Bassongo, he found Benga in the interior, where he was held captive by the Baschilele, who he claimed were cannibals.

"He was delighted to come with us, for he was many miles from his people, and the Baschilele were not easy masters." [2]

However, he told the *Columbus Dispatch* that he was waiting for a ship to come in when he ventured a short distance and spotted Ota Benga, along with a few members of his tribe. "They told me I was only a few miles from their settlement," Verner claimed, adding that he told them he did not have time to visit. In this contradictory retelling, he said he made arrangements with a chief to take Benga with him. "He was willing and even anxious to go with me, for the memory of his awful escape from the hungry cannibals had not been forgotten by him."[3]

In yet another account, he wrote that Benga had been captured in war by enemies of his tribe who were in turn defeated by government troops, who then held Benga. Benga elected to travel with Verner on learning that he "wanted to employ pygmies."[4]

The descriptions of their encounter would continue to change over the years. The only consistent themes were the threat of cannibals and Verner's role as Benga's savior. But even without knowing the specific details of their meeting, we can safely assume that Benga was prey for a merciless hunter. Whether or not Benga was captured and enslaved by the Baschilele, sold by a chief, or held by government troops, it appears that his life had already taken a tragic turn by the time he encountered Verner, possibly near Bassongo. This was a sparsely populated, largely uncultivated area of grassland, forest, and streams. It was also the site of a government post in the Congo interior, and just a few months before, a British inquiry in the Congo by the Foreign Service officer Roger Casement had confirmed many earlier reports of atrocities under Leopold's rule, including widespread enslavement, murder, and mutilation of the Congolese.

Casement, as a high-level British diplomat, raised the volume of what William Sheppard, E. D. Morel, and others had already alleged. Casement's credentials were unassailable. He had entered the consular service in 1893, and in 1903, after several deployments elsewhere, was dispatched to the Congo. In his report, "White Book, Africa, No. 1,

1904," he cited the horrors he had witnessed even as he seemed determined to present a balanced picture.

In his investigation of reports of dramatic depopulation Casement discovered natives who were "hopeless and listless, being debarred from trade and heavily taxed in food, fish and other produce." While government officials attributed depopulation to sleeping sickness, villagers principally blamed decidedly unnatural causes for the rapid population decline.

It was in the rubber zones of the upper Congo that atrocities were laid bare. Casement was immediately struck by the timidity of the people. On seeing him, villagers fled to the forest, taking their children and whatever household supplies they could grab. When he finally gained their confidence and asked why they had fled, a woman confided that they thought he was *bula matadi*, the term for a government official.

"Fear of this kind was formerly unknown on the Upper Congo," Casement observed, recounting a previous visit in 1887, when villagers had eagerly flocked around white strangers. "But today, the apparition of a white man's steamer evidently gave the signal for instant flight."

All around he saw a dispirited people.

"One of them—a strong, indeed, a splendid-looking man—broke down and wept, saying that their lives were useless to them, and that they knew of no means of escape from the troubles around them."

Men now came to him with missing hands, as Sheppard and others had documented, and also with reports that they had been castrated by government soldiers and sometimes by white state officials. Two villagers—one man and a boy of about twelve—told him their hands were beaten off with the butt end of rifles. Both claimed that the mutilations were witnessed by white officers, whose names Casement included in his report. On finding a teenage boy who had been shot and mutilated, Casement confronted an employee of a Belgian company, who brazenly acknowledged his offense. Casement appealed for his arrest, probably to no avail.

The widespread and wanton practice of mutilation "is amply proved by the Kodak," Casement assured his readers, and he submitted photographs of at least two dozen mutilated victims.

Also prevalent were illegal fines, levied "according to the whim or ill-will of the executive officers of the district." Government documents revealed officials' complicity in forced labor.

Casement gathered the testimony of workers routinely beaten and forced to gather rubber for no pay, or for only cloth and salt. As the rubber trees were increasingly plundered, the men were compelled to move deeper and deeper into the forest, some succumbing to attacks by wild animals and some others dying of starvation. When the rubber quotas were not met, claimed one villager, "the soldiers came to our towns and killed us. Many were shot, some had their ears cut off; others were tied up with ropes around their necks and bodies and taken away."[5]

Given the scale of the atrocities, Benga had almost certainly witnessed some of the carnage—the bloody raids of villages by the Force Publique or the Zappo-Zap, accompanied by mutilation, rape, and the brutal enslavement of men, women, and children forced to meet impossibly high rubber quotas. Most observers during this period noted a common sight: people chained by their necks and forced to work for the state. While Benga's personal experience in the Congo was not recorded, the incursions deeper into the forest for rubber and ivory would, for his people, mean greater exposure and vulnerability to state abuses.

And now, in this land of horror, Benga encountered an American shopping for "pygmies."

Casement's report was submitted to the British crown around the time Benga and Verner met. The report brought overnight fame to Casement, and international scrutiny to Leopold, who set up a commission to investigate the allegations. That year the commission, comprising a Swiss jurist, a Belgian appellate judge, and a Belgian baron, would set out for the Congo to investigate.

Meanwhile, as a white American man with the backing of Belgian and American officials, Verner was at liberty to move freely about the territory and prey on a vulnerable and traumatized people. The forest dwellers, already oppressed by their own countrymen and by their conquerors, were the most susceptible of all.

Sanctioned by the state, Verner could, by coercion or persuasion, orchestrate events and then narrate what happened to an unknowing public. While the land of Benga's birth, this was Verner's Congo, so if he chose to cast himself as a hero in Benga's life, who could challenge his account? McGee encouraged Verner to exploit the press "two or three times more freely than seems to you necessary."[6] Verner complied. In subsequent articles Verner claimed he had saved Benga from a tribe of cannibals. Indeed, his tale of befriending a companion amid a tribe of cannibalistic Africans veers strikingly close to Defoe's fictional characters Robinson Crusoe, who feared being "devoured by savage beasts" amid a "nation of negroes," and Friday. Crusoe was "called plainly by Providence to save this poor creature's life," and Friday becomes his servile companion, with whom he travels the world. Verner had apparently appropriated Crusoe's dramatic adventure, a favorite in his youth, as his own.

In one account, beneath the headline: "An Untold Chapter of My Adventures While Hunting Pygmies in Africa," a large portrait of a triumphant Verner, wearing a suit and bow tie, appears alongside pictures of his captives, including Benga, whom he claimed to have obtained for $5 worth of goods. But none of Verner's thrilling tales, relayed in his letters, articles, or books, expose the stark and incalculable inhumanity ravaging the heart of Africa. Verner was, to all appearances, unmoved by the suffering of his prey.

After obtaining Benga Verner advised McGee to send a statement to the prominent daily, weekly, and monthly publications to spread the news of his expedition. He also provided a local address where reporters could contact him. "As far as publicity is concerned the return by Europe and New York will of course conduce greatly that end."[7]

Verner also drafted a statement from the Wissmann Falls district of the Kasai region emphasizing the importance of his mission: "The anthropological character of the Pygmies is of extreme interest to the scientific world, and it is desired that opportunity be given to scientists from all over the world to see and study the Pygmies at the St. Louis Exposition." For this "unparalleled" opportunity he praised the Congo Free State and the United States government. Not only had Belgian officials made the scientific achievement possible by allowing the export of Congolese, but the United States had "signaled its approval" of the affair.[8]

Verner also indicated future plans to exhibit the Congolese at an exposition at Liège, "which can be easily done by having them to pass the winter in Florida or Cuba in tropical America."[9]

On March 21 Verner wrote to McGee again, to report that he, accompanied by a state official "of eminence and responsibility," had descended on a village.[10] Together they obtained another "pygmy." Verner said the African had been temporarily placed in a local mission. It was the first clear indication of coercion on Verner's part. There is little reason to believe that at the height of Leopold's reign, a native Congolese, in the presence of a high-level state official, was in a position to decline Verner's "invitation."

McGee effusively praised Verner's valiant efforts. "The more I have reflected on the distances and other difficulties you have had to overcome, the more have I been impressed with the clearness of your foresight and the soundness of your plans," he wrote.[11]

McGee also alerted Verner that a group of missionaries, including his former colleague William Morrison, had appealed to Secretary of State Hay and President Roosevelt to intervene to protect the Congolese from Belgian atrocities. McGee said the Belgian minister in Washington "has met the allegations by statements that, to say the least, reflect no credit on the complaints."[12] He was probably referring to a meeting in Washington a week earlier, at which a "Memorial Concerning Conditions in the Independent State of the Kongo" was drafted. The measure, which cited the Casement report and Morrison's speech to the Aborigines Protection Society, asserted the right of the United States to act on behalf of the Congolese people. Significantly, it won the support of Senator John T. Morgan, the ranking minority member of the Foreign Relations Committee, who had in the past supported Leopold's rule. A day later, E. D. Morel's Congo Reform Association was officially established in London.

After a meeting with the president, the missionaries decided to appeal directly to Congress rather than wait for the results of an investigation by the U.S. foreign minister, Townsend. On the basis of Verner's assertions, that investigation would have been a charade. While he was in Belgium en route to the Congo, Verner claimed, he had already met with Townsend and assured him he'd investigate matters for him.

"In fact," he reported to McGee from Belgium, Townsend "had already paved the way before my arrival, and he immediately went with me to the King's place, and to the Congo headquarters."[13]

From Townsend, the king, and Chevalier Cuvelier Verner had received "the warmest assurance" of cooperation and assistance, including free use of the state steamer.

McGee likewise reported that plans for the fair were proceeding well. The University of Chicago's Professor Frederick Starr had arrived with nine Ainu from Japan. The Patagonians were en route from Liverpool, and three hundred natives "including Igorottes and Negrito pygmies" had arrived the preceding Monday. Four hundred more were en route from San Francisco.

But the African "pygmies" were to be the signal attraction, and with the fair a month away and Verner a month behind his deadline McGee cared only that Verner complete his mission successfully. "I make but a single plea," McGee wrote, *get the Pygmies.*"[14]

To that Verner responded: "We are not going to fail unless death comes."

Not until April would McGee personally hear from Verner, who, the *St. Louis Post-Dispatch* reported, was rumored to have been ambushed "by a savage tribe of pygmies." [15]

From the Kasai region Verner wrote to McGee to report hostilities between state troops and the Congolese people that had compounded the difficulties he was having persuading any forest dwellers to return with him. He claimed that, with Benga at his side, he offered the villagers salt and guns, and appealed to village councilors who had previously sought his assistance in their dealings with Belgian officials.

As more of the villages came under Leopold's tyrannical reign there were growing demands for them to pay higher taxes in the form of ivory, copper, wild rubber, and other coveted resources. Lukengu, king of the Bushongo, had been imprisoned for not paying sufficient taxes. Ndombe, ruler of the nearby village bearing his name, was under mounting pressure to pay ever more, or face a similar fate.

Under the precarious circumstances, Verner found it especially difficult to persuade the shy forest dwellers to accompany him. They understandably harbored concerns for their families' safety amid the escalating violence. Verner was, after all, asking members of a tight-knit community to leave their homes and beleaguered loved ones to visit a fair in a foreign land with a white stranger.

Verner later recalled that the old men shook their heads gravely, the women howled through the night, and the medicine men "violently opposed" his scheme.[16] Yet Verner claims he changed their minds by simply supplying salt—which traders and company officials paid Congolese for their goods and which Verner claimed was more valuable than gold. Verner also claims he lent some of the men guns for hunting. Since hand mutilation was ordered by the state to ensure that ammunition would be expended solely to punish defiant workers, Verner's claim to have provided weapons to a conquered people is highly doubtful.

But somehow, one by one, Verner won over Malengu, then Lanunu, then Shumbu and Bomushubba. He later said more than twenty males in all promised to accompany him, but more than half of them "subsequently gave way to their fears." Most of the "Bitwa" ran away "but we succeeded in keeping some to their promise." In a handwritten contract dated April 25, 1904, that resembled those produced by Livingston, Verner said he was employing Bondongo "for twelve months from this date" at a rate of one pound of salt and two bolts of cloth per month. An "X" was said to serve as Bondongo's signature. The "witness" was John Kondola, the young Congolese orphan Verner had taken from the Congo in 1899.

On the morning of May 11 Verner, accompanied by Ota Benga and a band of eight other young males of undetermined ages, boarded a steamer for the long journey down the Kasai River to Leopoldville and the mouth of the Congo. On Tenerife, in Spain's Canary Islands, they boarded the steamer *Glenarm Head* bound for New Orleans.

Well before they arrived McGee optimistically listed them in the fair's official printed catalog of exhibitors: "Group of twelve men, women and children (en route) from Upper Kasai Valley, Central Africa expedition conducted by Rev. S. P. Verner."

Describing them as the aborigines of Africa, he wrote: "The pygmy derives from the smallest known variety of mankind, they are notable also for imperfect development of language, for skill and courage in the chase, and for timidity in the presence of larger men." [17]

Also in the catalog were "Red Africans," also said to be en route from the Kasai valley. According to the catalog, they were "Notable for reddish or coppery skin color, for fine physique and for intelligence and force; the ruling class or caste in the southern Congo country, especially in the territory of 'king' Ndombe, himself the leading representative of the type."

The delegation arrived in New Orleans on June 25. According to the passenger list its youngest member, Bomushubba, was twelve, followed by Lumbaugu (or Lumbango), who was said to be fourteen. "Otabenga" was said to be seventeen—significantly younger than Verner would later claim. John "Condola," one of the two orphans who had returned to the United States with Verner in 1899, is identified on the passenger list as Verner's valet, age twenty-two. Only five years earlier, Verner had claimed Kondola was ten, which would have meant he was fifteen in St. Louis. It is likely that Verner included Kondola in the fair exhibition out of desperation, since his delegation had fallen far short of the eighteen people he had promised to bring back.

Verner, by then thirty, is identified in the passenger list as a scientist and as married. With the exception of Kalammua, said to be twenty-four, married, and a cook, the rest, including "Otabenga," were identified as single.

Although the delegation had arrived nearly two months late and fell far short of the goal—and although not one woman, infant, or elderly medicine man had joined the party—Verner's African visitors were giddily greeted in St. Louis.

"African Pygmies for the World's Fair" was the headline in the *St. Louis Post-Dispatch* on June 26, even if days later, the newspapers would mock the exhibited Africans with one offensive headline after another: "Pygmies Demand a Monkey Diet: Gentlemen from South Africa at the Fair Likely to Prove Troublesome in Matter of Food" and "Pygmies Scorn Cash; Demand Watermelons." [18]

Verner himself would not arrive in St. Louis with his coveted acquisitions. Instead, he disembarked in New Orleans on a stretcher and was transported to a sanatorium. Some people suspected sunstroke. The British consul Roger Casement, who happened to be on the same ship heading to America, observed that many thought Verner was "cracked." [19]

Whatever ailed Verner was no longer McGee's problem. He dispatched J. A. Dorsey of the U.S. Geological Survey to escort Benga and Verner's other captured "pygmies" from New Orleans to St. Louis, and the show would go on.

McGee did, however, write to Verner to console him: "First and foremost I want to assure you of the heartiest sympathy in your disappointment. It is bad enough to be knocked out in any stage of the contest, but particularly hard to fall after the laurel and the plaudits have been earned but before they are bestowed."[20]

He reassured Verner that Dorsey had delivered his "little folk" in good condition. "They are temporarily installed on the grounds where they are attracting much attention, though less than they would receive if they were properly placed and clad under the direction of the only man in America competent to look after these things."[21]

McGee advised Verner to "divest yourself of all anxiety and sense of responsibility. Be good to yourself—and let yourself recover."[22]

SIXTEEN

THE ST. LOUIS WORLD'S FAIR

On a crisp and sunny April 30, 1904, President Theodore Roosevelt stood in the East Room of the White House surrounded by members of his cabinet, Supreme Court justices, ambassadors, and foreign dignitaries. At 12:15 P.M. he pressed a gold key on a telegraph machine, sending the order that officially opened the Louisiana Purchase Exposition in St. Louis. Within seconds ten thousand flags were unfurled from their masts, water leaped from fountains in Festival Hall, and a chorus of cheers rang out from the 200,000 gathered on the fairgrounds 700 miles away.

Six years in the planning and at a record cost exceeding $50 million, the fair covered 1,200 acres in Forest Park—the largest acreage ever designated for an exposition. The St. Louis world's fair commemorated the centennial of the Louisiana Purchase and the recent triumphs of the United States over the Philippines, Guam, and Puerto Rico, and celebrated the nation as the world's most advanced civilization.

As president of the fair, David R. Francis—who was a former

governor of Missouri and secretary of the interior and would later, during Grover Cleveland's administration, serve as ambassador to Russia—was determined to outspend and outshine even the spectacular Chicago world's fair of 1893. That fair had commemorated the four hundredth anniversary of Christopher Columbus's arrival in the New World and the fairgrounds had been wondrously washed with millions of white lights. Attendees would long remember the resplendent beaux arts architecture in the fair's shimmering White City.

Francis imagined his Exposition as a global village in which all of the world's people and their artifacts would be grandly displayed, to illustrate human development from the lowest to the highest civilizations. McGee had jumped at the opportunity to head the fair's anthropology department—and to showcase anthropology as a cutting-edge science.

By the fall of 1903 McGee had begun to dispatch agents around the world to bring back examples of humans and their artifacts. The anthropologist Frederick Starr, of the University of Chicago, was assigned to bring back Ainu from northern Japan. Professor George A. Dorsey of Chicago's Field Museum of Natural History, who held a doctorate in anthropology from Harvard, was hired to assemble a representative sample of Native American tribes. Verner would bring back the most highly anticipated attraction of all: African "pygmies," said to represent the smallest people and the least advanced civilization on earth.

In all, the Exposition featured some ten thousand people. They included two thousand Native Americans, among them the famous Apache chief Geronimo, at the time a federal prisoner of war. There was a Philippine reservation set on forty-seven acres with more than one thousand native Filipinos and one hundred buildings. The presence of Benga and his countrymen—along with the Native Americans; the Filipinos and Igorot; and the Japanese Ainu—was intended to highlight the United States' conquests, imperialism, and progress.

"While the buildings and the machines, the congresses and the beauty, the glamour and pomp of such a celebration and exposition shall pass into memory and every material evidence of it disappear, the measurement it makes of progress, noted as it is in the history of the world, must become a benefit to mankind, the value of which cannot be exaggerated," Secretary of War William H. Taft remarked in his opening day address. "It reduces the size of our world, in that it brings all nations into one small locality for a time."[1]

A month before Benga and his comrades arrived, fair officials had considered what would happen following the inevitable death of some tribe members on the fairgrounds. "There will undoubtedly be deaths among the Filipino and other tribes assembled at St. Louis," Ales Hrdlicka, director of physical anthropology at the American Museum of Natural History, matter-of-factly stated in a letter to Livingston Farrand, an anthropology professor at Columbia University also affiliated with the Museum of Natural History. Hrdlicka said McGee was in favor of his plan to keep as many of the bodies as possible, rather than make arrangements to send them home for burial: "They would come to the Columbia College, New York, and Professor [George S.] Huntington would utilize all the soft parts."[2]

He added, "The National Museum [the Smithsonian] would whenever possible get the brain, and the skeletons which would be prepared by Professor Huntington's men, would be the property of the American Museum [of Natural History]."

Hrdlicka offered to make arrangements with the St. Louis board of health.

Baron Ludovic Moncheur, the Belgian minister in Washington, presided over the opening of his country's pavilion. In a skillfully staged event he invited three hundred orphan girls—twenty of them "colored"—from St. Louis asylums and treated them to lunch on the fairgrounds. His display of benevolence, however, did not suppress a debate in the British Parliament that June: the debate resulted in Britain's urging Leopold to appoint an independent commission to investigate Roger Casement's allegations.

Meanwhile Benga and his fellow Congolese, although they had been late entering the global village at the end of June, proved enormously popular from the start. Even beforehand, there had been sensationalized news reports about them. Days before their arrival the *St. Louis Post-Dispatch* had begun to exoticize them: "Red pygmies and black, the dwarf tribesmen, concerning whom less is known than of any other people on the face of the earth, they come to St. Louis the first of their kind who ever visited the Western Hemisphere," one article said.[3] This article included a long list of "queer facts," among them: "They are reported to practice cannibalism," and "If caught young they are said to make excellent servants."[4]

It is likely that Verner provided at least some of these "facts" to fair officials. David Francis, in his published report on the fair, said that the Africans represented the lowest known human stage, and that a few of them, including Benga, had come from man-eating tribes. Benga, he wrote, is "notably cannibalistic," and he said that this explained Benga's filed incisors.[5]

"He confessed to feasts of human flesh but a few months before his departure from Africa, while his mouth watered at sight of some of the plump colored folk among the visitors at the Exposition," Francis added.[6] He also noted, "The physical types chosen for representation were those least removed from the sub-human or quadrumane form, beginning with the pygmy aborigines of Africa and including the negrito folk of interior Mindanao and other districts," from the Philippines exhibition.

Verner had explicitly said in his 1902 *Atlantic Monthly* article that cannibalism was not practiced among the so-called pygmies, but in St. Louis he no longer exercised such restraint. Instead he played up impressions of Benga's cannibalism—for example, in a first-person account of how he had brought "pygmies" to the fair published in the Sunday magazine section of the *St. Louis Post-Dispatch*. In that two-page article, he exploited Benga's pointed incisors, which were illustrated for maximum effect.

"Have you seen Otabenga's teeth?" the article began. "They're worth the 5 cents he charges for showing them. . . . Otabenga is a cannibal, the only genuine cannibal in America today."[7]

Of course, several years earlier, Verner had memorably claimed that Kondola—who was now also on the fairgrounds but did not have filed teeth—was a cannibal. But during the time Verner spent in the Congo he would have likely noticed that tooth-chipping—done by local craftsmen—was a common practice among young males and was no more consequential than ear piercing.

The headline of an article in the *Columbus* (South Carolina) *Dispatch* proclaimed: "A New Race of Africans Discovered and Brought to America: Among Them Are Cannibals and One Little Fellow Who Narrowly Escaped Being the Central Attraction at a Cannibal Feast."[8] That article featured a photograph of Benga, as well as one of Verner, who was described as "Rev. S. P. Verner the Explorer."

In its coverage of the fair, *Scientific American* described "Otto Bang" as a cannibal, apparently following the narrative provided by fair officials. The author of the article—which put his unscientific ideas and racial biases on full display—wrote of the Africans: "Their faces are coarse, features brutal, and evidence an intelligence of an extremely low order."[9]

Francis later conceded that although the nine Central African delegates had been billed as "pygmies," they could be so designated only "nominally."[10]

Kondola, whose age was given as twenty on the passenger list, was described by fair officials as nineteen and as belonging to the Batetela tribe. Benga, who on the passenger list was said to be seventeen, was now described as age eighteen and belonging to the Chirichiri or Badinga, while the others were said to be Mbuti, also called Bakuba. Lumbaugu (or Lumbango), who was described as age fourteen on the passenger list, was now said to be age sixteen and the nephew of Chief Ndombe.

Given the various descriptions provided for Benga and his fellow delegates, their ages and tribal affiliations appear to have been randomly ascribed. Kondola, who would later be identified in U.S. naturalization records as John Dundes Condola, gave his own birth date as April 5, 1892, which would have made him seven when Verner first brought him to the United States and twelve in St. Louis.[11] And at his adult height—five feet six inches—he would not, even by the so-called scientific standards of the day, have qualified as a true "pygmy."[12] Neither European nor American anthropologists would regard any adult male over five feet tall as a "pygmy."

Francis conceded that the only actual "pygmies" in the delegation were the four so-called Mbuti—Shamba, Malengo, Lumo, and Bomushubba, the last of whom was described as age twelve, and therefore, like Kondola and possibly others, not yet fully grown. But neither Francis nor Verner seemed troubled by such niggling technicalities. Francis said their average stature, including that of Ota Benga, was four feet ten inches. However, he did not account for their ages and did not suggest that, as children, they had not yet reached their adult height.

Benga proved especially popular with the public and the press. Reporters identified him variously as Otto Bang, Otabenga, Autobank, and Artiba. Of the group he was the most engaging with the crowds, and many spectators noted his sad eyes—and the sharp incisors that conveniently conformed to the stereotype of African cannibals.

Benga was mocked in one article for holding out his hand for money when his photograph was taken. Describing him as "Artiba, the cannibal," this article said: "He produced a very smart, civilized-looking purse and hid away his wage with his other wealth. He had nearly a dollar already. Then he lit his cigarette and inhaled in large breaths with the greatest delight, babbling volubly in the Baluba language."[13]

Before up to twenty thousand people at a time, Benga and the others danced and sang; their performance was billed as either a Mbuti social or cannibal dances. At times these performances were so popular that the police were called in to manage the crowds—the fair's organizers feared serious injuries. One incident occurred on July 16, "Anthropology Day," when the plaza "was the scene of a remarkable gathering of primitive race groups," participating in native sports and demonstrations, according to Francis. At some point, as Benga and the others danced while brandishing spears and bows and arrows before tens of thousands of people, pandemonium erupted.

"The pygmies so terrified a woman that she involuntarily cried out," reported the *St. Louis Post-Dispatch*. The guards swarmed toward Benga and the others, "who appeared as much frightened as the woman had been," the article said.[14]

Benga and his fellow Africans were also featured on "Children's Day," an event during which all the nations of the world were to sing and dance onstage in the plaza. Admission for children was free. "Cannibals Will Sing and Dance," announced the *St. Louis Post-Dispatch*. They participated in athletic games, including mud fights and a javelin toss, which Geronimo sadly observed from the sidelines.[15]

Throughout their time on display the African visitors were poked, prodded, pinched, and otherwise inspected by the crowds while their pet parrots and monkeys were taunted and burned with cigars.

"At first charmed by the kaleidoscopic novelty of strange signs and surroundings, the passing crowds and especially the insatiate photographers soon palled on the Pygmies and they held long and frequent palavers with Mr. Verner with the object of hastening their return," Francis later acknowledged.[16] Francis's observation indicates that fair officials were well aware of the visitors' discomfort and desire to leave the fairgrounds.

Behind the scenes the visitors were measured, photographed, and tested in what Starr described as "excellently equipped Laboratories of Anthropometry and Psychometry" on the fairgrounds. Portraits were commissioned by Chicago's Field Museum. A fictitious, provocative label for Benga's portrait read: "Subject: Pygmy showing teeth ground for flesh eating." [17]

Benga was also one of the individuals of whom plaster busts were made from life by Caspar Mayer, the sculptor for the American Museum of Natural History. Franz Boas, at the time a curator of anthropology at the museum, had written to McGee in March 1904 proposing to make casts of some two hundred of the displayed humans. He had already discussed the matter with Mayer, "whose work, I think, is remarkably good." [18] By August 9 Mayer was installed in the laboratory on the fairgrounds. "From a list of completed casts, it appears that Benga was his third subject, and Kondola the eleventh. Livingston Farrand of the museum had instructed Mayer to "make every effort" to get casts of the Patagonian tribes, adding that "those and the Pygmies I regard as especially valuable." [19]

The casts were made at a cost of $12 each, with plans to circulate sets of two hundred to museums around the country. In letters introducing Mayer to fairground exhibit directors, McGee said the casts were primarily being made on behalf of the museum "but with the hope that these may be multiplied in such manner as to find their way into all the museums of the country." [20] The effort, he said, would promote the interests of anthropology.

In October Mayer wrote to Boas to report that fifty-five casts had been completed: forty for the American Museum of Natural History and fifteen for the Field Columbian Museum in Chicago. [21] Dartmouth's Hood Museum was also among the institutions that acquired a set of casts, including casts of Ota Benga and John Kondola.

In addition to being measured and photographed and having his face encased in plaster, Benga also had what appeared to be a light-hearted exchange with Caroline Furness Jayne, an ethnologist from an influential Philadelphia family. The daughter of Horace Howard Furness, a Shakespearean scholar at the University of Pennsylvania, she was married to Horace Jayne, a biology professor at the same university. Her brother was a medical doctor and a fellow of the Anthropology Institute of Great Britain. Through him she would meet her mentor, Alfred Haddon, the noted founder of Cambridge's School of Anthropology, who encouraged her study of string tricks.

Haddon had played cat's cradle as a child and was surprised, during field studies in the Torres Strait, to find string figures "of savage peoples that put our humble efforts to shame."[22] Not only were the figures more complicated, but, he said, "they represented various natural and artificial objects in a state of rest or motion."[23]

In 1888 Boas published a paper on the Inuit that included a description of the method of string tricks—apparently the first such account. He found the game popular among the eastern Eskimo people, and he discovered numerous patterns. In 1902, Haddon, with W. H. R. River, published a paper recording a wide variety of intricate patters and shapes. A year later Haddon wrote a paper on Native American string games. But Caroline Furness Jayne would be the first to compile examples of the practice from around the globe. Haddon encouraged her to attend the St. Louis world's fair to investigate the practice among purportedly primitive people. There she visited the Native American, Philippines, and African reservations.

She described Ota Benga as "a bright little man" who showed her an intricate diamond pattern that she would identify in her book as "pygmy diamond." The illustrations, accompanied by a meticulous description and a photograph of a distressed-looking Benga, were included in *String Figures and How to Make Them: A Study of Cat's Cradle in Many Lands*, published in 1906 by Scribner and later reprinted by Dove.

Jayne said it was, to her knowledge, the first recorded description of an African string game. Given what had been written about Benga's people, she was clearly surprised by the discovery.

"The nature of the Batwas and their isolation in the heart of Africa would not lead us to expect to find among them a relatively complicated figure," she wrote.[24] The figure, she said, had much in common with a pattern found in the Carolina Islands, and was identical to the sixth movement of a mouth figure she found among the Eskimo. Ota Benga—whom she called "Ottobang"—is identified in her book as as a "Cannibal Pygmy" from the Kasai valley in the Congo.

When Verner was finally reunited with his charges on August 5 he found them gathered around a campfire, shivering and depressed. They were living in a tent on the frigid fairgrounds and wearing jackets and coats that they had somehow acquired. They had managed to get a few blankets from their Native American neighbors but needed more. In addition to the cold, they complained about the crude behavior of fairgoers, who laughed at them and physically attacked them. They wanted to go home.

At one point Verner, accompanied by Benga, gave a talk at the Davenport Academy of Science in Iowa. Benga's photograph and a diagram of his teeth would later appear in *Proceedings of the Davenport Academy of Science* in a long treatise on teeth-chipping.[25] Verner also visited Baron Ludovic Moncheur in Washington, D.C., where he was finally awarded his long-coveted concession, a triumph he announced in an officious statement to his friends, family, and colleagues.

As temperatures plummeted in St. Louis, the young Africans were left to endure the cold in only their loincloths. They attempted to stay in their huts, but angry spectators bombarded their quarters with bricks or rocks to drive them out.

"It required constant vigilance and half-cruel constraints to keep them out of close-fitting clothing . . . which would have interfered with the functions normal to their naked skins and brought serious if not fatal results," Francis divulged.[26]

But Verner, ever disingenuous, would later remark that the African visitors had been treated with the utmost respect. "They were not to be exhibited in dime museums or on the Pike, or in any other way than under the most respectable scientific auspices; a condition which was entirely carried out."[27]

In any event the African visitors' comfort was certainly not high on the list of McGee's considerations as he hosted the world's leading academics at the International Congress of Art and Science, held on the fairgrounds on September 19. Among the two thousand scholars attending that day were Franz Boas, the German sociologist Max Weber, and two university presidents: William Rainey Harper of the University of Chicago and Woodrow Wilson of Princeton.

In his presentation, "The History of Anthropology," McGee summarized the development of anthropology and the work of evolutionary thinkers who had singled out Caucasians as the beacons of enlightenment. McGee predicted that Caucasian enlightenment would spread around the world. Boas challenged the premise of the field and its assumptions, based on racial superiority, that he said merely rationalized popular prejudices.

But these high-minded debates were for the academic elite. For the general public, the sight of barely clad, presumably primitive people assembled across the fairgrounds was evidence enough of Caucasian superiority. The beings whom scientists had described as semi-human, cannibalistic dwarfs were no longer relegated to mythology or to anthropological field notes. The reality—that the delegation comprised captured African children—if considered at all, was understood as merely a means to a scientific end.

On December 1 the pavilions closed at 4 P.M., and by midnight the fairground lights had faded to black, ending a seven-month wonderland. Over that time eighteen million people had come to the fairgrounds, where many had been exposed for the first time to electric lights, moving pictures, the ice cream cone, and "pygmies." The fair brought representatives from sixty-two countries and colonies and world leaders, including President Roosevelt, who attended twice; vice president–elect Charles W. Fairbanks; China's Prince Pu Lun; Japan's

Prince Sadanaru Fushimi; the Mexican vice president, Ramon Corral; and Cardinal Francis Satolli.

The fair had played host to the first Olympic Games held in the United States, and twenty-seven nations had contributed to an art exhibition featuring eleven thousand paintings and sculptures. Fairgoers had been entertained but also educated in the "university of mankind" with its implicit lessons in evolutionary theory.

Benga's image would be immortalized in the life cast and bronze bust commissioned by the American Museum of Natural History and in photographic portraits made for the Field Columbian Museum, as well as in dozens of photographs taken by photojournalists and fairgoers. His image would also appear in books by Frederick Starr and Caroline Furness Jayne, and in scientific journals.

And Benga would help bring Verner the recognition he craved. Of the thousands of exhibits competing for attention, only a few were considered by fair officials to be prize-worthy. For the anthropology department, Kondola, who during the exhibition served as his fellow Africans' caretaker, won a bronze medal; Geronimo won a silver medal; and for his remarkable and memorable contribution to the fair, Verner won the gold. The intrepid showman would share the grand prize with the University of Chicago's Frederick Starr, who had exhibited nine Ainu men, women, and children from northern Japan, and who would soon join Verner in the Congo. Benga and his comrades were rewarded with gifts of fifteen cents each; Ndombe was sent $2 worth of salt.

SEVENTEEN

CONGO FIELD NOTES

As winter settled on St. Louis it was time for Verner to return his prizewinning delegation to the Kasai region. By the time they arrived in New Orleans Benga and the others contracted chicken pox, delaying their departure. There was another delay in Havana as they awaited a ship, followed by a two-week wait in Santa Cruz de Tenerife after they missed a ship to the Congo owing, according to Verner, to headwinds on the Atlantic.

McGee apparently denied Verner's request for additional funds. Verner said the decision would mean having to tap into his personal finances and that it "leaves Mrs. Verner and my children absolutely without means of support in the interior."[1]

While he noted that his wife was willing to sacrifice their interests to the honorable discharge of his duty, "I leave it to you as a man of honor [to determine] if it is fair to make her suffering the least for this series of events."[2]

Verner said he could not call on his family, who had already in the past "manfully" supported his African endeavors. He asked Mc-

Gee to pay his wife at least $75 monthly until he reached Ndombe and then for another two months afterward to allow for his return. "I must leave to you and to those gentlemen for whose plans she has suffered and endured more than I or any of us," he wrote, thereby relinquishing to McGee the responsibility to support his family.[3]

When McGee seemed to question his financial acumen, Verner reminded him that he was still young (he was then thirty) and that the educational value would benefit him in the future. He noted that McGee's opinion of him had weight with others, and if it was thought he could not handle such matters "I must be put down as hopeless."

Verner said if he or the Africans had been the recipients of the outlay of money for the expedition, "I might feel that we were all rightly subject to censure." However, he said the transportation and boarding necessitated by the unavoidable delays accounted for the additional costs. While Verner had initially proposed completing the mission for $1,000, he now, remarkably, recalled suggesting $30,000.

"The one great regret of my whole connection with this work is that I did not insist on making that thirty thousand estimate in writing and as a sine qua non for the acceptance of responsibility; with a guarantee of three thousand to myself," he complained.

Verner reminded McGee that other explorers faced similar challenges, noting that even Henry Morton Stanley had to draw a large sum from his personal finances and adding, "No doubt others also belonged to that unfortunate category."

He assured McGee that he would not use a cent of the Exposition's money. "As a matter of fact," he said, "my obligations to care for these people [the Congolese delegation] seriously crippled my efforts to prepare to do anything [in Ndombe] this time. At present I have no definite outlook for support there at all."

If he was able to make a living from the goods he had left at Ndombe to assure the king of his return, Verner would not consider his treatment by the Exposition "as anything less than liberal." If not, he said, he would suffer, but he would do so in silence. Verner was at least pleased that McGee had expressed personal fondness for him, "almost more than I deserve, seeing the difficulties I have put you to." But he again blamed himself for not insisting on $30,000. "That I regard as my main error—not the incurring of expenses for unavoidable emergencies."

Sometime during the spring of 1905 Verner, Benga, and the others were finally back in the Kasai region. Verner claims he tried to restore Benga to his village but, when he was unable to do so, placed him near Ndombe with the others he had brought back. There, according to Verner, Benga was adopted by a new village where he married a second wife. This account, like so many others offered by Verner, is questionable and has not been independently verified. Verner also claims that Benga continued to accompany him on trips through the woods collecting plants for the Missouri Botanical Gardens, while also searching for minerals, wild rubber, and ivory to sell from his new concession.

In December Verner was joined by the University of Chicago ethnologist Frederick Starr, who had been inspired by the African delegation in St. Louis. Starr's presence would provide an account of Benga in the Congo independent of Verner's, and a contemporary look at life among the forest dwellers. Nine years earlier Starr had translated the book *The Pygmies* by the French ethnologist Armand de Quatrefages, and now he wished to launch his own investigation in the African interior. In a newspaper interview before his trip, he offered the opinion that the forest dwellers were not "apish, as popularly believed." He wanted to prove that they had remained unchanged and were not "a degenerate people," as some suspected.[4]

Starr also planned to study the race of yellow and copper people Verner claimed to have discovered in the African interior. In an article in *American Anthropologist* on the so-called yellow Africans, Verner said they were found in Central and southern Africa along the Nile, Zambezi, and Congo Rivers. He said they were copper-colored and

Ota Benga and his fellow countrymen at the St. Louis World's Fair, 1904.

Papers of Samuel Verner, South Caroliniana Library Archives, University of South Carolina

Left: The *New York Times* article on September 9, 1906, that first exposed Benga's exhibition in the Bronx Zoo Monkey House.

The New York Times

Right: A portrait of Ota Benga taken by Manuel Gonzales during Frederick Starr's expedition in the Congo between 1905 and 1906. Starr noted that Benga's teeth were the result of tooth-chipping, a practice he found common among young males in the Congo. Verner untruthfully alleged that Benga was a cannibal.

Ota Benga (Plate XXVI) from PPC.S73, courtesy of the American Museum of Natural History

Samuel Phillips Verner, the former Presbyterian missionary turned explorer who was hired by organizers of the St. Louis World's Fair to bring "pygmies" to the fair. Ota Benga was one of the Congolese males he brought to the United States. Two years later, Verner left Benga at the Bronx Zoo.

Papers of Samuel Verner, South Caroliniana Library Archives, University of South Carolina

William Temple Hornaday, the zoologist and founding director of both the National Zoological Park in Washington, D.C., and the Bronx Zoo, where he exhibited Benga in the monkey house.

© *Wildlife Conservation Society*

William Sheppard, the Presbyterian missionary and explorer hailed as the "Black Livingstone" for his discovery of the Congo's Kuba kingdom. He also helped expose Leopold's atrocities in the Congo.

Reverend Robert Stuart MacArthur, the pastor of Manhattan's Calvary Baptist Church, was the first to publicly express outrage over Benga's exhibition.

Wilford H. Smith, the prominent lawyer and confidant to Booker T. Washington, appealed for Benga's release from the Bronx Zoo Monkey House cage.

Reverend James Gordon, the superintendent of the Howard Colored Orphan Asylum in Brooklyn, New York. Gordon led the protests against Ota Benga's exhibition and captivity in the monkey house. After securing Benga's release he provided him a home, first at the orphanage in Brooklyn and later at its farm on Long Island.

Reverend Gregory Hayes, the president of Lynchburg Seminary, became Ota Benga's guardian in Lynchburg, Virginia, shortly before his untimely death in 1906. Benga was sent back to the Howard Colored Orphan Asylum but returned in 1910 to reside with Hayes' widow, Mary.

Courtesy of the Anne Spencer House and Garden Museum, Inc. Archives

Henry Fairfield Osborn, a renowned paleontologist and eugenicist who played a lead role in the creation of the Bronx Zoo. He was among the zoo officials who supported Benga's exhibition in the monkey house. He later served as president of the American Museum of Natural History for twenty-five years.

Image #109272, American Museum of Natural History Library

Right: Mary Hayes Allen, who provided a home for Benga when he returned to Lynchburg in 1910.

Courtesy of the Anne Spencer House and Garden Museum, Inc. Archives

Left: Anne Spencer, who befriended Ota Benga while he was a student at Virginia Seminary, where she taught. Spencer would later achieve fame as a poet during the Harlem Renaissance.

James Weldon Johnson Memorial Collection, Beinecke Rare Book and Manuscript Library, Yale University

The July 1906 ship passenger record identifies Benga as Mbye Otabenga, the same name that Samuel Verner privately addressed him by in letters.

Courtesy of Ancestry.com

IMMIGRATION SERVICE
Form 1000.
(Ed. 11-12-1909—50,000)

3093 LIST OR MANIFEST OF ALIEN PASSENGERS [

Required by the regulations of the Secretary of the Treasury of the United States, under Act of Congress
Officer of any vessel having such passengers on boa

S. S. _Glenarm Head_ sailing from _Teneriffe, June 5_

NAME IN FULL.	Ages. Yrs. Mos.	Sex.	Married or Single.	Calling or Occupation.	Able to Read. Write	Nationality. Country.	*Race or People.	Last Residence.	Final Destination (State, City, or Town
Jennie Berliner	26	f	M	U.S. Citizenship	ye ye	United States	White	Teneriffe	Washin
J. F. T. do	1 11	m	S	do	no no	"	"	"	"
S. P. Verner	30	"	M	Scientist	ye ye	"	"	"	St Lo
John Condola	22	"	S	Valet	ye ye	"	"	"	"
Kalanna	24	"	M	Cook	no no	Congo	African	"	"
Lotuma	15	"	S	Farmer	no no	"	"	"	"
Lumbango	18	"	S	do	no no	"	"	"	"
Malengu	38	"	S	Huntsman	no no	"	"	"	"
Shamba	24	"	S	do	no no	"	"	"	"
Lumu	20	"	S	do	no no	"	"	"	"
Bomushutta	18	"	S	do	no no	"	"	"	"
Otabenga	17	"	S	do	no no	"	"	"	"

* "Race or People" is to be determined by the stock from which they sprang and the lang

March 3, 1893, to be delivered to the Commissioner of Immigration by the Commanding
rrival at a port in the United States.

Arriving at Port of New Orleans _____ June 25, 1904 _____ 23

By whom was passage paid?	Whether in possession of money, if so whether more than forty dollars or less.	Whether ever before in the United States and if so, when and where.	Whether going to join a relative; and if so, what relative, the name and address.	How in future to be transported by country if 3 years place which.	Whether a Polygamist.	Whether anarchist.	Condition of Health, Mental and Physical.	Deformed or Crippled. Nature and Cause.
Consul $ 500		Yes	Family	no	no	no	good	no
"	"	no	"	no	no	no	good	no
Himself $ 100	"	yes	St Louis Fair	no	no	no	good	no
S.P.N	"	"	"	no	no	no	good	no
"	"	"	"	no	no	no	good	no
"	"	"	"	no	no	no	good	no
"	"	"	"	no	no	no	good	no
"	"	"	"	no	no	no	good	no
"	"	"	"	no	no	no	good	no
"	"	"	"	no	no	no	good	no
"	"	"	"	no	no	no	good	no

Frank Syms
Master

The passenger list for Samuel Verner and the African delegation en route to the World's Fair in 1904. Ota Benga appears last.

Courtesy of Ancestry.com

MRS. GORDON, MOTHER OF THEM ALL.

Mary Gordon, house matron of the Howard Colored Orphan Asylum.

Verner with Kondola and Kassongo in the Congo.

MR VERNER AND THE BATETELA BOYS

In Central Africa, before the boys were Americanized

"generally more intelligent" and "less emotional," than darker Africans. Of course it is likely that the "yellow negroes" were products of voluntary and involuntary sexual liaisons between African women and others, including Europeans and North Africans.

Starr said Verner's discovery of an unknown race of yellow negroes "has awakened a widespread desire among scientists for a more extended knowledge in regard to them, which can only come from careful and prolonged research."

Starr appeared eminently qualified to embark on such an inquiry. Unlike Verner, who appeared chiefly motivated by commercial interests, Starr was a recognized ethnologist. The forty-six-year-old native of Auburn, New York, was a popular and charismatic lecturer who had already earned distinction as a scientist before sharing the grand prize with Verner at the St. Louis world's fair.

He had already conducted field studies in Mexico, Guatemala, Korea, the Philippines, Cuba, Liberia, and Japan. Among his many published books were *Indians of Southern Mexico: An Ethnographic Album* and *In Indian Mexico: A Narrative of Travel and Labor.*

With an undergraduate degree from the University of Rochester and a Ph.D. in geology from Lafayette College, he obtained academic appointments at Coe College in Iowa; Chautauqua University in New York; and Pomona College in California, where he served as a professor of geology and anthropology and dean of the science department. In 1888 he was hired by the American Museum of Natural History to work as an ethnologist; three years later he was hired by the University of Chicago to organize anthropology instruction, and he became a popular lecturer there.

Starr's Congo expedition field notes, photographs, articles, and ethnologies would reveal colonialism and global complicity in the plight of the Congolese and offer glimpses of Benga negotiating the country's treacherous terrain near the twilight of Leopold's reign.

Starr left New York on September 23, 1905, and made the obligatory stop to meet with Belgian officials, who promised to provide transportation and assistance in the Congo, as they had for Verner. Starr no doubt would be obliged to vow discretion in exchange for entry into Leopold's dominion, even if he would later claim that "it was understood by them that I should speak freely and frankly of everything which I should see. On their part, the state authorities expressed the liveliest satisfaction that an independent American traveler should visit the Congo Free State."[5]

By then the state was under mounting pressure, compounded by the publication of Mark Twain's satire *King Leopold's Soliloquy.* While ridiculing Leopold, Twain praised Sheppard—Verner's former missionary colleague—for exposing the atrocities. A book on the Congo tragedy by one of America's most famous writers fueled public outrage and put more pressure on President Roosevelt and Congress to act. Also, the inquiry by Leopold's commission into the atrocities unexpectedly confirmed the British consul Roger Casement's allegations of forced labor, mutilations, killings, and overall abuse of the Congolese. The surprising rebuke provoked Leopold to intensify his public relations efforts; meanwhile, the Congo Reform Association published the findings as a pamphlet.

Starr made stops in Dakar, Freetown, Accra, and other cities along the African coast, and arrived in Leopoldville in mid-November. He explored villages along the Congo River, and arrived in Ndombe on December 29 for his reunion with Benga and Verner. He would stay at Verner's concession, which was called Mount Washington; Starr complained that its name was "curiously and painfully American." He also grumbled because it was some thirty minutes by hammock from Ndombe. Starr made the trip accompanied by Manuel Gonzales, a photographer from Mexico City, who would take hundreds of photographs, some of which would be exhibited and published in a book. A striking portrait of a beaming and boyish Benga, baring his pointed teeth, would appear in Starr's *Congo Natives: An Ethnographic*

Album, published in 1912. Benga, with his hair shaved on both sides, looked far more youthful and vivacious than he would less than a year later at the Bronx Zoo.

Starr arrived fully prepared to document native life. In addition to Gonzales, he took a phonograph machine to make cylinder recordings, a graphophone on which to play them; materials with which to make casts and impressions, and tools to take measurements. As a physical anthropologist, he was a proponent of anthropometry, in which measurements were taken of the cranium, limbs, sexual organs, and other parts of the human body. Its adherents believed that relevant distinctions could be found and that these could explain varying levels of intelligence and achievement along racial lines, a theory that has since been discarded. Starr had already taken measurements of Benga, among the other "primitive" people gathered in St. Louis. In the Congo he would, with Leopold's blessing, observe and take impressions, casts, photographs, and measurements of as many as a thousand Congolese soldiers.

During his study of the forest dwellers, Starr noted the characteristics of "pygmies," saying French anthropologists agreed that the height of an adult male should not exceed 1,500 millimeters—or roughly four feet eleven inches, while the English set the limit at five feet. "Our Batua," he said, "lie between."

He said the forest dwellers lived primarily by the chase and gathering wild food. While he found geographic variation, he said they were generally characterized by their lives in the forest, the constancy of hunting with a bow and arrow, an absence of agriculture, their shyness and distrust of outsiders, and their "parasitic relation" to their larger neighbors, who were often wary or disdainful of them but nonetheless relied on them for game.

"Today the pygmies are mere fragments, scattered and separated, but retaining with tenacity their ancient life," Starr observed. "Little in stature, scrawny in form, with a face shrewd, cunning, and sly, the pygmy is a hunter."[6]

He described their settlement in a forest clearing as a ring of rounded homes measuring 1,695 millimeters—about five and a half feet—high, situated around a central open space. The houses were constructed of a framework of poles, stuck three to four inches into the ground, and bound together at the top. Across the vertical poles, at regular intervals, were horizontal poles forming "a square mesh work," which was covered with a thick sheet of large leaves held down by a square mesh of tied *kodja*, or rattan.

At the center of each house was a hearth with charcoal and ashes. The inhabitants slept on beds made of bamboo sticks and piled firewood on the opposite side of the house. The Batua, he said, made fire by friction—by "whirling an upright stick between the palms, the lower bluntly pointed and resting with pressure in a notch cut in a lower stick laid on the ground." They did not appear to engage in agriculture or weaving and their favorite article of clothing was made from the skin of a large baboon.

Similar observations were made by German anthropologist Ludwig Wolf during his expedition in the Wissmann Falls region from 1883 to 1885. He found reserved, shy "African dwarfs" who were notable hunters and lived in clearings in the forest. He remarked that they had the task of providing a daily supply of palm wine and game to the neighboring Bakuba king. Noting their well-developed bodies and their average height of 1,400 to 1,440 millimeters (about four feet seven or eight inches), he said that "pithecoid characters were never present."[7] Wolf also noted that they did not engage in cults and buried their dead.

In his Congo field notes Sidney Langford Hinde made repeated references to "the little people of the forest," describing them as "sturdy and independent" nomadic hunters who "run along a game path with perfect ease, which to an ordinary man would be impossible unless bent nearly double." Their agility had enabled them to ward off earlier expeditions by Arab slave traders. "On seeing the flash of the firing gun (muzzle-loading) they drop, and running in, hidden by the grass, spear their opponent while he is in the act of reloading."

He called their intimate knowledge of poisons and their bows and arrows "deadly engines in hunting or war."[8]

Perhaps British anthropologist Colin Turnbull best described the spiritual and cultural world of the forest dwellers. During the 1950s Turnbull spent years living in the Ituri forest with people he called the Mbuti. His observations of these small forest dwellers bear striking similarities to descriptions of Benga by those who knew him.

Turnbull characterized their environment in the forest as a damp parallel universe, a "shady world with light filtering lazily through the tree tops" and the air filled with the trumpeting of elephants, the cooing of pigeons, and the chattering of monkeys.[9]

There the Mbuti lived in thatched huts, and roamed the forest in small hunting groups, moving swiftly and silently as they stalked their prey with short handheld spears and bows and poisoned arrows. He described the people of the forest as fearless but peaceful and said they loved their children, revered their elders, and mourned and buried their dead. What distinguished them was that they lived by their wits as hunters and gatherers and had an intense love of nature, which they regularly celebrated through dance and song.

Turnbull described their celebrations of the forest as "the most joyful sound of all . . . as they sing a lusty chorus of praise to this wonderful world of theirs—a world that gives them everything they want. This cascade of sound echoes among the giant trees until it seems to come at you from all sides in sheer beauty and truth and goodness, full of the joy of living."[10]

It was a ritual that Benga would bring to his life in America.

Like Wolf, Turnbull observed that forest people typically did not believe in evil spirits, but nonetheless were generally feared by outsiders who saw them as alien people with special powers.

One of the earliest references to so-called pygmies is found in Egypt during the Fourth Dynasty, in the expedition record of an

Egyptian explorer trying to find the source of the Nile some 2,500 years before the Christian era. Preserved in the tomb of Pharaoh Nefrikare was a report of his commander, Herkouf, who entered a great forest to the west of the Mountains of the Moon and discovered a people of the trees—a tiny people who sang and danced to their god. Nefrikare sent an order for Herkouf to bring one of the "dancers of God" back with him.

Later records show that the Egyptians became familiar with the diminutive forest dwellers who were, then as now, scattered throughout Central Africa. Later, in Pompeii, they were depicted in mosaics, living in huts in the forest A thirteenth-century map in Hereford Cathedral, England, also accurately located them in Central Africa, but represented them as subhuman beasts.

Up until the nineteenth century many explorers continued to ascribe superhuman or subhuman characteristics to them. Some claimed they had tails. Now Benga, despite his gentle nature and apparent intelligence, was the victim of romanticized myths and persistent prejudice.

Starr examined the teeth of nine hundred soldiers across the Congo Free State. He provided three pages of detailed drawings of various types of teeth modifications in "Ethnographic Notes of the Congo Free State: An African Miscellany," published in *Proceedings of the Davenport Academy of Sciences*. Diagram 45 featured a drawing of Ota Benga's V-shaped teeth, a modification that Starr noted was "not uncommon among Basoko, Mongo, and the populations of Lac Leopold II and the Vele."[11]

Unlike Verner, who fallaciously associated the custom with cannibalism, Starr elaborated on "tooth-chipping" among many in the Congo, suggesting that it was a common practice.

"Knocking out, pointing, and otherwise modifying the teeth is common among Congo peoples," he wrote.[12] "In the higher Congo it is found among most tribes and in some is practiced upon practically every man." He added that *Basongo meno*—a term loosely applied to various tribes along the Kasai River that would be likely to include Benga's—"all have their teeth pointed." [13]

He said tribal differences accounted for the distinct ways the teeth were chipped, and added, "So common is the practice, that even in art it is represented." [14]

While this is commonly called filing, it is actually performed by chipping with implements similar to a small hammer and chisel, a procedure Starr observed. "The operator's finger is firmly held behind the tooth which is being chipped, as a support; the fee is small, only three to five metaku (brass rods)." [15] The operator was considered an artist. Starr noted several words for the practice, including *tula nsangu*, *munsangu*, and *sonsa*.

In some regions the modification was considered a tribal mark, but it could also be a family custom or "individual caprice," Starr said. Where the practice was vital, he said, several types could occur in a single village or family. He also said it was generally considered a test of bravery and noted that among the Lokele, "no girl would marry them unless their teeth are made beautiful." [16] So whereas Benga was dehumanized and characterized as a cannibal on the fairgrounds in St. Louis, he would be considered courageous and appealing in his native Congo.

Starr provided more detailed observations of the practice, and of the small forest people he called Batua, in his book *Congo Natives: An Ethnographic Album,* published in 1912.

Fleeting images of Benga, set against a backdrop of chain gangs, forced labor, flogging, and overt slavery, intermittently appear in Starr's field notes. In an entry that conveys appalling indifference, Starr noted a flogging of ten men by a *chicotte*-wielding *capita*, a state-appointed overseer. Many critics of Leopold's state mentioned beatings with the *chicotte* as a particularly brutal form of torture, but Starr was unfazed.

"The Capita gave 25 blows to each," Starr wrote, noting that the men lay facedown. "It seemed to me that his first blows were rather nerveless, but he soon got into practice."[17]

He added: "Some took them like men, others wiggled and squirmed and pled. Usually this seemed to inspire the capita to his best efforts."

He attributed the "discipline" to rebellion and mutiny. "The ten had refused to chop wood—or at least had failed to do so," he wrote. Perhaps the environment had so normalized the degrading discipline of grown men that Starr would consider employing the practice himself. In one entry he complained about his workforce of forty-two men. "I hate to think of discipline, but such a set of shirks ought to be disciplined," he wrote. "We go through the farce of calling them together and assigning tasks and they go—some do."[18]

At one point it becomes clear that one of the workers is Benga, who was assigned to the household staff as a "helper in room" and to do "table work." It's unclear if this meant that he would set a table or make one. Starr includes him on the "proper payroll," but does not indicate how much he or the others were paid.[19]

Starr's impression of "Otabenga" as "quick, lively, intelligent and brave" agrees with Caroline Furness Jayne's impression following her observation of Benga doing string tricks at the St. Louis world's fair. Starr also noted that Benga reveled in hunting and trapping small animals and birds.[20]

Starr's altogether positive depiction of Benga is especially noteworthy given his derisive remarks about those he deemed inferior. In his book on the indigenous people of Mexico, he described them as "ignorant, timid, and suspicious."[21]

By early January Starr was ill with fever, and as he recovered in mid-January he prepared a long list of artifacts for Verner to collect for him. The list was characteristic of Starr's interest in objects of everyday life; it included cooking and drinking vessels, dishes, gourds, torches, lamps, and "ornaments of every kind: lip, nose, ear, cheek, plugs, pendants, necklaces." Also included were pottery, toys, games, native clothing, cloth, clubs, slings, amulets, pipes, musical instruments, and baskets. In a letter to his mother, Starr said Verner took thirty men with him and planned to be gone for one month. On his return he would go away again in another direction. Verner's assistance in the collection of these artifacts would, years later, be a source of contention.

During Verner's absence Starr oversaw the building of two new houses and the repair of another, and began drafting a new course he'd teach at the University of Chicago, "The Peoples of the Congo." He created his own "zoological garden" by adopting striped mice, "pretty little birds," and a monkey that he described as "an affectionate little creature, but very like a spoiled baby."[22] He also dismissed most of the hundred people in the workforce, saying, "I could see no utility in either his or my paying a hundred men 'just for looks' and I dismissed seventy of them on Saturday."[23] He listed "Otabenga" as among the "necessary force" he retained, an indication that Benga was not among the thirty people who accompanied Verner during his expedition for Starr.[24]

While Starr indicated the assigned tasks for seven others, there was no assignment next to Benga's name. Assignments included cook and manager, houseboy, table and room boy, sentry, and general helper.

In an earlier letter to his mother Starr had reported on the recent unrest in the area, which resulted in Lukengu's being sent to a chain gang. "He is now peaceful and restored to his power," Starr wrote.[25] Ndombe, he said, had remained a friend of whites. Starr also said he felt safer than he would feel in Chicago or New York. "It would be an extraordinary thing for negroes to kill a white man, under any circumstances, in the Congo."[26]

He also reported that Verner was having "great success" collecting ethnographic objects among the Baluba, Bakuba, Bateke, and Zappo-Zap. In the meantime, he said he and Gonzales had been busy "buying things, receiving visitors, making studies, taking photographs," observing that "the twenty-four-hour day is very fast."[27]

On February 15 Starr received a letter from Verner, who was in Djoko Punda, a town near Stanley Falls and the location of a large factory. Verner reported that he was ill and Starr indicated his annoyance that Verner had not shipped or even packed any of the artifacts that he had collected. Starr dispatched ten men to Djoko Punda that morning. Verner would arrive in Ndombe the following day, provoking Starr to write that "all was upset for one entire week by the arrival." Referring to Verner as "the patient," he described him as talking incessantly of his condition, "groaning," and "drooling."[28]

"Bad as it sounds, I could not feel any particular sympathy," Starr wrote. "He would be limping in great apparent pain and then would go rushing across the place completely forgetful." In other words, Starr thought Verner was a faker.

Starr had already ignored Verner's claims about Benga's cannibalism and would later question the plausibility of some of Verner's other accounts of adventures in the Congo. He especially doubted Verner's tale of being rescued by Kassongo, who Verner claimed had saved his life by sucking poison from his leg. How, Starr asked, would the African not be poisoned as well? He now questioned Verner's capricious limp, which may have been faked to support his persistent claim that his aborted missionary service and extended hospitalization were due to a severe leg injury.

Only a few days after Verner's return, Starr was already impatient for him to leave. Verner said he'd be gone another month to collect among the Baschilele, the Bachoko, and the Bampende. "I hope he will get away because his presence upsets everything we are doing and his crowd of work people tire me,"[29] Starr wrote. He said that while he hated to rush a sick man, if he was to stay on course "he *must* start soon and we *must* work."[30] On February 28 Verner would leave for another month while Starr stayed behind exploring villages, collecting, and "making pictures faster than we can develop them."[31] He also entertained officials of the Kasai Company, and members of the Baluba who came to dance.

By then Verner had collected about one thousand articles and Starr another seven hundred in addition to the photographs and phonographic recordings. "And my class course advances—when Verner is *not* here!"[32]

While Verner was out collecting, Starr visited villages and observed native dances, burials, family life, hairdressing, and teeth-chipping, all the while taking detailed descriptive notes. In his study of more than nine hundred state soldiers he noted, among other things, the size of their sexual organs, and the characteristics of their pubic hair. In some cases he imposed western ideas of masculinity on teenage boys who impressed him as feminine owing to their plucked eyelashes, shaved eyebrows, or other cultural practices. In March he reported some success measuring the Batua but complained that "unfortunately, most of them are off in the forest after rubber."[33] He had already measured eleven men and two women who were not as small as he had hoped.

On March 18, two days before he left Ndombe, he wrote to report that the entire town had moved before he and Gonzales had a chance to document it in photographs. "Houses, walls, all were in movement," he wrote. "All were carried away."[34]

By the time Starr left the Congo on March 22, 1906, he had, over the course of fifty-three weeks, logged a total of eight thousand miles, visited twenty-eight villages, and collected cast impressions and some seven hundred images. There were pictures of a goat sacrifice, grave sites, street scenes, men carrying rubber, and sad-eyed children with distended stomachs at a factory. One hundred of the images would be published in his book *Congo Natives*. Many others were turned over to Underwood and Underwood, a well-known distributor of stereoscopic and other photographic images. In 1910 an exhibit of the life-size portraits illustrating Congolese fashions—such as tribal marks, tooth-chipping, head bandaging, and ear piercing—would be awarded the grand prize at the Brussels International Exposition.[35] Many of the portraits are of men bearing thick chains and padlocks around their necks, a sign that they were not free. Starr may not have intended the chains and padlocks to be as arresting as the men's elaborate facial scarification. Starr left the photographs at the Congo Museum, today the Royal African Museum, in Tervuren outside Brussels, with duplicates deposited at the University of Chicago and the American Museum of Natural History; the AMNH still retains them in its archives.[36]

In addition he returned with recordings, among the earliest aural documentation of Congo music, accompanied by detailed descriptions of musical instruments and Baluba and Bakuba songs. At least one of the songs was sung by Chief Ndombe's eldest son. On his return to New York Starr took the cylinders to Columbia University to assist with the production of permanent cylinders. He had hoped to release them commercially but could not, owing to their poor quality.

Starr's ethnologies, recordings, and additional photographs would be divided among Indiana University, Columbia University, and the University of Chicago. Starr had also, with Verner's assistance, amassed a collection of some 3,500 artifacts that he would sell to the American Museum of Natural History for thousands of dollars. Museum officials could not provide the exact price. To Verner's chagrin, his assistance collecting for Starr would go unacknowledged in museum records and in Starr's *Congo Natives*. Starr, in his introduction, explicitly said that his expedition party comprised two people: himself and Gonzales. In his acknowledgments he thanked Chevalier Cuvelier, the Belgian secretary general for foreign affairs, and the Belgian prince Albert de Ligne for making arrangements; and Belgian officials based in the Congo. Also acknowledged were missionaries and the Kasai Company. He did not disclose that his entire expedition had been financed by the Congo State. Verner's last name was included among a list of writers whose work was cited "without specific reference to those authors."

While Benga's humanity was conspicuously, and ironically, enshrined in Starr's work, Verner's hospitality, his assistance collecting artifacts, and his role in inspiring Starr's expedition would go largely unrecognized. Years later Verner continued to appeal to the American Museum of Natural History to credit his role in the expedition, but to no avail.

EIGHTEEN

LEOPOLD'S LOBBY

The expedition not only augmented Starr's already impressive credentials and personal fortune, but also would provide him with a prominent platform for defending Leopold's rule. On his return, Starr emerged as one of Leopold's most trenchant defenders. In a series of fifteen articles published in the *Chicago Tribune* he would lend his eminence as a scholar to dismiss the king's critics.[1] Under headlines like "The Truth About the Kongo as Told by an Unbiased American Educator," he noted how the expedition had afforded him an objective close-up look at conditions in the interior that had been widely condemned in newspapers and magazines.

Before embarking on his expedition, Starr claimed, he read the literature of the Congo Reform Association, and he went to the Congo expecting to witness "all kinds of horrors."

"I supposed that mutilations, cruelties and atrocities of the most frightful kinds would everywhere present themselves. I expected to find a people everywhere suffering, mourning, and in unhappiness," he wrote.

Instead, he found a Negro population "far happier than I had dreamed it possible." In the Congo, he insisted, "Life is easy. Wants are few."

He did report that he had repeatedly witnessed state-imposed floggings, chain gangs, and forced labor, and he essentially corroborated what Sheppard, Morel, and Casement had reported. But, employing a sort of tu quoque argument, Starr said the same conditions could be found in the U.S. South.

"Flogging, chain-gangs, prison, mutilation, heavy taxation, hostages, depopulation, all these I saw," he divulged, confirming Sheppard's claim that chain gangs could be found at every state post. He described Africans employed in "all sorts of work" joined together by rings around their necks. But contrary to reports, he said the rings were of a "light iron" not exceeding two pounds. He said it was a "very mild form of punishment" that did not arouse his sympathy: "To grieve over the weight carried in the form of chain and ring is simply ridiculous."

He also downplayed the widely practiced floggings with the *chicotte*, a stiff whip made of rhinoceros hide that Leopold's critics described as an especially cruel form of torture. Starr trivialized the practice as "a rather mild and simple punishment" that "hurt but little." As for reports of slavery, he said it still flourished but was "difficult to deal with" and "scarcely worth the candle."

Starr also explained away Roger Casement's report corroborating accounts of widespread mutilations. He said the mutilations were a traditional native custom and not limited to the Congo Free State, or to Africans. He noted that the British force had recently decapitated a hostile chief. He casually remarked that "most of the difficulty" with Congo natives stemmed from the demands on them to gather rubber. "The native hates the forest; he dislikes to gather rubber," Starr matter-of-factly remarked.

Starr also failed to understand the fuss over taking hostages, particularly the practice of taking men from their villages to collect rubber. He noted that the great explorer Henry Morton Stanley had used female hostages to provide food supplies, without provoking a similar outcry.

Given his indifference to the harsh treatment and his habitual reliance on negative stereotypes of non-Westerners, his characterization of the Congolese as "quick and bright" and "remarkably intelligent" was striking. He also noted that many Congolese spoke numerous languages with ease and often quoted from their thousands of proverbs showing "great keenness and shrewdness, deep observation and insight." "No people with a mass of proverbial philosophy, such as the Bantu and the true negroes have, could be considered stupid," he said.

He found Congolese children especially precocious. "Children of four or five, in shrewdness, comprehension, and intelligence, are like our ten-year-olds," he wrote. "As a fact, boys of sixteen and girls of thirteen are frequently ready for marriage. A man of twenty-five is in the prime of life."

However, Starr said the most striking characteristic of the Congolese was "emotionality," invoking a familiar depiction of Africans and their descendants by his white elite contemporaries. The African was, he said, "one instant joyous, the next in tears. . . . In disposition variable and emotional, he quickly forgets his sorrow."

Observing that the Congolese laughed, sang, and danced, he deduced, "The native is born to dance."

Attempting to neutralize criticisms made by missionaries, he noted the elaborate mission compounds, and said that the missionaries had become "so filled with a complaining spirit they are incapable of seeing good."

He also offered an insight into the disciplinary practices exerted by the white man in the Congo: "Alone in a population so unlike himself, his only safety rests in his commanding at once fear, respect, obedience. He frequently possesses government power."

With few white women present, Starr said, a white man would typically select a black concubine shortly after he arrived. "He considers her an inferior being," Starr drily observed, "but treats her like a doll or toy. . . . Where he goes, she goes." He also observed that many white men did not like to walk, and so were typically carried in a hammock by two to four black men.

He noted that tribes in the Kasai region, where he resided with Verner, "are poor carriers [and] indifferent workers."

Starr insisted that there were no grounds for American intervention and that what he found in the Congo was no worse than what occurred in the U.S. South, or in the Philippines.

"When our hands are clean and when we have given the Philippines their well-deserved independence and free government, and let them to work out their own salvation then and not till then, should we intervene in the Congo Free State for reasons of humanity," he argued. Moreover, he said interference would strain the United States' relations with France and Germany, and should not be considered "unless we are ready to undertake the policing of the whole of Africa."

Up until the time when international pressure resulted in Leopold's relinquishment of the Congo, Starr continued to insist that many of the alleged atrocities had never occurred, or were ancient. His book *The Truth About the Congo*, a compilation of his *Chicago Tribune* articles defending Leopold, would be published in 1907.

At the conclusion of his journey, Starr received a letter from the Belgian prince Albert de Ligne, who looked forward to receiving his printed report. "You have seen every thing with your own eyes, and been able to appreciate how things are in the numerous districts which you have visited," the prince said. "Owing to you, many errors will be dissipated, many things put right."[2] In another letter, he said that Starr's *Chicago Tribune* articles had been "sympathetically appreciated" by the Belgian press.[3]

Verner also continued to lobby for the state. Over the summer, in articles published in the *Washington Post* and the *Baltimore Afro-*

American, he praised Leopold as "a real king who, as a monarch of finance and captain of industry, puts [John D.] Rockefeller and [John Pierpont] Morgan into the shade."[4]

Contesting claims by reformers that Belgian officials were trying to deceive the public by concealing actual conditions in the Congo, Verner told the *Washington Evening Star* that Leopold's policies were not to blame for any of the country's existing problems.[5]

"They come principally from weaknesses and mistakes of individuals in the field," Verner contended.[6] "The general effect of the government has been progressive and beneficial."

His more recent role in the king's media campaign did not go unnoticed. Reformers like E. D. Morel and Morrison were incensed. Morrison, in a letter to Morel, considered the need to discredit Verner publicly, adding: "Some doubt the man's sanity, but this you need not refer to, of course."[7] Senator Morgan would receive an anonymous letter alleging that Verner had been withdrawn from the Presbyterian mission because of his conduct and personal life. It also divulged that he had entered a sanatorium "for mental trouble."[8] As already noted, earlier that year Casement had confided in a letter that many considered Verner "a bore" and believed he was "cracked."[9]

But Leopold's emissaries were eager to encourage Verner, particularly given his status as a former African missionary working in the same Presbyterian mission that condemned Leopold's state. Who better to undermine the allegations by Leopold's missionary critics?

Verner's praise of the cruel, corrupt king was nothing new. In 1899, on returning from his missionary work in the Congo, Verner had told the *Washington Post* that the alleged evils of Leopold's civilizing mission were "largely exaggerated." He said that while gin and rum had taken their toll on the population, the Berlin conference had proved beneficial by preventing the importation of firearms and intoxicants. This claim was disputed by reports by Arthur Conan Doyle and others that ships reached the Congo loaded with guns and explosives and left stocked with ivory, rubber, and minerals. However, in his *Pioneering in Central Africa,* Verner hailed the despotic Leopold as an "enlightened monarch." [10]

Verner had become an even more fervent advocate as Leopold's emissaries sought to neutralize the criticism leveled by the missionaries and by the British consul Roger Casement's report. Casement's report had resulted in intense global scrutiny. In July 1904 Leopold would finally yield to pressure from the British Parliament and appoint an international commission to examine conditions in the Congo. The commission arrived in Boma in October and would travel through the Congo until the end of February. Leopold's emissaries simultaneously circulated pamphlets titled "The Truth About the Congo" and planted newspaper articles denying Casement's claims. To save face, officials were arrested and one Belgian national was sentenced to five years in prison for ordering the shooting of more than 120 Congolese.

While protests in Britain had been gathering steam for several years, Leopold was especially troubled by the growing tide of protest in the United States, where missionaries and prominent citizens like Booker T. Washington and Mark Twain took to the podium and appealed to the White House to condemn his brutal reign.

Over the summer Verner had privately met with Ludovic Moncheur, the Belgian minister to the United States, who followed up with a letter expressing his delight with Verner's efforts.

"I am well aware of what you have already done for the defence of the just cause of the Congo against prejudicial and unfair criticism," Moncheur assured him. "I wish to thank you for it and to say that I have kept the Government duly informed." [11]

Moncheur offered suggestions for how Verner might increase his chances of securing a concession. He noted how Leopold's critics used the press and lecture circuit to allege abuses by the king. Could Verner not counteract with a series of lectures, complete with slides, for which expenses would be defrayed? Moncheur asked. Or perhaps Verner could directly challenge missionaries in statements to the press, or by writing a letter denying the allegations—a letter that Moncheur could then quote.

"You are about the only man in this country who can be relied upon to be fair and to act in fairness to the State," he said.[12]

Moncheur scoffed at critics like Booker T. Washington who, merely because they had traveled to Africa, presented themselves as experts. "I am afraid that the public pays more attention to the trash of some of these fellows," he said.

While Moncheur would still have to convince his superiors, he said, Verner was an "evermore deserving recipient of consideration and official favor."[13]

Verner heeded the advice and went on a speaking tour arranged by a New York agent, J. B. Pond, who had represented the showman P. T. Barnum as well as Henry Morton Stanley. As one who had lived among so-called pygmies in Africa, Verner could also draw a crowd. In the meantime, he could provide a useful service to Leopold by touting the prospects for business in the Congo.

One of Pond's circulars, with the heading "Empire Building in Central Africa," billed Verner as "The Most Eminent Living American Explorer of Africa." A photograph showed Verner in Africa, with Benga in the foreground, a symbol of capitulation and conquest. The circular indicated Verner's desire to make a living exploiting the Congo atrocities. Beneath the photograph McGee, identified as former president of the National Geographic Society, was quoted as saying, "Verner impressed me as more nearly in the class of Rhodes than any other African worker." It is not known if McGee had offered such an endorsement or knew he had been quoted.

Another circular, which appears to have been produced by Verner himself, notes his award at the St. Louis world's fair, his membership in scientific societies, and his work "opening up the country of the cannibal Baschilele." It includes a long list of implausible endorsements from the late president McKinley, the British prime minister, Frederick Starr, and the missionary William Sheppard. Sheppard allegedly stated: "Mr. Verner has done more at his age for the African race than any other white man in the world." [14]

Verner also continued to churn out articles for magazines including *The World's Work, Harper's Weekly,* and *The Forum,* extolling Leopold's benevolent rule and the abundant opportunities in the Congo for American businessmen. In one article he praised Leopold as "an instance of the renaissance of royal efficiency. In him have reappeared Ferdinand of Spain, the spirt of Elizabeth, the power of Catherine, the ambition of Charlemagne." [15] He marveled at the industry and ingenuity of a small Belgian nation that "controlled 10,000,000 savages with fewer than 2,000 whites." [16]

Dismissing the critics of the Belgian state, he said he knew many of the officials personally, some intimately. "They are gentlemen, and men of rare ability and the assertion that they are guilty of unmentionable crimes and atrocities is simply a malicious falsehood." [17]

In fact, Verner asserted, while natives who preferred idleness had been urged to work, they were, in general, treated better than those in any other African colonies, including the French, Portuguese, British, German, and Spanish territories. He insisted that the widely reported mutilations were perpetrated by Africans themselves as punishment for crimes. "The white men do their best to stop these crimes," he insisted, while preposterously claiming that the subjugated and debased Africans felt far safer in regions populated by whites.

Under headlines like "The White Man's Zone in Africa," "White Race in the Tropics," and "Belgian Rule on the Congo," he touted the country's natural resources and the wealth to be amassed from white domination. While Casement and the missionaries decried the horrors of the rubber industry, Verner lauded the fortunes it produced. He said the area he assessed yielded about $8 million a year but was "probably capable of producing from the wild sources alone, five times as much." [18]

This created new opportunities for the "right men" to make great wealth without the outlay of much capital.

"The gathering of the rubber is a simple process," he said of the backbreaking work. "An incision under the bark in the afternoon produces a lump of hard rubber by morning. This is one case where money grows on a vine."[19]

Noting the untapped resources, he said he met a Kentuckian who had shipped several loads of mahogany home in less than a year's time "with the aid of two hundred native employees, without the use of mule or steam."

"Within a few years," he predicted, "one can live a civilized life there without drawing on the outside world for anything but newspapers." To accomplish this, he proposed placing African natives on reservations and abolishing taxation. "The profits of exploitation are so high that the government can be operated on an economical basis without resort to native taxation at all."[20]

He asked rhetorically: "Can white families live and increase in tropical Africa? And ought the white race colonize those regions? Like Stanley, I answer, Yes."[21]

In December Verner was rewarded with a long-coveted concession in Ndombe. Now Starr's meritorious service to the Belgian nation would also be recognized. He was given the Order of Leopold, Belgium's highest knighthood.

But as protests gathered momentum, Leopold's officials saw a need to intensify their lobbying. Colonel Henry I. Kowalsky, a famously flamboyant San Francisco lawyer who counted celebrities and underworld figures among his clients, was hired as Leopold's American lobbyist. For his efforts he would be paid 100,000 francs a year, or roughly $500,000 in today's dollars.

NINETEEN

BENGA'S CHOICE

arriet Verner was concerned. It had been ten months since her husband left St. Louis to take the Africans back to the Congo, and he had not yet returned home. By then the couple had two children: Mary Elizabeth, born in 1901; and John Bradshaw, born in 1902. In October Harriet wrote to McGee to say that her husband was "practically stranded" on the upper Kasai by a lack of money.[1] Implicit in her letter was that fair officials were responsible for his plight, a case that Verner had already made in his letter to McGee.

Given the money already allocated for the expedition—$8,500 plus another $1,500 set aside for unforeseen expenses—McGee didn't understand why Verner could not afford to return home. Fair officials, he told Harriet, had "more than complied" with their obligations to her husband. Still, McGee did not want to see him suffer. During the fair he had grown fond of the man who had lived next door to him in St. Louis and who had followed through on a difficult task. He appealed to the fair's president, David Francis, for funds.

On October 7 Francis expressed befuddlement. "Why does he not return?" he asked Harriet Verner.[2] Nonetheless he agreed to advance $500 in credit and asked "how soon and in what means" could he send it.

But three months later, Verner was still in Luebo. His wife wrote to him on January 24, 1906, complaining that she had expected him back by then. Verner explained that Starr had made him an attractive offer, which affected his plans to return.

Verner was trying to get home, "not [as] a pauper—but in a decent condition all around and as soon as possible."[3] With the concession of land awarded by the government Verner hoped to establish a rubber, ivory, and palm oil collection station at Ndombe and use it as a base for exploration and development. He believed that with American financial backing, he too could cash in on development in the African interior.

By then Verner had built something of a national reputation as an expert on "pygmies," and he would have been especially well known in St. Louis, where he was regularly reported on throughout the fair. So in June 1906, when it had been a year and a half since he left his wife and the children, his extended stay in Africa provoked rumors that he had gone bankrupt and abandoned his family. McGee told Verner that he had "vigorously and scornfully" denied such an allegation posed by a reporter, and assured him it did not stem from anything said by the Exposition Company.[4]

That summer, while Verner tried to improve his financial status, the Kasai was a region of forced labor and a hotbed of unrest. Whereas trade had been limited prior to 1893, by 1899 Leopold for the first time opened the area to merchants, bringing a number of factories and traders, and increasing the need for labor. By 1904 the area was swarming with state and company officials, police, and independent fortune hunters like Verner. But merchants began complaining that they were competing with the state for the rubber and ivory that villagers were increasingly required to provide. The state had already put fourteen independent trading companies in the Kasai basin into a state trust, which enabled Leopold to retain 50 percent of the profits.

The keen competition for rubber and ivory, and Leopold's increased attention to the Kasai region, fueled reports of endless atrocities committed by state troops. In 1903, after the first year of the trust, the Kasai Rubber Company alone estimated that it had collected 565 tons more rubber than it had the previous year, an increase that had entailed rising death tolls and worsening despair. That year, fresh from a trip to the Congo, Morrison, in an address to the United Service Institution, again highlighted the many atrocities that had already been outlined in missionaries' reports. He specifically appealed for redress for the once regal Baluba and Bakuba people in the Kasai region, who had been reduced to starving, hopeless laborers.

That same year British vice-consul Armstrong toured the Basenji villages near the site of a state post and the province's most important highway.[5]

"There is no free labour," Armstrong said. He said that about every six weeks, each man was required to take to the state post a large basket holding some twenty-five pounds of rubber. It took roughly thirty days to collect the quota, during which time, he said, the workers were "subjected to the gravest abuses." He said the workers spent thirty-eight out of forty-five days in the compulsory service of the state. For a basket of rubber the chief received one kilogram of salt, nominally worth one franc, for the entire village.

The "incessant call" for rubber, food, and labor left little time for rest or peace of mind. Armstrong cited deplorable living conditions, with none of the European amenities promised by Leopold's civilizing mission. "The people live in a state of uncertainty as to the advent of police officers and soldiers, who invariably chase them from their abodes and destroy their huts."

He went on, "I must say that during more than nineteen years' experience in Northern and Central Africa, I have never seen such a miserably poor lot as the Basenji in this State."[6] Leopold's independent commission of inquiry would release similar findings on October 31, 1905—an unanticipated development that vindicated critics of the state.

Meanwhile, Verner, in the midst of the regional crisis, sent only news of his personal financial woes when he wrote home.

From McGee, by then director of the St. Louis Public Museum, he sought an advance for a promised collection of specimens. While McGee sent a letter of credit for $500, it is not known if the items were ever deposited.

Verner disclosed neither the forced labor nor the fact that a female student at the Presbyterian Mission school in Luebo had become his regular companion.[7] As usual, Verner could sift through all the moments that made up his African adventures and select which ones to share with the outside world.

By June Verner was ready to return to the United States. As he made his round of good-byes, he claimed Benga asked to return with him. It would not be difficult to understand why, even considering the humiliation and discomfort Benga had endured in St. Louis. Caught now in a cycle of unrest, he could weigh that earlier humiliation against the present genocide of his people. Perhaps in America he could, like Kondola, learn to read and write. Perhaps he could be free and someday return home. However, even though some such calculus was possible, it is not known whether Benga willingly accompanied Verner back to the United States.

In one account Verner, once again casting himself in the role of Benga's savior, claimed that Benga threatened to kill himself if he didn't bring him along. In another Verner claimed he was concerned that Benga would be re-enslaved and so elected to bring him; he also said that Benga's return was made possible by the sale of a gift of ivory from a Chief Mwiila. Given Verner's troubling history of fabricating stories to ennoble himself or fatten his wallet, any of his assertions must be considered alongside the possibility that he recognized Benga as a business opportunity. Verner was perpetually desperate for money and had already demonstrated his willingness to exploit

Benga, along with Kassongo and Kondola—for example, by alleging that they were cannibals—to advance his own career. "Benga the cannibal" could at once benefit Verner financially and enhance his reputation as an African explorer. Verner had also demonstrated his willingness to use the force of the state to exert his will.

There are no independent accounts of the actual circumstances of Benga's return to the United States. The only documentation of the trip back to America is a receipt for thirty-five British pounds for a chimpanzee Verner sold in Sierra Leone, and a letter Verner wrote on July 17 from a hotel in Liverpool, England, to a shipping and travel agent, seeking passage to America for himself, two chimpanzees, and an African "pygmy." Benga would make his second voyage to the United States with a man intent on achieving renown as a scientist and explorer by insisting that his African companion was a cannibal savage.

TWENTY

A MUSEUM MOST UNNATURAL

On July 20, 1906, Verner and Benga set sail from Liverpool, England, on the SS *Armenia*, a tri-level ship that made weekly voyages between England and New York. The 512-foot passenger vessel was built in 1895 by the famous Belfast firm Harland and Wolff, designer of the luxurious *Titanic*.

During his first voyage to Africa in 1895, Verner had given his occupation as clergyman, and in 1903 he gave it as teacher; but this time, at age thirty-two, he identified himself as a scientist, indicating that he planned to build on the reputation he had made as a prizewinning exhibitor at the world's fair. The passenger list identifies Benga as Mbye Otabenga, age twenty-two, a widower, and Verner's servant. The cabin accommodations are not specified.

The ship arrived at New York's Ellis Island on July 30, 1906. The two checked into the Belleclaire Hotel on Seventy-Seventh Street near Broadway on Manhattan's Upper West Side.

On Thursday, August 2, 1906, Verner left the Belleclaire and strolled down five tree-lined streets of handsome town houses and luxury apartment buildings. It is not known if Benga accompanied him. Verner approached the American Museum of Natural History, the mammoth castle-like brownstone and granite edifice on at Seventy-Seventh Street overlooking Central Park. There he hoped to see Hermon C. Bumpus, the former Brown University biology professor who four years earlier had become the museum's first director.

Verner had initially reached out to Bumpus in 1904, fresh from his success at the St. Louis world's fair and as he was about to return Benga and Benga's countrymen to the Congo. Verner had wanted to know whether Bumpus wished him to collect specimens for the museum during his stay in the Congo.

"As to my capacity for such work," Verner wrote on St. Louis Exposition stationery, "I have been awarded the grand prize here for my recent Expedition to Africa—the highest award given."[1] Bumpus had declined; but now, two years later, with Verner at his doorstep, he agreed to a meeting.

Bumpus was initially ill at ease. He knew little about Verner beyond what he was told that morning—that Verner had graduated from the University of South Carolina and had supplied the National Museum with a large collection of African ethnological material. Verner now had tons of objects, of which he would take some to the Shaw Museum in St. Louis; he hoped to sell others to Bumpus.

"He is a queer fellow," Bumpus wrote in a letter to Clark Wissler, who that year succeeded Franz Boas as curator of the museum's ethnology department. "Not a Chesterfield, but after some discussion with him he impressed me as having many good features."[2]

One good feature was apparently Ota Benga, whom, along with two chimpanzees, Verner wished to leave at the museum while he traveled to St. Louis. Bumpus said that while he was unfamiliar with Verner's ethnological work, "he tells me that his paper on the stature of the pigmies has received favorable comment."

Bumpus wrote, "He may be a crank with whom we wish to have

nothing to do, but I hated to take chances."[3] So Bumpus told Wissler that he had agreed to temporarily take charge of "his pigmy" and chimpanzees.

"This gives me time to write to you and find out something about him," said Bumpus, who also noted that if Wissler was amenable, he'd consider helping Verner arrange to pursue doctoral studies at Columbia University. Bumpus then wrote to Walter Hough, who headed the ethnology department at the Smithsonian, to ask whether Verner would make a suitable assistant at the museum.

In the meantime, Bumpus became the temporary guardian of Benga and would later regret ignoring his initial impression of Verner as somewhat odd.

We can hardly imagine what went through Benga's mind as he roamed the building that housed the remains of dinosaurs, insects, meteorites, and other prehistoric specimens. By then the museum, with its cavernous halls and vaulted ceilings, was among the nation's most esteemed institutions. It was conceived by Albert Smith Bickmore, a former student of Harvard's Louis Agassiz, and quickly won the support of the city's leading citizens, including Theodore Roosevelt Sr., William Dodge, and J. Pierpont Morgan. The governor of New York State, John Thompson Hoffman, signed the act that incorporated it in 1869, and its first exhibits were opened in 1871. By 1872 it had outgrown its space at the Central Park Arsenal, and a year later architects Calvert Vaux and Jacob Wrey Mould were commissioned to design a new building. Both men had already left their mark on the celebrated Central Park. Vaux was the park's codesigner, and Mould contributed to a number of its best-known structures, including Tavern on the Green and Bethesda Terrace.

The pair began drawing plans for a sprawling five-story building with four enclosed courts, its interior bathed in an unusual red hue for which Mould would become renowned. President Ulysses

S. Grant would lay the cornerstone in 1874, and three years later his successor, Rutherford Hayes, presided over the official opening.

Morris K. Jesup, a cofounder of the museum, in 1881 became its third president. He was credited with placing it on a solid financial footing and launching, in part with his own funds, its golden age of global expeditions. Jesup, a retired banker and railroad financier, was still president in 1906 and had already begun to oversee the museum's impressive collection of prehistoric specimens, including a two-hundred-ton meteorite. In 1897 a diplodocus, the museum's first dinosaur, was excavated by the Zoological Society's own Henry Fairfield Osborn.

Frederic Ward Putnam, a curator who would go on to head Harvard's Peabody Museum, hired Franz Boas in 1895 as assistant curator in the department of ethnology. There Boas would embark on what is arguably the most important expedition in American anthropology. From 1895 to 1902, the ambitious North Pacific Expedition, funded by Jesup, uncovered the life and culture of the first immigrants to the New World in Siberia, Alaska, and northwestern Canada.

Benga was, during his stay, the building's only living resident, but he had not been its first.

Nine years earlier the museum had housed six Inuit from Greenland who had been brought there by explorer Robert Peary to be studied by the staff. The visit was prompted by a request from Boas, whose book *The Central Eskimo*, the first extensive ethnological study of Canadian Eskimo, was published by the Smithsonian Bureau of Ethnology in 1888. As Peary prepared to return to Greenland Boas asked him to bring back one middle-aged Eskimo, whom he hoped to study for a year. He said the study would be of great scientific importance. Peary, apparently in an effort to impress Jesup, his patron, brought back six.

Some ten thousand people gathered at the Brooklyn Navy Yard pier to greet Peary, the six Eskimo, and an Antarctic meteorite that was perhaps ten thousand years old. By the second day thirty

thousand people had visited the pier hoping for a glimpse of the
foreign delegation. Peary's party headed to the American Museum
of Natural History, where they were, like specimens, housed in the
basement. Although some visitors were granted access to view them,
many were disappointed to learn that they would not be on display,
so, according to one news account, "they had to content themselves
with a glimpse through a grating above the basement."[4]

The guests from Greenland soon became ill with what appeared
to be colds, eliciting amused commentary from the *New York Times*,
which would later similarly mock Benga.

"The unfortunate little savages have caught cold or warmth," the
writer quipped, "they did not know which, but assuming it was the
latter their sole endeavor yesterday was to keep cool."[5] By November six members of the delegation were in Bellevue Hospital battling
pneumonia. Most were returned to the museum and placed in drier
quarters on an upper floor, but by February all were back in the hospital, where one of them, a man named Qisuk, died on February 17,
1898. His orphaned son Minik was distraught.

"He was dearer to me than anything else in the world," Minik
later said.[6] Recalling his father's affectionate care during his own illness, he said, "How he would smile if I was a little better, and how he
would sob, with big tears in his eyes, when I was suffering."

Minik also lashed out at Peary, who he claimed had lured him
and the rest of his delegation to America under false pretenses.

"They promised us nice warm homes in the sunshine land, and
guns and knives and needles and many other things," recalled Minik.
"My mother was dead, and my father would not go without me, so
the five of us said a last farewell to home and went on Peary's ship."[7]
The five were joined by Uisaakassak, a young man from another village.

Following Qisuk's death the remaining five were moved to the
home of a museum staffer, where on March 16 Atangana, the wife
of Nuktaq, died. Alfred Kroeber, a twenty-two-year-old doctoral

student at Columbia University who would go on to become one of the field's most important cultural anthropologists, studied Nuktaq's behavior after his wife's death. He recorded his observations in a detailed report on Inuit grief.

Peary, who had his sights set on the North Pole, had not visited the Greenland Inuit since he deposited them and the meteorite at the museum, and he steered clear of the embarrassing publicity following their deaths.

Sometime in March three of the four remaining Eskimo were moved to upstate New York, to the country home of William Wallace, the museum's superintendent of buildings. Only Minik, who was still in fragile health, remained in New York City living with Jesup. By May 14 Nuktaq died, followed ten days layer by Aviaq. For a month Uisaakassak lived with Matthew Henson, Peary's African American assistant, aboard the *Windward* off Canal Street in Manhattan. Uisaakassak finally departed for Greenland on July 2, leaving only Minik behind with William Wallace and his wife Rhetta, this time in the Highbridge section of the Bronx.

Many newspaper articles ignored the personal tragedy that had led to Minik's unofficial adoption by the Wallaces. One article, bearing the headline "Taming a Little Savage," suggested that he was lucky to be in America rather than in his barren Arctic environment.[8] It was the kind of insensitive reporting that years later would characterize news coverage of Benga at the St. Louis world's fair and then at the Bronx Zoo.

As the controversy over the Inuit died down, a new one emerged. Wallace, a trusted museum employee, was accused of misappropriating funds, and on January 11, 1901, he resigned after twenty years of service. Another shoe would drop a few months after Benga arrived. On his rural property in Lawyersville, New York, Wallace operated a macerating plant that was used by the museum to bleach the bones of its animal specimens. In January 1907 the *New York World* ran a full-page article in its magazine, claiming that the remains of Minik's father had been processed in Lawyersville and were on display at the American Museum of Natural History.

"Give Me My Father's Body" read one headline.[9] "It makes me cry every time I think of his poor bones up there in the museum in a glass case," Minik charged. In addition to excoriating the museum staff, Minik also condemned Peary for never returning to offer his assistance after luring the group to America.

At the time of Qisuk's death Minik was just eight years old, probably too young to read newspaper reports about what would become of his father's remains: it was decided that Bellevue Hospital would use some of the remains for the dissecting room, while the skeleton would be preserved and mounted in the American Museum of Natural History."[10] Nor would Minik, at the time, know of "The Eskimos of Smith Sound," Kroeber's detailed observations of the six as they battled tuberculosis. It was published in 1899.

Wallace, for his part, alleged, like the *New York World,* that the museum had exhibited Qisuk's remains; he also claimed that the museum had faked Qisuk's interment by burying a log wrapped in cloth. His allegations were questionable, given his controversial resignation from the museum, but his account was corroborated by Boas.

Another gruesome development was that Dr. Ales Hrdlicka, one of the researchers on the team, wrote an article detailing his study of Qisuk's brain. He identified Qisuk as a male Eskimo about forty-five years of age who was chief of his tribe in the area of Smith Sound, from which he was taken by Peary. Hrdlicka said he himself was present for an autopsy performed at Bellevue Hospital by Dr. Harlow Brooks.

A preliminary report was published in 1899 in *Proceedings of the American Medico-Psychological Association*, and was followed two years later by "An Eskimo Brain," published in *American Anthropologist*, the journal of the American Anthropological Association. The latter was accompanied by full nude frontal and profile photographs of Qisuk and Minik on their admission to Bellevue Hospital with tuberculosis. It also included head measurements and several photographs of Qisuk's cerebrum. The incontrovertible identification of Qisuk and Minik was dehumanizing—they were regarded less as human beings than as scientific specimens—and also denied them the anonymity typically afforded subjects of scientific studies.

Hrdlicka said the brains of the three other deceased Inuit remained in the medical department at Columbia University, and would be reported on in detail.

The controversy would culminate in 1909, the year Peary finally reached the North Pole. The ensuing fanfare afforded Minik another opportunity to publicly condemn Peary and the museum. By then Minik said that Bumpus no longer denied having his father's remains, but refused to release them to him for a proper burial. Peary's wife sought to quiet the troublesome Minik by offering him a one-way ticket to Greenland. Before boarding the ship on July 10, Minik cried, "You're a race of scientific criminals," adding, "I am glad enough to get away before they grab my brains and stuff them into a jar." [11]

Minik would eventually return to the United States, where he died in 1918 during the influenza pandemic at the age of twenty-six or twenty-seven. He had never recovered his father's remains.

Perhaps the long-simmering controversy resulted in more hospitable arrangements for Benga. Bumpus said he would stay in a museum guest room. Verner told Bumpus to feel free to take Benga home with him "if you seriously wish to have him near you" for closer observation. [12]

In a letter to Bumpus of August 4 Verner noted that he had intended to get Benga better garments "but having put this off until my intended last visit, I was obliged to let that remain one of the privileges of someone of your museum staff. The little rascal has spoiled every new suit by doing his work in them, as vanity is well developed in him." [13]

He added that any expenses should be billed to him and that Benga was naturally "rather cleanly."

"But do not spoil him," he urged. "My experience with his race is that it is easy to do this! Still I err on the side of kindness always." [14]

He enclosed a note for Bumpus to read to Ota Benga. In it he tells Benga that he is well and will return in a few days. He advises him to be patient and appeased. [15]

Two days later Verner wrote again to offer his services to Bumpus. In addition to his ethnographic material already stored at the museum, he could offer the chimpanzees "provided we can arrange for my occasional use of them in lectures." He also offered to prepare notes on the vocabulary and grammar of the "pygmies," and provide full maps of his local discoveries as well as other ethnic reference material.

"The point is whether you can go as far as to offer to pay my expenses to and at New York for a month until the remoter questions can be settled, I to place myself under your instructions as to work for that period," he proposed. [16]

He suggested a monthly salary of $175—the equivalent of roughly $4,605 in 2014—"which I think is fair," he reasoned. Verner added that it would be convenient for him if that amount could be deposited in advance.

To expedite the matter, he enclosed a promissory note for Bumpus to sign, with instructions to deposit the money in the First National Bank of Tuscaloosa in Alabama. The agreement would give Bumpus ownership of his property "until the date of one month after the sale sum is paid to the said Bank." [17]

In a letter to Wissler, Bumpus confided that Verner's proposition came as somewhat of a shock, given that he had met with Verner for only several minutes. Bumpus nonetheless asked for Wissler's thoughts on employing Verner as either a student or a temporary assistant in African ethnology. Bumpus said he knew nothing about the worth of Verner's collections at the Smithsonian or elsewhere, and believed that one of the chimpanzees had early signs of tuberculosis.

"In any event," he said, "I should of course not engage him, even temporarily, without your full knowledge and approval, and I think that it would be impossible for him to do anything at the Museum before your return."[18]

He enclosed Verner's letter for Wissler's review.

Bumpus also sought a recommendation from Walter Hough, director of the Smithsonian ethnology department, asking, "Is he a person that could make an acceptable assistant here?"

Hough's impression of Verner was mixed. He said that Verner had indeed contributed valuable African treasures to the museum in 1899 and that, as a collector, "I have no hesitancy in expressing a favorable opinion."

However, he noted that Verner had "become temporarily insane" and been confined for a while, a reference to his hospitalization in Baltimore.

On August 10 Bumpus wired to Verner: "Regret that cannot agree." He then composed a detailed letter explaining why, making no mention of Hough's confidential claim that Verner had gone insane. Instead he said a monthly salary of $175 "would be quite impossible for us to arrange," even temporarily, since it was far more than other museum officers earned. He also said he had written to Wissler for further advice and would contact Verner after hearing from Wissler. Bumpus advised Verner to dispose of his material however he saw fit, and noted that one chimpanzee appeared to be in an advanced stage of tuberculosis and was likely to die soon. He advised Verner to approach the Zoological Park about the possible sale of the other.

Bumpus was far more enthusiastic about Ota Benga. "I have bought a duck suit for the Pigmy," he said. "He is around the museum, apparently perfectly happy and more or less a favorite of the men."[19]

Bumpus had other pressing matters as he and his staff continued to make preparations for the unveiling, in the museum foyer, of busts of ten eminent American Men of Science. The busts had been financed by Jesup, and the subjects included naturalists William Baird; John Audubon; and Louis Agassiz, the famous Swiss American scientist and Harvard professor who had described Africans as a "degenerate and degraded race." The ceremonious unveiling on December 29 would be presided over by J. P. Morgan.

Meanwhile Verner, as Moncheur had suggested, tried to line up lectures and solicited the help of McGee, who eagerly complied. In a letter to the Society of Pedagogy, McGee described Verner as a "genius" who had brought a typical "pygmy" to the United States. Verner, he said, "is better acquainted with the Dark Continent than any other American known to me, and his knowledge probably exceeds that of Sir Harry Johnston or any other of the noted British explorers."[20] In another letter he said Verner was not a scientist, but "his grasp of general principles is good and constantly growing." McGee said Verner had undertaken what was, in his view, "among the most successful ethnologic expeditions ever sent out."

Verner, he added, "is of the most substantial Scotch-Irish Presbyterian stock, tempered with American admixture." He noted that Verner was something of a genius, adding: "Like other geniuses, Verner is somewhat erratic."[21]

Four days after his upbeat letter to Verner, Bumpus wrote again. This time he reported that his African guest was "somewhat restless and is doubtless rather counting on your arrival at an early date."[22] Benga had by then made his displeasure with his accommodations clear. He attempted to escape the museum by blending in with an exiting crowd. A guard spotted him and brought him back. Bumpus said he had read Benga a letter dated August 9 that Verner had sent him. In it Verner tells Benga that "Chief Bumpus" loves him, that Benga should be smart and careful, and that he himself will return and not dwell for long. Bumpus did not indicate how Benga responded.

Two days later, Bumpus indicated that circumstances had worsened.

"Ota Benga restless," Bumpus typed in a cryptic note directed to Verner in care of the National Museum in Washington, D.C. "Chimpanzees need attention. When can you reach New York?"[23]

TWENTY-ONE

FONDLESS FAREWELL

Already saddled with an agitated African and a dying chimpanzee, Bumpus might not have imagined that more trouble would arise from his brief encounter with Verner. But on August 18 he was visited by a sheriff with a warrant for Verner's arrest, for writing a bad check. It is likely that Verner also still owed the Cunard company for the voyage for himself, his cargo, and Benga.

For months more Bumpus would be enmeshed in Verner's legal and emotional problems, even after a sheriff returned to impound the boxes of African artifacts that Verner had left in his care. Verner's financial problems would emphasize the urgency of his request for Bumpus to pay him a $175 advance and of his negotiations with the Zoological Gardens to sell the chimpanzees.

On August 27 Verner wrote Bumpus a farewell letter, saying that he had "arranged to place the African in satisfactory hands and hope to get him away today."[1]

With an outstanding warrant for his arrest, Verner slipped into town quietly and arranged to retrieve Benga from a museum side door.

Given Bumpus's eagerness to cut his ties with Verner, he probably didn't care where Benga and the chimpanzees would go. He had reached out to Hornaday to assist with negotiations for the sale of the chimpanzees. It would be five days before Verner turned Benga over to the zoo during a meeting with Hornaday and Madison Grant. In the interim, if the account he gave to a reporter can be believed, Verner attempted, in vain, to seek temporary shelter for Benga at the Salvation Army and at a police precinct.

The same day that Verner retrieved Benga from the museum, he was quoted in a long article in the *Washington* (D.C.) *Evening Star* defending the Congo Free State. In addition to continuing charges of atrocities—forced labor, mutilation, and murder—the Congo Reform Association alleged that Belgian officials were trying to "veil the eyes of the public" concerning actual conditions. James Gustaves Whitely, the government's consul general, adamantly denied the charges, as did Verner. Identified as a scientist and missionary who had worked in the Kasai region where atrocities had been reported, Verner maintained that any problems in the Congo stemmed from "weaknesses and mistakes of individuals in the field."[2]

He insisted that "the general effect of the government has been progressive and beneficial."

Verner also continued to submit articles for publication. In one unpublished article, "Pygmy and Chimpanzees," he said that although he had, after the St. Louis world's fair, been detained in the Congo for more than a year "soley against my will"—an apparent reference to his financial difficulties, for which he had blamed the fair's officials—things had turned out "more happily than I dared to hope."[3] Not only was Verner home safe and sound, but he had brought back "some very interesting things. Among these latter the most interesting are a pygmy and two chimpanzees, the famous anthropoid apes."

He said that after trying in vain to place Benga in a suitable home, he decided to bring him to America. "To leave him would be to expose him to almost certain re-enslavement, for none of his tribe were in that country for hundreds of miles, and slavery is the certain lot for one so isolated." In this account he did not claim that when he started home, Benga threatened suicide. He said a present of ivory from Chief Mwiila covered the cost of Benga's journey "and now I shall watch his future development with much interest."

He said one chimpanzee had already learned to eat with a spoon "simply by imitating the pygmy."

In addition to his collections, Verner claimed to have opened up a region the size of England, "which had been previously closed against the white man; a territory extremely rich in rubber and ivory and fairly densely populated by intelligent and interesting tribes—as African natives go." He also claimed that he had discovered a number of Batwa villages "and a fund of knowledge as to the history and traditions of these people was acquired." But most important of his discoveries, he said, was the condition of the natives, and their relations to the "white invasion, which was done in the most minute and detailed way, and the results of which are to be laid before the Governments at Washington and Brussels."[4]

A day after Benga left the museum, Grant notified him that negotiations regarding the two chimpanzees had failed over the required two-week quarantine. He said the Zoological Society was, however, prepared to take the healthy chimpanzee.

On August 31 Hornaday wrote to tell Verner that Grant had forwarded his letter and that he indeed wanted a meeting. Two days later, on Saturday, September 2, 1906, Hornaday met with Verner and Grant, and during this meeting Benga was placed in the care of the Zoological Gardens.

By early September news reports revealed that Leopold had been meeting with Thomas Ryan, a New York businessman and partner of Daniel Guggenheim. Ryan and Guggenheim had already formed the American Congo Company and the International Rubber Company, and were looking to gain ground in the Congo. Asked what the meetings were about, Ryan declined to comment. By then Leopold, hoping to win back dwindling U.S. support, planned to grant lucrative concessions to prominent U.S. businessmen.

Three weeks later, as controversy swirled around Benga's exhibition at the zoo, Verner continued negotiations with Grant that were finalized when Verner instructed Hornaday to send $75 to the Guardian Trust Company and keep $200 for him. With his debt paid, Verner was able to return to New York to retrieve Benga and meet with officers in the newly formed American Congo Company about business opportunities in the Congo.

Verner was still attempting to establish a formal relationship with the American Museum of Natural History. On September 16, during Benga's second week of internment, Verner asked to be included on Bumpus's lecture schedule for the season.

"There are peculiar reasons why the delivery of one of these lectures might help me in New York," he said.[5] He added that it had been a "considerable disappointment" when Bumpus was unable to help him, "though the disappointment was more because of hopes raised by chance words than of the destruction of long-cherished aims." He felt that Bumpus had misled him. Indeed, Bumpus had initially seriously considered hiring him but had made no promises. By the end of August there was no hope of Verner joining the museum staff, given the financial and legal troubles that he had brought to its door.

But Verner still did hope, even as a sheriff served Bumpus with a warrant to impound the twelve remaining boxes Verner had left at the museum.

"This has been done," Bumpus's secretary informed Verner a day later.[6]

Verner wrote to Bumpus to apologize for troubling him: "When my last few letters have been forwarded I hope we can look at each other only with the eyes of that love at first sight which brought about so curious a train of consequences—but with the added affection of a more sympathetic and accurate knowledge!"[7]

Verner assured Bumpus that he would, in the distant future, hear enough positive things "to take the taste of this thing out."

However, by October 5 Verner's letters to Bumpus took on a confrontational tone. That day he wrote to ask what Bumpus had told a representative of the Guardian Trust Company.

He expressed outrage over the bank's summons of attachment, and said that he only wished to settle the matter, "otherwise I might try to enjoy the effort of breaking Mr. Williams head," a reference to the bank representative seeking collection.

He said he was in New York permanently and did not expect any amenities from Bumpus "and shall not seek any of the privileges you alluringly held out to me." However, in a rather menacing aside, he said he was at liberty to conduct research at the museum, noting that it was a public institution.

Bumpus was startled. He wrote to Verner a day later, saying that he had repeatedly tried to reach him at the Hotel Belleclaire, but was informed he was no longer there. "The substance of your letters naturally surprises me, since my behavior toward you, and the time and expense that I have devoted to your interests, would rather argue against unfriendly acts on my part."[8]

But Verner would continue to harbor ill feelings toward the museum director even after Bumpus's fatal heart attack in 1908. Three years later, he expressed his hostility toward Bumpus in a letter to his successor, Henry Fairfield Osborn. But for all his troubles, Bumpus had, during Benga's one-month residence at the American Museum of Natural History, avoided the kind of public controversy that followed the deaths of the Inuit, or that would reverberate for the Bronx Zoo a century later.

PART III

FREE

TWENTY-TWO

WEEKSVILLE REFUGE

From the moment Benga set foot on American soil he had been held up to public ridicule by those determined to prove he belonged to an inferior species. Now, at the Howard Colored Orphan Asylum in Brooklyn's Weeksville section, he would be surrounded by elite African Americans determined to show that blacks could be fully integrated into American life as respectable and self-sufficient citizens.

Named for James Weeks, a stevedore from Virginia who in 1838 bought a plot of land in the ninth ward of central Brooklyn, by the 1850s Weeksville had become one of the largest African American communities, a picturesque suburb bounded by present-day Fulton Street and East New York, Troy, and Ralph Avenues. Its population had swelled to nearly seven hundred after the 1863 draft riots made it a refuge for blacks fleeing Lower Manhattan.[1]

Hundreds sought safety in Weeksville and Flatbush, where, according to an account in the *Christian Recorder*, "the colored men who had manhood in them armed themselves and threw out their pickets every day and night, determined to die defending their homes."[2]

By the close of the century Weeksville was known for having more African American property owners than any other northern community. It had its own cemetery, churches, school, and social service and civic organizations. Until the 1860s it had been the national headquarters of the African Civilization Society. Founded in 1858 by forty black citizens of New York and Brooklyn to "promote the civilization and christianization of Africa"—and of people of African descent—this society stressed "self-reliance and self government, on the principle of an African Nationality, the African race being the ruling element of the nation, controlling and directing their own affairs."[3] The society's founders included Martin R. Delany, the brilliant journalist, abolitionist, Civil War officer, and physician widely considered the father of black nationalism. He was one of the first three African Americans admitted to Harvard Medical School, but although he enrolled in 1850, he was dismissed a month later owing to protests by white students. He went on to apprentice with a doctor. Other members included Henry Highland Garnet, a prominent abolitionist orator who advocated rebellion and the return of African Americans to Liberia; Reverend Richard H. Cain, pastor of Brooklyn's Bridge Street Church; and Henry M. Wilson, a graduate of Princeton's theological seminary. The organization published *Freedman's Torchlight*, one of the nation's earliest African American newspapers, and was instrumental in opening schools for black children throughout the South.

An indication of the community's feisty independence was a meeting held at the African Civilization Building in 1869 to protest the hiring of a white teacher for Weeksville's Colored School No. 2. In a letter to the board of education, the petitioners said they were "sorely aggrieved that you have made this appointment, felt by us to be antagonistic to our educational and social interests." Noting the lack of black teachers in white schools, the petition said, "If you have a right to choice in the physical complexion of a teacher for your children, so have we. . . . If your choice is worthy of respect, so is ours."[4]

Weeksville counted among its residents doctors, lawyers, ministers, educators, and businessmen. It was home to Moses Cobb, who was born into slavery in 1856 and became the first black policeman in what was then the city of Brooklyn. Another notable resident was Dr. Susan Smith McKinney, the first African American female physician in New York State and the third in the country. She graduated at the top of her class from the New York Medical College for Women and went on to found the Women's Homeopathic Hospital and Dispensary, later renamed Memorial Hospital for Women and Children. She served as the official physician for the Brooklyn Home for Aged Colored People in Weeksville, where she was also a board member from 1892 to 1896.

Other prominent residents included noted educator Charles Dorsey, a graduate of Oberlin who came from a successful family of Philadelphia caterers. A longtime principal of Brooklyn's Colored School No. 1, he was secretary of Howard Colored Orphan Asylum's board of managers until his death in 1907. His widow continued to serve on its auxiliary committee. Charles Dorsey's brother, Thomas Dorsey, graduated from Harvard Medical School and moved in elite circles in Washington, D.C.

T. McCants Stewart, one of Brooklyn's most affluent citizens, was also a Weeksville resident. A native of Charleston, South Carolina, he had attended Howard University and later the University of Southern California, where he received a bachelor of laws degree in 1875. He moved to Brooklyn in 1885, became corresponding editor of the *New York Freeman*, and resumed his lucrative law practice. In 1893 he was appointed to the board of education, and three years later he was a cofounder of the Legal Rights Union, which provided counsel to African Americans who could not afford representation. Other cofounders of the union included Dorsey; Timothy Thomas Fortune,

publisher of the *New York Age*; and Howard's longtime superintendent, Reverend William F. Johnson.

In 1884 the orphanage relocated into a handsome three-story
brick building on Dean Street between Troy and Albany Avenues,
on land purchased from the city. This was where Benga would reside. The building was designed by William A. Mundell, a prominent Brooklyn-born architect who by age twenty-four had already
designed, in the style of a Renaissance palazzo, the gleaming cast-iron
Long Island Safe Deposit Company building at Front and Old Fulton
Streets in Manhattan. His landmark Brooklyn buildings included the
Hall of Records, the Alms House in Flatbush, and armories in Park
Slope, Fort Greene, and Williamsburg.

Howard's new home was brightly lit and well ventilated with
twenty-eight windows on each floor and a top-floor skylight. Visitors
were greeted in a gracious wainscoted reception area. The home also
featured a sixteen- by eighteen-foot dining room for the children, a
twenty-nine- by thirty-two-foot schoolroom, and two smaller class-
rooms. The girls' and boys' dormitories were roomy—each measuring
eighteen by sixty-three feet—and a smaller nursery had an adjoining
nurse's room. The building cost $35,000—more than $800,000 in today's dollars—and indicated the orphanage's ascent.

Publisher T. Thomas Fortune was among the speakers at the
opening celebrations, which lasted several days and brought blacks
and whites from across the city to Weeksville.

An article in the *New York Times* in 1894 noted Howard's commodious environment, and its "excellent care and teaching."[5] Physicians visited the children twice a week, and summer instruction
included sewing and cooking. At the time Howard housed about 150
youngsters, aged three to sixteen years.

In addition to the main building, a large annex had just been
completed for use as an industrial school and for entertainment; and a
large corner lot had just been purchased.

"It will give plenty of room for the asylum to grow when it has the money always necessary for such development," the *Times'* article said. "It is very comfortable and spacious now, but is well filled by nearly 150 children," who, the *Times* noted, ranged in color "all the way from café frappe to black coffee."[6]

Around the same time that Howard was moving into its new home, Weeksville's Berean Baptist Missionary Church moved into a new building on Bergen Street between Utica and Rochester Avenues. In 1900 the Zion Home for Colored Aged, Howard's former neighbor, would also move into a new building, on St. John's Place and Kingston Avenue, bringing Booker T. Washington to Weeksville to preside over the opening ceremony.

By the time Benga arrived the thriving community still had its own churches, old-age home, and cemetery, but its Colored School No. 2 was integrated and renumbered P.S. 83. By then Howard's board was also integrated, and William Hoople, a white Congregational philanthropist, had been elected board chairman in 1902. That year a restructuring was prompted by a scandal over alleged financial improprieties that resulted in the resignation of Johnson, who was by then eighty-two years old. He died a year later. Attempting to win the confidence of donors, the board was transformed from one that had been predominantly black and female to one that was all male and multiracial. The advisory board members now included the city comptroller and borough president. Among the black board members were Mount Olivet's M. W. Gilbert; and S. W. Timms and George Sims, who had joined Reverend James Gordon, superintendent of the Howard orphanage, in protests to arrange Benga's release. Wilford H. Smith, the lawyer who had represented Benga in those protests, was on the advisory board, as was Robert MacArthur of Calvary Baptist Church, who by 1909 became a trustee. Reverend Adam Clayton Powell, who in 1908 became pastor at Harlem's Abyssinian Baptist Church, and Reverend William T. Dixon, pastor of Concord Baptist Church, would also join the board's executive committee. In 1906 a thousand worshippers celebrated Dixon's forty-third year as Concord's pastor with remarks delivered by Gordon.

When Benga arrived Howard was bursting at the seams with 265 young residents. Between 1902 and 1906 the number of occupants had more than doubled (from 116), and the orphanage had to turn away three times as many indigent children for lack of space.[7] Benga, one of 152 male boarders, would be among the fifty-three new males taken in between October 1906 and 1907.[8]

In the annual report ending October 1907 the board president, William Hoople, said that $25,000 was urgently needed to relieve this situation, and that Howard planned to rent an additional house to comply with board of health requirements. "There may be some reader who will glance at our report and see the deep necessity of lending a helping hand," he said.[9]

Still, Benga probably marveled at his new residence, with its all-black staff of six teachers; its several nurses and administrators; and its full slate of physicians and dentists on call, including specialists in radiology and diseases of the chest, throat, nose, ear, and eye. Many of these doctors and dentists lived nearby and "willingly and graciously respond to our call at any hour of the day or night," Gordon said.[10]

According to a fairly straightforward *New York Times* article, it was hoped that Benga would be civilized at the orphanage. "The teachers in the orphan asylum realize that they have a difficult problem, but they are hopeful of Ota Benga," the article said. One problem was that Benga, although he was the size of a child and was in an institution for children, was actually a man. But the article did not note the improvement over his cohabitation with apes. The article also noted that while Benga was as "gentle as a child," he was impatient of restraint, and that this could pose difficulties at the orphanage. In this regard, however, the writer ignored the fact that at Howard Benga would not be a caged attraction in need of restraint, but a welcome guest.[11]

At the time, the larger boys occupied a third-floor dormitory, while the 113 girls and younger children of both sexes lived on the second floor. However, Gordon gave Benga his own room, one that had been used as the sewing room, on the main floor. He said Benga would eat with the staff in the kitchen, located in the basement.

In the *Times* article Gordon appeared to relieve Verner of any responsibility for Benga's degrading and harrowing experience at the zoo, saying, "He brought the little man to us at our suggestion, and we are quite convinced that he has done all he could for the pigmy and that his treatment in the Zoological Park, where he was put in the monkey cage, was not intended to degrade him, but rather to supply him with amusement until the professor could come back from a trip South." [12]

Whether Gordon actually believed Verner bore no responsibility, or merely sought to placate the man who, he stressed, had not surrendered his guardianship and would eventually return Benga to Africa, is not known. But Verner had previously sought a letter from the mayor of Birmingham releasing him of responsibility for Kassongo's death, and may have requested from Gordon a similar statement that would hold him harmless. Gordon also said Verner told him that Benga, in his native tongue, said "he was pleased to be with black people and free from the witchcraft of the white man." [13]

On his first day, Gordon said, Benga had already learned a surprising number of English words and was being taught to write his name. Benga repeated his name and tried to imitate the writing.

One staff member—named Egypt, and a native of Africa—attempted to communicate with Benga, but to no avail.

Gordon had feared that Benga would be unmanageable but now said that "he is more intelligent than many people I know." [14] He said Benga was alert and interested in everything around him. "So far he has been very sensible, and we have a hope that at last he has found a refuge."

By his second day there were reports that Benga was smitten

with a Howard nurse, Miss Upson. According to the *Brooklyn Eagle*, Benga took Gordon by the hand, pointed out the window at her in the courtyard, and insisted he wanted her for his wife.

"He's been here one day, and he's certainly dead in love with Miss Upson," Gordon was quoted as saying. "I don't know what I'll do about it."[15]

From the start Gordon had designs for Benga's future. He indicated that he planned to send Benga to a southern seminary where he would be trained as a missionary. Verner would eventually return to take Benga back to Africa, but the idea of making him a missionary, while mocked by some reporters, was not as far-fetched as they believed. Among Howard's summer teachers was Mohouga Carparsa, a native of Africa who had resided at the asylum since the age of ten. Her brother had been sold to a French consul, with whom she traveled to the United States. Carparsa planned to return home as a missionary once her education was completed.

In the meantime Gordon said he and his attendants would take Benga out for walks and allow him to get his bearings. "We hope to arouse his ambition and to make him feel that he at least ought to know as much as the children."[16]

During his first week Benga was smoking a pipe, shaking hands, and saying, "How de do."[17] On Sunday James Gordon took his young protégé to Fleet Street Memorial A.M.E. Zion Church, where, at the conclusion of the service, he introduced "the young African boy" in his charge.[18] It appeared that either Verner was still translating for him or a reporter used creative license, insisting that Benga no longer wished to return to Africa, because "he has a suspicion that he would be made very welcome there; in fact, he thinks the cannibal tribe to which he belongs has the pot already on the fire for him."[19] With Verner fading from Benga's life, this would be one of the last references to his alleged cannibal past.

At Howard, Benga was under the watchful eye of Mary Gordon, the superintendent's wife and house matron from 1902 to 1914. Reared in Philadelphia, she stressed respectability, decorum, professional aspirations, and Christian values. She also conformed to Victorian ideals of chastity and was determined to combat negative stereotypes of blacks. Accordingly, a custodian caught kissing a teacher in front of the children was threatened with dismissal. Benga, a young healthy male surrounded by female adolescents, would certainly merit her close attention.

Even so, Howard's familial character defied its institutional setting. Visitors to Howard, including Booker T. Washington and inspectors from the Charities Board, noted the loving atmosphere created by Mary, who was often affectionately referred to by former wards as "dearest mother," "my own sweet mother," or "darling mother."[20]

Wrote one: "Some day you may have just cause to be proud of us, for I know I don't intend to spend the rest of my days in the kitchen."

A city inspector noted that conversation was permitted in the dining room, an indication that such a liberty was uncommon in similar settings. "One notable feature of the home is the spirit of cordial relationship and friendliness evident between staff and children," he wrote. At Howard, children accused of wrongdoing were tried by a jury of their peers. "Nothing resembling military discipline prevails."

Booker T. Washington was similarly struck by "the natural bearing of the children," remarking that "a natural relation seemed to exist between them and their instructors."

Mary Gordon routinely tracked discharged wards and when one was accused of theft, she intervened on his behalf, saying, "I am his mother in love, trust and purpose." She then arranged for him to live with her brother in St. Louis, Missouri, where he became a farmer. She also granted his request to take her last name, and in letters he referred to her as "his mother," and she to him as "her boy."

During Benga's first week at Howard Mary Gordon took him to the Hippodrome, accepting an invitation that had first been directed to Hornaday while Benga was at the zoo. Seated in a box beside Mary Gordon, the former elephant hunter applauded and chortled his approval, at times shouting, "Fine!" and "Nice!" as the elephants performed tricks on a large stage that could hold a thousand people.

He sported a new suit that, a reporter commented, made him look like a Thompson Street "Beau Brummel."[21]

At one point, Benga was asked by a Hippodrome official to appear onstage surrounded by animals, a request that Mary declined. She said that Benga did not like going out and feared crowds. Given his experience at the zoo and the world's fair, that was not surprising and could well have signaled post-traumatic stress syndrome. The condition would not be uncommon for someone who had experienced early trauma in the Congo, followed by the trauma of being caged, heckled, and attacked at the zoo.[22] After the show Benga did, however, go backstage to pet the animals.

Meanwhile, Verner did not appear ready to release the reins. After reading about Benga's trip to the Hippodrome, he wrote a letter to the editor of the *New York Tribune* urging New Yorkers not to spoil Benga. He also appealed to "the intelligent and serious part of the public not to believe the tales told about Ota Benga and myself."[23] He said he and Benga would travel back to the Kasai region together if Benga survived scientific and reportorial investigation and elementary education. Verner continued to perpetuate his tales of rescuing Benga from cannibals—tales that had begun with his arrival at the world's fair.

"I saved him from the pot and he saved me from poison darts and we have been good friends for a long time," Verner wrote. "I beg New York not to spoil him."[24]

Weeks later Verner was angered by a request from a reporter for an interview with Benga. The reporter wanted Verner to serve solely as Benga's translator. In a letter dated October 16, Hamilton Holt, the managing editor of the *Independent*, wrote to Verner to express his surprise at "the heat" of Verner's reply.

"You could have easily refused," said Holt. "I did not want an article about him *by you,* and was not aware (as I should have been I presume) that you were his guardian."[25] He added: "I thought a story of his life in his own words would be interesting. Where the 'dishonorableness' of the transaction lies, I fail to see."

By early 1907 Verner was working as an agent for the American Congo Company, one of two firms formed by financiers Daniel Guggenheim and Thomas Ryan. Guggenheim had become a ruling power in U.S. and Mexican mining and smelting and also had interests in Chile and Canada. Thomas Fortune Ryan was co-owner of a patent for extracting rubber from the guayule plant. The men now hoped to expand their operation into Leopold's Congo.

In December 1906 a concession agreement with Leopold gave their new Société Internationale Forestière et Minière du Congo a ninety-nine-year lease for prospecting rights. More specifically it granted them a six-year royal concession to prospect for minerals in the Congo. They could then, for another ninety-three years, continue to work on already exploited mines. The deal placed the Guggenheims in control of mineral exploitation in all of the undeveloped Congo. Leopold maintained a 25 percent share and the Belgian kingdom another 25 percent, with the rest divided between Guggenheim and Ryan.

Meanwhile Verner said the letter of introduction from U.S. secretary of state Hay, written for his trip to the Congo, had helped him secure a $50-a-week job as a subway ticket agent in New York City, enabling him to send for his wife and children. About a month into his residence in New York, Verner's path crossed Ryan's. Verner claimed he was invited to meet the man who was " 'a power behind the throne.' I thought I was in fairyland," he wrote of the invitation.[26] The meeting led to an introduction to Senator Nelson Aldrich, who wished to see the development of the Congo Free State. Verner was eventually invited to Ryan's Fifth Avenue home, where he met with Ryan, Guggenheim, and Aldrich to discuss business dealings that

Verner claimed totaled more than a billion dollars. "At least one dream had come true," he later wrote.

He was awarded a retainer that enabled him to help his ailing father. "My African obsession had always looked to my family like a wild dream," he wrote, "and the fact that I could not help much was a most distressing fact." Verner now claimed a retainer far more lucrative than what was given to his idol Henry Morton Stanley. Counting his blessings, he said the fates had sent him three kings: Leopold, Ndombe, and now Ryan.

"It sounds like a story from some weird romance, but it is the truth, the whole truth and nothing but the truth," he wrote.[27]

However, his fairy tale would come to an abrupt end. An exposé that December by the *New York American* described Leopold's influence-peddling, drawing greater scrutiny to the business dealings of men like Ryan and Guggenheim.

The series of articles in the *New York American* stemmed from the release of letters exchanged between Congo state officials and Henry Kowalsky, the man Leopold had hired to represent him in the United States but had since been released from his lucrative contract. Some people speculated that Kowalsky, angered by Leopold's refusal to renew his contract for a second year, sold the letters to the newspaper; Kowalsky claimed they had been stolen.

Among the revelations was Kowalsky's huge salary in addition to a promised bonus of 100,000 francs in bonds if "the American Government does not make any declaration harmful to the Congo State, and if Congress passes no unfavourable resolutions before the end of the next session." It was disclosed that Kowalsky had bribed Thomas G. Garrett, who was on the staff of the Senate Foreign Relations Committee, to block a protest resolution. In a letter to Leopold, Kowalsky said Garrett had personally stood at the committee room door "and held back the demanding, howling missionaries, ministers, and religious cranks."[28] A copy of Garrett's handwritten letter on U.S. Senate stationery, requesting payment, appeared on the front page.

In another letter to Leopold, Kowalsky bragged of a $1,000 bribe paid to an unnamed journalist who he claimed was a close friend of President Roosevelt. He said that the payment had yielded hundreds of thousands of dollars worth of publicity promoting Leopold's cause.

In addition to detailing the efforts to bribe U.S. officials, the articles highlighted the atrocities that reformers had alleged for years, accompanied by photographs and graphic headlines such as "Infamous Cruelties," and "Torture of Women and Children."

The exposé—by the same Hearst newspaper that had criticized Benga's exhibition at the zoo—quickened the pace of Leopold's spectacular fall. Even U.S. senator John T. Morgan, who in 1884 had introduced a resolution recognizing Leopold's claim on the Congo, agreed it was time for him to go. He supported U.S. Senator Henry Cabot Lodge's resolution calling for an international investigation of conditions in the Congo. Secretary of State Elihu Root finally, if belatedly, agreed to support Great Britain's efforts to end Leopold's reign in the Congo.

Still, near the end of Leopold's rule there, Verner set out for the Congo as an agent of the American Congo Company, to find sources of native rubber and to oversee the construction of buildings and the recruitment of labor. In February 1907 Benga spurned Verner's offer to return with him to Africa. The invitation to rejoin Verner came through a letter directed to Gordon from A. T. Wilkinson who said he was writing on Verner's behalf. He said he expected to leave the country shortly to meet Verner in Europe "and I will be very glad to take the Pygmy in my charge." [29]

Wilkinson told Gordon that Verner was too pressed with business to personally take the matter up with him. Gordon's reply could not be found, but a week later Chris Chisholm of the American Congo Company wrote to Verner to confirm that he had spoken to Gordon and that Benga had decided to remain in America. Gordon had told him that Benga was perfectly capable of judging for himself

what was in his best interest. "He thinks that his wishes in regard to
the matter should be complied with," Chisholm said.

Chisholm assured Verner that he had relayed his message that he
felt responsible for Benga and would himself want to hear from him.
Gordon replied that he would have Benga write a letter to Verner.
While it is likely such a letter was written, it has not been located.
Such a letter would provide Benga's reasons for staying, and also for
not returning home with a man who had brought him so much igno-
miny and pain.

Verner would proceed on his trip to the Congo as an agent of
the American Congo Company. He spent most of this third trip
to the Congo studying the business of collecting wild rubber, especially the kind derived from the *Landolphia* vine, and experimenting
with practices that might improve the yield in the exploitation of this
natural resource.

The *Washington Post* reported that Verner had left on the *Kai-
ser Wilhelm der Grosse* a day earlier, without Benga. The article said
that Benga "refuses to go back to the jungle until he is qualified to
teach." [30]

In one of the most creatively concocted narratives yet, the *New
York Sun* reported that Benga had been "such a hit" that Hornaday
had engaged him as assistant keeper of the monkeys. "In a little while
Ota, who is of a sensitive nature, discovered that because he wasn't a
member of the Monkey Keepers' Union Local No. 1, the other keepers were pestering him by hanging cards on the cages of the primates'
house, which drew great crowds." [31] The *Sun* also claimed that Verner
had gone to Brooklyn to consult Benga about his future, and that
Benga "told him frankly that if he stayed in this country and went to
college he might grow up to be a great man like [Booker T.] Washington, after which he could go back to the Congo Free State and make
a great hit as the father of his country." [32]

Gordon told a reporter that the Baptist Ministers Association
intended to send Benga to the Virginia Theological Seminary in

Lynchburg once his English improved. According to the article in the *Washington Post*, those who went to the orphanage to steal a look at Benga were disappointed. "He refuses to be looked at since his experiences in the monkey cages," it said.[33]

Meanwhile, sometime between the end of September 1906, when he arrived at Howard, and October 1908, Benga had taken the name Otto Binga, as recorded in Howard's annual report for the year ending October 1908. It is not known if the new name was intended to free Benga from the stigma of his exhibition, or simply to ease his transition by being more Americanized. Gordon identified him as "the African boy, who was rescued from the monkey cage in the Bronx Zoological Gardens."[34]

That fall Benga visited the Virginia Theological Seminary in Lynchburg as a ward of the New York State Colored Baptist Convention, of which Gordon was president. The national organization traced its roots to 1880, when delegates from eleven states founded the Baptist Foreign Mission Convention in Montgomery, Alabama, with the goal of establishing missions in Africa. Six years later, the National Baptist Convention of America was established; it was followed seven years later by the National Baptist Education Convention. The three bodies merged in 1895, creating one of the nation's largest and most influential religious organizations.

The Virginia Theological Seminary and College, nestled in the foothills of the Blue Ridge Mountains, had been founded by African American Baptist leaders to train men and women as teachers, ministers, and missionaries. Reverend Gregory Willis Hayes, its second president, a graduate of Oberlin and a nationally recognized orator, became Benga's newest benefactor.

By 1906, as head of the National Baptist Convention Education Board, Hayes was a lightning rod in debates among black educators over whether to accept white patronage and its insistence on an exclusively industrial education for blacks. Hayes, like Booker T. Washington, had been born into slavery, had overcome his circumstances, and advocated self-help, but he vigorously opposed the Tuskegee president's racial conservatism. Whereas Washington counseled patience and submission in the face of political and social slights, Hayes opposed anything short of full racial equality. He insisted that blacks determine their own course. An ardent black nationalist, he would use his elite Oberlin education and prominent platform to promote what some considered a radical vision.

But in December 1906, shortly after Benga's arrival in Lynchburg, Hayes, at age forty-four, died suddenly of Bright's disease, an inflammation of the kidney that could arise slowly from high blood pressure, or suddenly after strep throat. Whatever the cause, he left behind a devastated widow with five young children, and a visiting protégé who was sent back to New York.

Benga returned to an acutely overcrowded Brooklyn orphanage whose population had swelled from 222 to 276. Of that number, 152 were male. To relieve the overcrowding, the board looked to a farm in St. James, Long Island. At its October 6, 1906, meeting, just a week after Benga moved into the Brooklyn orphanage, Howard's board had voted, twelve to three, to purchase this 160-acre farm. The board agreed to pay $10,000 down on a purchase price of $25,000. It was hoped that the site would house an industrial school modeled after Booker T. Washington's Tuskegee Institute. By the fall of 1907, thirty-five of the male wards, including Ota Benga, were sent to St. James.

TWENTY-THREE

ST. JAMES

S t. James was a sleepy village with a scenic bay, amid rich farmland and rolling hills, roughly two hours from New York City by the Long Island Railroad. It was located on the north shore of Long Island in Smithtown, which had been founded in 1665. The addition in 1873 of the Long Island Railroad station brought a wave of wealthy New Yorkers who by the turn of the century had erected palatial mansions as summer retreats.

Among these millionaires were Thomas Caldecott Chubb, founder of the insurance company; the fur merchant John Riszits; and a justice of the Brooklyn supreme court, William Jay Gaynor. Gaynor was a neighbor of the Howard farm: he summered at a sprawling estate later known as Deepwells Farm, on North Country Road near Moriches Road, that he purchased in 1905 and continued to use after he was elected mayor of New York City in 1909—while Benga lived in St. James.

Gaynor enthusiastically supported Howard's farm in St. James, and wrote a letter to raise funds for the construction of buildings.

"The enterprise is of the highest merit," he wrote, noting that his own home was located in the neighborhood. "Everyone broad enough to look at humanity in a broader spirit than that of mere race or sect should contribute to it, if his means permit," Gaynor said, adding that Gordon—Howard's superintendent—was "in every way competent and worthy of your confidence." [1]

The farm—on Mills Pond Road, halfway between the railroad and Moriches Road, was to be the site of an agricultural school. It was hoped that the shift in emphasis would ensure more funding, owing to the preference for that model for black students among the mostly white elite patrons of Negro education.

Gordon ended 1907 brimming with optimism about the future of the orphanage. "We feel sure the Asylum has made many new friends," he said. "Instead of having thirty-five boys in training for the various industrial pursuits, we ought to have a thousand of these unfortunate children in the school, teaching them the various trades, so they may become respectable, self-sustaining citizens." [2]

The farm would allow Howard to "develop enterprises impossible within our cramped quarters in the city."

Gordon crowed about the community's enthusiastic support of Howard. A drill team, the "Boys Brigade," had been started by a community volunteer and, according to Gordon, was among the finest in the city. A Christmas dinner of turkey, vegetables, fruit, and dessert, with a present for each child, was provided by other generous patrons. The financial report showed that $13,218.55 had been paid on the farm and another $5,000 had been paid for equipment, supplies, and repairs. Donations, large and small, had poured in from churches across the city, and from as far away as Westchester.

Gordon said that he was "glad to report that the colored people (my people) are greatly aroused by seeing the needs of an institution of this character, and are sacrificing more and more each year towards the support of it."

At the farm, the potato crop yielded more than nine hundred

bushels, and this figure was expected to increase to three thousand the following year. A ten-acre field was being cleared to plant corn. Baby, the farm's first calf, had been purchased. Gordon said the health of the boys had been "phenomenal." Aside from a broken finger incurred during a game of baseball, and a few sprains, no child had been ill since the farm opened.

Gordon now hoped to raise $150,000 to erect buildings and purchase equipment necessary to make it a great industrial school for one thousand Negro youngsters in the North.

"In faith and hope, we have crossed the Red Sea," proclaimed William Hoople, the board chairman. "Let us now enter the promised land with a new enthusiasm."[3]

In his annual 1907–1908 report Gordon noted that Benga was at the farm, working a half day and going to school a half day. "He has been converted and baptized, and says he expects to go to Africa to preach to his people."[4]

Three of the boys were hired out for $8 to $10 a month. "They are getting along very nicely, and the people are very much pleased with their services," he reported.[5]

Gordon said the institution had been warmly embraced by the residents of St. James, who saw it as a source of needed labor, given the scarcity of available workers in their rural area.

By then the farm housed an average of forty boys, two farmers, a cook, a matron, and a schoolteacher. The plan was to relocate the entire male population from Weeksville—which by the fall of 1908 numbered 173—to relieve the chronic overcrowding there. The total orphanage population had again increased, from 265 the previous year to 302.[6]

Benga, believed to be in his young adulthood and without the comfort of his culture or people, was likely to have had a lonely life in rural Long Island.

St. James in 1907 was still mostly farmland but also had a silent movie theater and a string of inns and hotels like St. James Park,

Gould's, and Peter Myers's that during the summer months swelled
with visiting New Yorkers. Notable figures in show business summered in St. James, including Irving Berlin, Ethel and John Barry-
more, Buster Keaton, Lillian Russell, and William "Willie" Collier,
who, from 1906 to 1907, was starring on Broadway in *Caught in the
Rain*. Around 1890 Collier, already a famous vaudeville actor, had
purchased the village's old one-room schoolhouse on Three Sisters
Road to use as a clubhouse and performance space. The building,
set in a gulch in a hilly wooded area near the bay, became the heart
of the New York actors' colony. Collier and his actress wife, Louise
Alcott Collier, for a time lived in a nearby Queen Anne house.

Those entertainment figures who did not purchase or rent homes
often stayed at the Shore Inn on Harbor Road at the bay, operated by
retired vaudevillians Anthony and Sophie Farrell. The inn featured
all-night parties, a casino, and spring water for swimming.

Stanford White, of McKim, Mead, and White, married Bessie
Smith, a descendant of Smithtown's founder, and in 1885 began work
on Box Hill, a fifteen-thousand-square-foot neoclassic showplace on
St. James's Carmon Hill. It overlooked a foxtail-lined bay with flocks
of ducks. White designed other homes in St. James, including his
sister-in-law's octagonal mansion next door. Following his death in
1906 he was buried in the cemetery at St. James Episcopal Church,
which had been erected in 1853, the year he was born. His son, Lawrence, also an architect, continued to reside and design structures in
St. James.

By the turn of the century the area had become known as
"Boomertown," as real estate companies tried to lure New Yorkers to
live there year-round. The first two decades of the twentieth century
also saw a rise in anti-immigrant activity, bolstered by the arrival of
the Ku Klux Klan.

African Americans, who had made up roughly 20 percent
of Smithtown's population during the slavery era, were less than 5
percent of the population after emancipation in New York in 1827.

Whereas there had been a total of 215 African Americans in Smith-town in 1830—nearly 15 percent of the population—they numbered only 130, less than 5 percent, by 1900.[7] In contrast, the white population during that same period had increased from 1,471 to 2,383. So Benga and his black male schoolmates at Howard were awash in a sea of whiteness, and they joined the class of workers who served as farmhands and servants to the wealthy.

During the first year Howard's farm added to its livestock six calves, seventy-five chickens, eleven ducks, and twenty hogs and harvested eight thousand cabbages. It planted thirty acres of pota-toes, twelve acres of corn, and additional acres of turnips, carrots, and beets to feed the stock, wards, and staff. However, by the year's end, because of a drought, the crops had not yielded as much as expected. Instead of the anticipated yield of four thousand to five thousand bushels of potatoes, the farm had produced only 2,200 bushels—and only half of that was marketable. Howard hoped to have better success with the new corn crops planted on twelve acres.

"We will have enough cabbage to supply the inmates of the asy-lum and the farm until about April," Gordon noted in the report for the year ending October 1909. "We have a few hundred to sell."[8] Meanwhile planned construction at the farm had been delayed, al-though an effort to raise $10,000 for a building in St. James contin-ued. Thus far Howard had raised only $116 for its building fund.

The inability to build more facilities had delayed plans for more housing and also for a barn to house the livestock and store crops. "The old stable has almost fallen down," Gordon reported. "It is in-deed unsafe for our horses."[9] In the meantime it was propped up as they tried their best "to make it stand a while longer."

In addition, the optimism expressed by Howard's board the pre-vious year had been dimmed by the realities of limited funding for building and by the inadequate equipment due to its burgeoning pop-ulation and deteriorating facilities. The board was also reeling from the sudden death of its president, William G. Hoople, which Gordon said "was a great shock and loss to us." Howard had also lost its vice president, Reverend William T. Dixon, whom Gordon described as "a strong race man, a friend to the orphan, and an ardent supporter of the institution." [10]

In the annual report for the year ending October 1909 R. M. Whiting, the new board president, noted how unfavorably Howard's rudimentary living conditions compared with conditions at white orphanages, which had "capacious and well tiled" toilets, bathrooms, and laundry rooms and modern plumbing, appliances, kitchens, and dining facilities. He said that while Howard's residents were kept clean, well clothed, well fed, and educated at the Brooklyn asylum, the furnishings were "of the most primitive." [11]

By then it had 292 residents, 164 of them boys, and the focus was not on expansion—although the previous year's report had set a goal of a thousand students—but rather on providing adequately for those already in its care. In Weeksville Howard was under pressure by the board of health, the buildings commissioner, and the state Charities Board to make repairs and to improve the "very dilapidated condition" of its facility.[12] The farm was being operated solely by the residents, with no foreman but "only the man we left in charge when we were not there."

Gordon reported that despite the problems, most of the boys seemed happy and proud of their home. Three, however, had left without permission. "As our home is not a reformatory," Gordon said, "we have no way of keeping them if they want to leave."

But the three had been traced, including Ota Benga, "our African boy," who Gordon reported became "dissatisfied on the farm." [13]

By the fall of 1909 Ota Benga was working for $10 a month—the equivalent of roughly $256 today—at a nearby farm owned by William J. O'Berry. The 1910 census identifies O'Berry as a forty-eight-year-old farmer on Moriches Road who was born in New York to Irish immigrants. O'Berry's household included his forty-one-year-old wife, Anna; and his thirty-three-year-old brother-in-law, Oscar Field. An "Otto Bengal" is identified as a black male, age twenty-four, who is said to be a servant stable groom. The census indicated that Benga could read and write. By then Benga had taken classes, but how much he could read and write is not known. The census taker probably recorded his reply to the question.

Gordon said Benga was still hoping to raise enough money to return home. In 1910 a third-class ticket from New York to Liverpool, England, would have cost about $37.50, the equivalent of $900 today. He would then still need to get to the Congo. Verner and Starr had traveled on the government steamer, which Benga would almost certainly not have access to.

Given Benga's assumed age, which was based on information provided by Verner, Gordon said that Howard's officials had no control over his money. He also said that O'Berry had assured him he would encourage Benga to save most of his earnings, after buying adequate clothing. At $10 a month, then, it would take Benga four months to purchase a third-class ticket from New York to Liverpool, without allowing for his daily living expenses.[14] However, Benga appeared determined to work his way back home rather than rejoin Verner. That decision could have stemmed from any of several reasons, including a simple desire to maintain his independence. Whatever the reason, it is clear that he did not wish to reunite with the man who had brought him to America, and ensured his degradation, even if that meant forgoing a free journey home.

With the O'Berrys, Benga may have enjoyed more commodious living quarters than those at Howard's farm. The O'Berrys lived in a gracious Queen Anne house, one of several on their four-hundred-acre farm east of Stony Brook Harbor. The farm had been in the family since 1852, when William O'Berry's father, John, purchased what was part of the Nathaniel H. Smith Homestead. The land had been settled by Adam Smith, a son of Smithtown's founder, in what was then called Sherrawog—so named by the Native Americans there. O'Berry became one of Suffolk County's most prosperous farmers, and would raise his nine children on the property.

In 1894 William and Anna's eldest son, Loftis, commissioned New York architect Stanley S. Covert, who designed a white, three-and-a-half-story, ten-room Queen Anne house with a wraparound porch and an octagonal cupola. The elegant house was complete with stained-glass windows, high ceilings, oak banisters, and ornate moldings. Loftis had inherited money from an uncle and namesake who had made a fortune on patents for a stove used on ships. One of Loftis O'Berry's extravagant pastimes was racing horses. His horse Soldier was well known in Suffolk County for winning races, and could well have been among the horses Benga cared for. The St. James Driving Park, a mile-long racecourse used for training and trotting horses, was considered one of the finest in the country.[15]

Whether Benga, who by then spoke some English, had opportunities to mingle with other blacks is not known. Howard's farm was close to O'Berry's, but no other blacks listed on the census were in the immediate vicinity of O'Berry's home. The 1900 census shows sixty-eight black females, thirty-four of whom were over the age of fifteen, in all of Smithtown, so there were few opportunities for female companionship—especially since at least twenty of those thirty-four females appear to have been married.[16]

While Benga spent his days in Long Island trying to earn his passage back home, British vice-consul Wilfred Thesiger was touring the Kasai region investigating reports of abuses. Thesiger would be the first foreign diplomat to go into the interior, and he relied heavily on William Sheppard to be his guide and translator. Sheppard took him to observe for himself the plight of the once-mighty Bakuba people, who by then were forced laborers for the state.

"The work is compulsory," said Thesiger, adding, "it is also incessant." He said although there had been no incidents of sleeping sickness, the once prosperous Bakuba population was quickly diminishing

ST. JAMES   213

as a result of overwork and food shortages. Many were starving despite their previous role as agriculturalists in one of the richest food-producing regions in the country. "Under the present regime," he said, "the villagers are not allowed to waste time in cultivating, hunting or fishing,—time which should be occupied in making rubber." [17]

He said one villager told him that the men went out to the forest hungry and returned home sick and dying. The Bakuba were sent to the forest to cut down and disentangle high-growing branches, divide them into lengths, and carry them home, a process that was continually repeated. He said accidents were frequent, since the Bakuba were large and unaccustomed to climbing trees.

Everywhere he saw armed *capitas* employed by the Kasai Rubber Company to enforce labor and the rubber tax, noting, "They can do as they please, so long as they insure the rubber being brought to the proper place." [18]

On October 18, 1908, the Belgian parliament voted in favor of annexing the Congo as a Belgian colony. This was only after King Leopold II had given up any hope of maintaining a substantial part of the Congo Free State as a separate crown property. The government of the Belgian Congo was arranged by the 1908 Colonial Charter, with executive power resting with the Belgian minister of colonial affairs, assisted by a colonial council in Brussels. The Belgian parliament would exercise legislative authority over the Belgian Congo, with the governor-general holding the highest colonial administrative rank. A year later Leopold, who had been gravely ill, died of cancer.

Verner's career in the Congo would also come to an end. On his return he prepared a circular in which he claimed credit for, among other things, "the founding of the American Congo Company," and four expeditions—including one in 1906 during which he said he had opened up the country of the "cannibal Baschilele." He also claimed to be a member of many scientific societies and said he now hoped to inform his countrymen about "the vast labor building a civilized empire in the last stronghold of savagery." Among the numerous people allegedly offering words of praise were Hornaday, McGee, Starr, and Sheppard. As noted earlier, Sheppard remarkably and implausibly was quoted as saying: "Mr. Verner has done more at his age for the African race than any other white man in the world." [19]

Meanwhile Sheppard was at the center of a lawsuit brought by the Congo Free State for an article he had published that year outlining the same abuses Thesiger had witnessed. Sheppard had served as the British vice-consul's guide and translator, and Thesiger had merely reported what Sheppard had written in that article.

Sheppard's article, in the *Kasai Herald,* detailed the unrest in Kasai and the forced labor of the Bakuba, or Kuba, gathering rubber for the Compagnie du Kasai. They spent their days in the forest cutting rubber as guards patrolled their villages to ensure that they would waste no time cultivating their farms, which had once produced corn, tobacco, and potatoes, but now were weed-choked and incapable of feeding their hungry children.

Sheppard could not have known that his article, published in a small newsletter circulated among a few hundred Presbyterians, would gain a global audience. A trial for libel was set for May 1909 in Leopoldville, and Sheppard trekked through the Kuba villages on foot looking for witnesses to testify. In August Morrison and Sheppard arrived at Leopoldville, where they would await their rescheduled September court date with twenty Kuba witnesses, who in the end were denied an opportunity to testify. Émile Vandervelde, head of the Belgian Socialist Party, volunteered to defend Sheppard and Morrison for no fee.

Observing the trial were U.S. consul William Handley and his assistant, who had been dispatched by President Howard Taft to Leopoldville (Kinshasa) to attend it. The charismatic Vandervelde made it clear that the trial was not between the Company and Sheppard, "but between the company and the natives." [20]

Judge Charles Louis Gianpetri handed down his verdict on October 4, 1909. Sheppard was acquitted of the libel charges, but the Compagnie du Kasai, which had made millions of dollars from forced labor, was merely fined forty-two francs for the costs of the trial.

While reformers had hoped for more, the trial transformed Sheppard into an international celebrity. Many newspaper accounts noted his legendary history of hunting hippos, discovering the Kuba kingdom, and cofounding a mission in the heart of Africa.

At the end of 1909 Gordon wrote to Verner, who by then was working on the Panama Canal, to report that Benga was still working on the farm. "He has a bank account, and is saving his money to go back home or to do whatever is thought for him," Gordon said.[21]

Gordon said the educational project had "proved to be a failure," given Benga's age. "It was simply impossible to put him in a class to receive instructions, from a literary point. . . . I have done the best I could in trying to develop him, from every standpoint, and I find that the only thing to do is to let him work."[22]

Soon afterward, in January 1910, Benga made his second pilgrimage to Lynchburg, Virginia. That spring William Sheppard settled in Staunton, Virginia, seventy-four miles away. Sheppard would never return to Africa—a fate that Benga desperately hoped would not befall him.

TWENTY-FOUR

SOUTHERN COMFORT

Lynchburg, Virginia, in January must have been a physical and psychological lift for Benga, who had endured four winters in the colder Northeast. Whereas St. James was quiet, quaint, rural, and sparsely populated, Lynchburg was a picturesque city of nearly thirty thousand people, with electric streetcars, sumptuous mansions, sycamore trees, and soaring hills overlooking the James River.

In 1757 John Lynch—a Quaker, the son of Irish immigrants—set up a ferry service across the James River to reach the colonial village, which would be authorized as a town in 1786. By the start of the Civil War Lynchburg, owing to its location, the river, and its tobacco, was a major transportation and trading hub and one of Virginia's largest and most prosperous cities.

By the early 1800s many Quakers left because they were opposed to slavery, on which Lynchburg's thriving tobacco industry relied. An inspector of Lynchburg's tobacco factories noted that all of the workers were enslaved men, women, and children. "Their nimble fingers do not stop although upon your entrance every eye wanders to your face." [1]

The Quakers' early resistance to slavery alienated them from their white neighbors but also accounted for the higher proportion of free African Americans in Lynchburg than in the rest of the state. The first census of Lynchburg, taken in 1816, shows an overall population of three thousand, with nearly half—1,200—African American. Of the African Americans, 250, or roughly 20 percent, were free, compared with 8 percent for the state.[2] As free people of color they were required to register at the courthouse and carry their "free papers" at all times, but they operated businesses as barbers and craftsmen.

Still, Lynchburg had a flourishing and conspicuous slave market; African Americans were routinely advertised in the *Lynchburg Star* and later in the *Press*, and openly sold at auctions on Main Street in front of the Indian Queen Tavern, between Seventh and Eighth Streets; and later at Main and Ninth Streets, in the heart of the city. Observers described bare-breasted women being auctioned for $1,000 or more depending on their physical condition.

So woven into the fabric of the city was Lynchburg's slave market that one of its leading citizens was also one of its most prosperous traders. Seth Woodroof, who served on the city council from 1859 to 1866, ran advertisements seeking to purchase up to 150 people ages ten to twenty-five, and he constructed a brick building on Commerce Street, in the business district, to warehouse his human stock between auctions.[3]

But even as the town was built by the labor of the enslaved, by 1825 some, eager to reduce the population of African Americans, founded a colonization society to send free blacks back to Africa. Thomas Jefferson had broached the idea in 1776 when he asked the Virginia general assembly to provide for the return of emancipated blacks. Colonization societies were established across the South, with auxiliary societies founded in places like New York where funds could be actively raised. In Lynchburg, through the efforts of its Emigration Society, some 150 African Americans were sent to Liberia.

When Benga arrived in 1910 the city's population, as noted above, had climbed to thirty thousand. For most of the past century the population had been evenly divided between blacks and whites, but by 1910 steel and iron had replaced tobacco as the leading industries, decreasing the demand for the agricultural skills of the formerly enslaved. So while African Americans had been more than half—53.1 percent—of the population in 1881; they were little more than a quarter, or 27.7 percent, in 1910. Between 1890 and 1910, while the overall population increased, the number of blacks dropped from 9,802 to 8,200, a loss of 1,602.[4]

But African Americans already had roots in Lynchburg and had established twenty-two churches there and in the adjoining towns. In addition to its black Baptist and Methodist churches, its colored public schools and orphan asylum, and the Virginia Theological Seminary and College, Lynchburg was home to the Virginia College and Industrial Institute, an annex of the historically black Morgan College of Baltimore. African Americans held agricultural and industrial fairs and operated a number of successful businesses, including the People's Undertaking Company.

As an African guest of the Virginia Theological Seminary and College, Benga could blend visibly, if not culturally, into the city's proud African American community of eight thousand people. Those who remember him say his teeth were capped, but it's unclear if that was done in Weeksville, where Howard had an affiliated dentist, or Lynchburg. The dental procedure is not recorded in any of Howard's annual reports but could have been performed independently. In any case, his teeth would not arouse curiosity, as they did in St. Louis and the Bronx.

From the start Virginia Theological prided itself on its fierce independence from white Baptists, even if at some point the issue would divide the trustees. It had been founded by black Baptists during the nineteenth annual Virginia Baptist State Convention, held in Alexandria. In 1886 Reverend Phillip Fisher Morris, pastor of Lynchburg's Court Street Baptist Church and a delegate of the Baptist Foreign Missionary Convention of the United States, offered the resolution that authorized the establishment of what was originally called the Virginia Baptist Seminary.

In outlining the elements essential for the elevation of the race, the group's education board, chaired by Morris, said Negro education should emphasize: "(1) Race pride. (2) Race respect and ancestral reverence. . . . (3) Self-reliance. (4) Confidence in one another, and (5) Faith in one another's ability, honesty and trustworthiness to lead, and respect for the leadership."[5]

A Lynchburg resident with degrees in law and theology from Howard University, Morris would become the first president of the coeducational school created to train ministers, missionaries, and public school teachers. In July 1886, lawyer James H. Hayes of Richmond was appointed to obtain a charter for the school, and plans for the building and site were made during the 1888 session of the Virginia Baptist State Convention.

The school was incorporated by an act of the general assembly of Virginia on February 24, 1888, and in July the cornerstone of the first building was laid in an open triangular plot in the southwestern part of the city. Centrally located in the state and served by three major railroads, the school came into being the same year that the city's historic Diamond Hill Baptist Church was dedicated, which was also the year that electric cars replaced horse-drawn carriages. The Diamond Hill church would play a significant role in the city's African American community.

On January 18, 1890, the Virginia Baptist Seminary's first class—thirty-three students, with Professor R. P. Armistead as the instructor—was held in a temporary frame structure composed of two rooms, each measuring twenty-five by twenty-five feet. None of the early buildings are still standing, but contemporary photographs and maps show an imposing three-and-a-half-story brick Second Empire building with a five-story central tower, along the western side of Garfield Avenue. The building, later named Hayes Hall, was constructed between 1888 and 1911.

During his brief tenure Morris struggled to raise funds and to build consensus for his vision. In 1891 some trustees were troubled by a pact he had made with the American Baptist Home Mission Society: he had agreed to take $1,100 from the society for teachers' salaries and a matching grant from its "friends" in exchange for its right to inspect school operations, to dismiss teachers it deemed unfit, and to recommend replacements. Virginia Baptist would join two dozen of the society's affiliated schools, including Wayland Seminary in Washington, D.C., and Richmond Theological Seminary and Hartshorn Memorial in Virginia.

The agreement set the stage for a long battle between the "cooperationists"—those in favor of working with the white American Baptist Home Mission Society—and those vigorously opposed to giving that society a say in school affairs. Cooperation would mean adapting to the society's insistence on a purely industrial curriculum. In the midst of the debate, Morris resigned as president in 1891, but he remained on the school's board of managers until 1899. In 1898 he left Court Street Baptist Church and founded the Eighth Street Baptist Church.

In 1891 the Virginia Black Baptists appointed Reverend Gregory W. Hayes, a Presbyterian who was a graduate of Oberlin, to succeed Morris. One trustee hailed him as "that power and friend to the race and all true lovers and friends of the Virginia Seminary."[6] Hayes would preside for sixteen years over Virginia Theological, where his eloquent oratory and fierce commitment to liberal arts education and African American autonomy earned him national acclaim.

With an all-black faculty and staff, Hayes resisted the trend toward purely industrial training for blacks—modeled after Tuskegee—and insisted on offering the same options available to white students. His position would place him at odds with some school trustees who feared losing the financial support of the white-run Baptist Home Mission Society.

During Hayes's tenure enrollment climbed to 408 and the school enjoyed an enviable reputation among African Americans across the country. Hayes traveled extensively throughout the East Coast to raise money and recruit students from cities like Washington, D.C., New York, and Philadelphia.

Gregory Willis Hayes had been born into slavery on a plantation in Amelia County, Virginia, and was three when the Civil War ended. His family then relocated to Richmond, where his father worked as a carpenter and saw to it that the five children were educated. Hayes would prove to be a brilliant student at Navy Hill School and by the age of twelve attended Shooley Mountain Seminary in New Jersey. A few years later he attended Oberlin College, from which he graduated in 1888 with a degree in mathematics.

For many African Americans, Oberlin was an oasis in a racist wilderness, a place where talented African Americans could soar as high as their talent and ambition allowed. While it was not the first to accept African American students, it would, beginning in 1835, regularly admit them, achieving a number of firsts in various fields. Prior to the Civil War Oberlin enrolled more African American students than any other college or university. George Vashon would in 1844 become the first black Oberlin graduate and go on to become a founding professor at Howard University and the first black admitted to the New York State bar. Oberlin's distinguished alumni included Blanche Kelso Bruce, the first to serve a full term in the U.S. Senate; Mary Jane Patterson, the first black woman to receive a degree; and John Mercer Langston, Ohio's first black lawyer, who created the law department and served as acting president at Howard University, and was a consul general in Haiti.

By the time Hayes arrived, the school had already secured its reputation for attracting talented African American students. During his time at Oberlin he had become known as a stirring orator and was selected as the senior class speaker. One press account called his delivery "second to none" adding that "some among the audience who had heard Frederick Douglass, compared Hayes' delivery to that great orator."[7]

A few years later his fiery speech to the graduating class at Richmond Normal School provoked a reporter to call him "bitter" and "severe," although this reporter added: "But at the close of his speech his eloquence brought down the house as he depicted our sweet land of liberty."[8] Hayes became the first president of the National Baptist Education Convention, which in 1895 joined the Foreign Mission Convention and the American National Baptist Convention to become the National Baptist Convention of the United States of America. By 1906 it had more than 2.2 million members in the continental United States.[9]

While Virginia Theological Seminary would thrive under his leadership, his politics—in particular his concept of black self-determination—would put him at odds with many Baptists, white and black, who favored a more moderate course.

By the time Benga arrived, the school still offered courses in the liberal arts and science, including English literature, history, Latin, chemistry, physics, and psychology. Its accomplished faculty included Bernard Tyrell, a Yale graduate and pastor of Diamond Hill Baptist, who was named dean of theology; and John Robinson, a graduate of Lincoln University and Boston Law who taught linguistics. Long before Benga's arrival the school had also attempted to cement ties with Africa.

In 1898 John Chilembwe, a native of Nyasaland (now Malawi), in east Central Africa, enrolled at Virginia Theological under the auspices of the secretary of the Foreign Mission Board of the National Baptist Convention, and a Roanoke, Virginia, pastor.[10] From the inception in 1880 of the Foreign Mission Convention, Virginia's black Baptists had played a key role in the organization's formation and later expansion and its emphasis on Africa. Of the six missionaries sponsored for work in Africa between 1883 and 1884, five were from Virginia and the sixth was from Mississippi.[11] The black Baptists would take pride in being the first national organization to send African Americans to Africa as missionaries, rather than as emigrants.

Hayes had taken Chilembwe under his wing and together they formed the African Development Society, with the goal of purchasing land and promoting economic development in Central Africa. During his time at Virginia Theological Chilembwe was exposed to a culture of self-empowerment and pride that he hoped to transport to his homeland. He returned to Africa in 1900, receiving his bachelor of arts and bachelor of divinity degrees in absentia in 1901.

With support from the National Baptist Convention Chilembwe established his own mission, Providence Industrial Mission, in 1904. Two African Americans would serve in it. By the time Benga returned to Lynchburg Chilembwe had established five churches with 800 members and 625 students and had emerged as a vocal opponent of British colonialism and a leader in his country's struggle for independence.

A few months before Benga's arrival, James E. East, a native of Huntsville, Alabama, graduated and set sail for South Africa, where he would become one of the leading missionaries of his day. He was joined by his new wife and former classmate, Lucinda Thomas, with whom he would have seven children; four of them born in Africa. Over the next decade the Easts built a church with six hundred congregants in Rabula, South Africa. On his return, James East became an influential corresponding secretary of the National Baptist Convention's Foreign Mission Board.

It's not known whether Benga ever had the opportunity to meet either of these missionaries in whose footsteps his patrons hoped he would follow. Unlike them, he would not have the benefit of Hayes's inspiring mentorship. However, throughout his time in Virginia he would be surrounded by an impressive array of African American educators and leaders. When he returned three years later Mary Hayes had completed an interim tenure as seminary president and had been succeeded by James R. L. Diggs. Like Gregory Hayes, Diggs was an outspoken advocate of liberal arts instruction. He had graduated from Wayland Seminary in Washington, D.C., had then earned bachelor's and master's degrees from Bucknell University and a Ph.D. from Illinois University, and had taught Latin, French, and philosophy at Virginia Union University. In addition to belonging to the African American intellectual elite Diggs was an uncompromising civil rights activist. He was a founder of the Niagara Movement, a group of pan-African intellectuals formed by W. E. B. Du Bois, with whom he was closely associated. At the height of Booker T. Washington's fame, the founders of Niagara had boldly challenged his leadership and asserted the right of African Americans to vigorously pursue political, economic, and social equality. In a portrait of its members, posed before Niagara Falls, Diggs can be found standing at the far right end in the top row, peering confidently into the camera. Sporting a trim beard and mustache, his hat set far back on his head, the forty-year-old Diggs appears far younger than the others.

In 1909 Diggs had urged Du Bois to write a history of Reconstruction from the Negro point of view. Until then, the Reconstruction-era African American congressmen, governors, and the like had been crudely stereotyped in the popular press as corrupt buffoons.

"Southern writers present our white brothers' side of the question," Diggs wrote, "but I do not find the proper credit given our people for what of good they really find in those trying days." [12] Du Bois agreed the idea was a good one and the following year presented a paper, "Black Reconstruction and Its Benefits," at the annual American Historical Association meeting. He would later elaborate on it in *Black Reconstruction in America*, his historical treatise on the period that shed light on the achievements of African

Americans. Among these was their election to high office as U.S. congressmen, senators, governors, and state legislators. Many of the gains were erased during the bloody post-Reconstruction backlash.

In 1911 Diggs was followed by Robert C. Woods, who had been Hayes's student and protégé and would aggressively build on his legacy. Under Woods the school expanded its acreage, faculty, and student body, and erected three new buildings. By then the school had an orchestra and a football team and sponsored a number of social events, including picnics. Its annual graduation at Court Street Baptist Church had engraved programs and prominent speakers.

So Benga, with his halting English and little more than a rudimentary education, found himself in an academically rigorous environment surrounded by black intellectuals who were dedicated to attaining racial equality in the United States and abroad. Accordingly, their students were held to the same high standards as white students at top colleges.

A survey of the required curriculum in 1917 found that it included three years of Latin and Greek and one year of German.[13] Such an environment would be daunting, even overwhelming, for many American students. Now a person who had spent most of his life as a hunter was thrust into the vortex of a vigorous debate over the course of education most suitable for Africans and their descendants. While Benga might have found greater satisfaction in the woods or on a farm than he could find learning Latin, such thinking would be deemed heretical among the school's academic elite.

Benga would, however, find a kindred spirit in one of his instructors. Annie Bethel Spencer was not quite twenty-six when Benga arrived at Virginia Seminary. She had been born on a farm in Henry County, Virginia, to mixed-race parents. Her father, of black, white, and Seminole Indian ancestry, had been born into slavery in 1862, and her mother was the biracial daughter of a wealthy Virginia aristocrat and his enslaved mistress. In America, where "one drop" of African American blood outweighed such nuances of ancestry,

Annie Spencer was considered African American, a designation she proudly embraced.

Spencer spent her early years in Martinsville, Virginia, and after her parents' separation moved to Bramwell, West Virginia, where she was placed in foster care with an affluent black couple. However, her mother did not want her to attend the colored school in this poor mining community, fearing she'd be exposed to the underside of life. So what reading she learned she attained by being read to at home and mimicking what she had heard. By 1893 Annie, then eleven and practically illiterate, enrolled in the Virginia Theological Seminary and College, where she would receive the classical liberal arts education that the school was then noted for.

Although she struggled at the beginning, she eventually made an impression on Gregory Hayes, who was president during her entire time there. He selected her to be his assistant Sunday school teacher and also to teach his classes when he went away, as he frequently did to raise money for the perennially cash-strapped school. She and Mary Hayes would become lifelong friends. Annie also caught the eye of Edward Spencer, a student six years her senior who tutored her in math and science while she helped him with languages.

In 1899, at age seventeen, she graduated as the school valedictorian, and two years later she married Edward Spencer, the city's first parcel postman. Annie, who favored pants over frilly dresses and poetry over formal religion, continued to delight in simple folks and solitude.

In 1903 the couple moved into a clapboard Queen Anne home at 1313 Pierce Street that Edward had designed and built. The lot was on land that Annie's great-great-grandfather had purchased in 1867; it had once been the site of a Confederate camp and military hospital, and during Reconstruction was the site of a freedmen's school and a black Methodist church. Several generations of the family would live in as many as a dozen houses on the lot.

The Spencer home, with its bountiful well-tended garden, floral-papered walls, and stylish Victorian-era furnishings, became a favorite refuge for Benga. In the decade and a half before Spencer would become a famous Harlem Renaissance poet and founder of the city's chapter of the NAACP, she and Benga probably connected over their shared reverence for nature and her passionate commitment to human rights. Spencer, with her lilting southern accent, would have been likely to discuss the latest additions to her garden, which featured, seasonally, lilacs, poppies, daisies, wisteria, roses, daffodils, narcissus, peonies, honeysuckle, chrysanthemums, nasturtiums, petunias, sweet peas, snapdragons, and tiger lilies. While tending her garden she was likely to have inquired about the vegetation in Benga's native land. They may also have spoken of his captivity in the zoo, but their conversations were not preserved in letters or poems that survived the period, or in family lore.

From her cozy Pierce Street haven, Spencer, with family and friends, could retreat from the racial tensions of their time. Between 1900 and 1918 Virginia would pass a series of laws regulating racial interactions on streetcars, in neighborhoods, and even in prisons. By state decree, any person with even one-sixteenth Negro blood was considered colored. As a black woman who savored literature, Spencer would not be allowed to patronize the city's Jones Memorial Library, which opened in 1908 and was named for a Civil War soldier and philanthropist; his widow, Mary Frances Jones, stipulated that the library was "wholly for the use of white people without respect for religious distinction." [14]

The city's African American citizens had only the segregated Dunbar High School Library, with its sparse collection of tattered books. In 1924 Spencer would become the librarian at Dunbar High School, near her home; she worked there for twenty years and augmented its three books with those from her own collection.

Never one to tolerate injustice, Spencer attempted to move around, over, or under it. She would hitch a ride on an ice wagon or walk across town rather than board a segregated streetcar. While some thought her mode of transport beneath her, she found it more dignified than submitting to second-class citizenship.

But the poetry fashioned from a life of slights and protest celebrated nature and beauty through an exploration of biblical and mythological themes. She explained her artistic credo in Countee Cullen's anthology *Caroling Dusk*: "I write about the things I love. But have not civilized articulation for the things I hate." [15]

Following James Weldon Johnson's discovery of her poetry in 1919 she would, on his advice, change her name from Annie to Anne, and be published in his anthology *The Book of American Negro Poetry*, and later in the *Norton Anthology of American Poetry*. A short time later Edward would construct a writer's retreat for her in the garden behind their home, where she would spend much of her time. She named her small cottage sanctuary Edankraal, a composite of Ed, Anne, and the Afrikaans name for enclosure.

Benga's friend and mentor would join the celebrated community of leading African American artists and intellectuals, among them Du Bois, Langston Hughes, Paul Robeson, Marian Anderson, and Countee Cullen, whose achievements defied the hardwired racial attitudes of their day.

TWENTY-FIVE

HOME

I n Lynchburg he was known as Otto Bingo. At least one Lynchburg native attributed this change to a name that appeared in
a letter from the orphanage, but whether that was due to a ty-
pographical error or misreading, it was the new name by which he
became known.[1]

Four years earlier Benga had left a grieving Mary Hayes following the death of the seminary's president Reverend Gregory W.
Hayes. She was thirty-two at his death, with five young children,
including Hunter, an infant son. Benga returned to live with Mary
and her family, which now encompassed seven children and her new
husband, William Patterson Allen, a thirty-one-year-old lawyer from
nearby Danville.[2] Mary Rice Hayes Allen would give birth to one additional child, bringing the total to eight.

Benga lived with the Allens in a rambling yellow house across
the road from the Virginia Theological Seminary, surrounded by
woods and overlooking the valley below. There he was given his own
room at the end of a hall. Mary proved as devoted a patron as her late

husband had been. A fierce advocate of the underdog, Mary would bring to their friendship, from her own intimate encounters with injustice and grief, a bottomless well of empathy.

The birth of Mary Magdalene Rice in 1875 in Harrisburg, Virginia, was the stuff of secrets, scandal, and taboo. Her mother was Malinda Rice, who at sixteen worked as a maid in the home of a Confederate general, John Jones, and his wife. Mary's father was General Jones. What made the arrangement unusual was Jones's open acceptance and adoration of his beautiful auburn-haired, beige-skinned daughter, whom he paraded through town, while ignoring her darker brother Willie. Defying convention, Jones took young Mary to the town's whites-only ice cream parlor, taught her how to read, exposed her to poetry, and saw that she was well educated. While privilege and an attentive father enhanced her self-esteem, they also inflamed her sense of injustice and racial solidarity.

A month before her tenth birthday she bade a wrenching farewell to her young mother, who lay in a pine coffin in the parlor. Mary was taken in by her mother's brother and his wife, and while considered an orphan in the eyes of many, she was still actively supported by Jones. He saw to it that she received the best education afforded colored women of her era. At the age of sixteen she became a student at Hartshorn Memorial College in Richmond. Founded in 1883 by the American Baptist Home Mission Society, it was one of the first schools established exclusively for African American women. Since it admitted only advanced students who could already read and write, many were products of privilege. Named for its wealthy Rhode Island benefactor, the school offered industrial, normal, and college tracks, with the college curriculum modeled after Wellesley College.[3]

After excelling in and completing the normal track to prepare for work as a teacher, Mary advanced to the college curriculum; her courses included Latin, pedagogy, and music. It was during her senior year that she met Professor Gregory Willis Hayes.

Mary had been selected to present a gift to Virginia Theological Seminary's distinguished president, who had come to address the students. Even without his notable oratory, Hayes would have made an impression. In 1894 few black schools were run by African Americans. Hartshorn, headed by the imposing Lyman Beecher Tefft, was not among them. As Hayes spoke Mary was inspired by his bold declaration that black people must control their own destiny. She wrote a letter thanking him for his speech, calling it the best she had ever heard.

Hayes would almost certainly remember the striking coed, and in his reply confided that the white-run Baptists were attempting to turn Virginia Seminary into an exclusively industrial school. He already resented their insistence on monthly reports, and he found the latest demands intolerable.

"I am determined our Negro students will have the opportunity for both industrial arts and liberal arts," he told her. "I will fight for this to my last breath."[4]

A romance quickly developed between them, and the following year, on May 3, 1895, they were married in Richmond at the home of Hayes's parents. Rice was twenty and Hayes, thirty-two. The gap in their ages and experience was bridged by their unwavering commitment to the struggle for equality and social justice for African Americans.

Following the wedding Hayes and his bride moved to Durmid Hill, just outside the Lynchburg city limits, where they lived in a charming two-story house with spacious rooms, a mahogany four-poster bed, and a wisteria-laced porch. The house is probably the one where Benga first lived during his first brief stay in Lynchburg, and it was a regular stop for race leaders passing through town, including Du Bois. For Mary and Gregory, it was a refuge from the storm raging over the future of the seminary, its leadership, and black education.

That summer Hayes would barely survive a tumultuous debate among the trustees over whether to grant him another term.

During the early years of their marriage they would endure the heartbreaking loss of two infants. One was stillborn and the other—Gregory Willis Hayes Jr., their third child and first boy—would die during his first week of life, before Hayes could get home to see him. But between 1903 and 1906 the couple would have three more children, one of whom would also have his father's name.

While they belonged to the African American elite that Du Bois called the "talented tenth," the two were not part of Lynchburg's established aristocratic circles. Lynchburg, given its higher than average population of free blacks, lured accomplished African Americans from other cities. With twenty-five black fraternal organizations and fifteen churches, there were ample opportunities for elitism. In 1910, of the city population of 8,299 blacks, 3,068 belonged to secret societies.[5] Relative to Virginia as a whole, Lynchburg also had a higher percentage of black children attending school, and a higher number of black professionals; the forty-one teachers in the city's elementary and secondary schools earned comparatively higher salaries than those in other parts of the state.[6] But Mary would gravitate to Annie Spencer, with whom she shared radical racial politics and a disdain for elitism, especially among blacks.

At the time of Benga's enrollment the school would continue to enjoy a period of expansion under President Diggs and then Robert C. Woods. Under Woods's direction enrollment climbed to six hundred and the school expanded, adding three new buildings and acquiring more lots and cottages.

Benga took elementary courses alongside children believed to be less than half his age, but outside the classroom he became a trusted teacher and companion to neighborhood boys. For Gregory, Hunter, and Wilelbert Hayes, who were born between 1903 and 1906 and lost their father before his memory could become indelible, Benga became a father figure and hero.

Often barefoot, though wearing western clothes, Benga would lead a band of boys—including the three Hayes boys and Annie Spencer's son Chauncey—and teach them the secrets of the forest, including how to shave the tips of hickory wood to sharp points to make spears, or how to make bows from vines. With Benga the boys also learned how to gather blackberries and spear fish. The man they called Otto Bingo also taught them how to hunt wild turkeys and squirrels with a bow and arrow and how to trap small animals. They learned to forage for roots to make sassafras tea and marveled at his ability to collect honey from the bees without being stung.

Years later Hunter recalled with amusement how Benga rolled on the ground, overcome with laughter, after Gregory stuck his hand in a hive as he had watched Benga do. Unlike Benga, Gregory was stung, and ran home crying to his mother.

In his scrappy Congo-infused English, Benga regaled the boys with stories of his adventures hunting elephants, pantomiming how he stalked them—"Big, big," he'd say with outstretched arms—and recounting how he would celebrate a kill with a triumphant hunting song.

In Benga they found an open and patient teacher, a beloved companion, and a remarkably agile athlete who sprinted and leaped over logs like a boy. And with his young companions Benga could uninhibitedly relive memories of a lost and longed-for life and retreat to woods that recalled home.

Benga also delighted in eating, and at the sound of the noon whistle at the cotton mill, he would drop what he was doing to race home and fix his lunch. "Gotta go cooka eat," he'd say.[7]

He especially relished Mary's cooking and she happily indulged him, often specially preparing for him the baked yams that he so enjoyed. He delighted in the hog-killing season, and enthusiastically joined the men in the time-honored communal ritual that took place throughout the South—and nowhere more than Lynchburg—and that had many of the characteristics of his own hunter culture.

The slaughtered hog would be placed in a barrel and then boiled over hot sandstones to soften the bristles. With the hog splayed on a long table, Benga would go to work, vigorously scraping it to remove the hair, which he then used for ticking. With the hog hung by its feet, and cut from bung to throat, he'd clean its insides with a sharpened broomstick.

The hog would then be divided into parts and products: bacon, belly, ham, shoulders, feet, ears, sausage, spareribs, neck bone, tail, brains. The fat would be used for soap and the small intestine for chitterlings. What wasn't cooked for the day's feast was salted, dried, and seasoned and days later hung in the smokehouse to be preserved for future meals. The ritual, for the hunter, surely evoked home.

In Lynchburg Benga had found a surrogate home and family and would learn their customs, and the contours and boundaries of their binding blackness. When he crossed into neighboring Cottonwood, a white working-class community, he was heckled and pelted with rocks. "He would come back and ask why they did that," Chauncey recalled years later. "He didn't understand." [8]

However, long before he arrived in Lynchburg Benga had seen that scowl of scorn; he had seen it on the faces of the *chicotte*-wielding *capitas*; in the jeering crowds in St. Louis, and among the spectators outside the cage at the Monkey House.

The experience in Lynchburg probably triggered memories of earlier trauma.

A study on shame and post-victimization released in 2011 found that individuals who, like Benga, had experienced shame-related trauma risked developing severe psychological symptoms, and also that "shame is more likely to be evoked in these individuals, increasing the risk for re-traumatization." New trauma, the authors of this study said, caused "a significant increase in the frequency of post-traumatic stress reactions to the original trauma." [9]

Whether Benga internalized shame or blamed his oppressors, he would know that he was not free. He learned to live within the carefully drawn lines of Lynchburg's black community and practice customs its people had crafted from memory and centuries-old oppression. In their sermons and spirituals he may have recognized a sorrow as familiar as the forest dew. They were the descendants of a people who knew the despair of displacement and the loss of language and of friendships, family, ritual, sights, scents, and sounds.

These people, cobbled together from a far-off continent and made anew, sang of being "r'buked and scorned," and yet drew him to their bosom. Some had lost loved ones to slavery; some bore the children of their enslavers. Yet with all of their travails, they had made room for a homeless stranger.

Still, they did not know the piercing rupture; the vacuous eternity of alienation that many of their forebears had known—and that the man they called Bingo now knew. While they were burdened and disdained in America, it was the land they had tilled and spilled blood on, the land where they created life and buried their dead. For all the rejection and hardship, they were home.

Benga had only memories, and no one but he could know what form they took. Was his sleep troubled by nightmares of being stalked by howling mobs, or being caged with apes? Was he haunted by visions of murdered loved ones, or of starving, tortured, chained Congolese? Did he dreamily drift into joyful gatherings of kin and clan, only to awaken alone?

Some nights, beneath a star-speckled sky, the boys would watch Benga build a fire and dance and sing around it. Chauncey, Gregory, Wilelbert, and their friends were enraptured as he circled the flame, hopping and singing as if they weren't there. They were no older than ten, too young to grasp the poignancy of the ancient ritual, or the urgency of Benga's refrains.

TWENTY-SIX

FREE

Mammy Joe's general store on Garfield Street, across the road from the Hayes home and a holler away from the seminary, was a popular gathering place for Lynchburg's African American community. It was also a haven for children who frolicked in her adjoining hayloft.

Mary's daughter Carrie remembered it as a childhood refuge, "our place for hide-and-seek and for eating Mammy Joe's cookies, a place we'd go and fall laughing into the hay-covered floor, clucking chickens strutting around us."[1]

So adored was Mammy Joe, whose real name was Josephine Anderson, that Mary named her seventh child Carrie Anderson Allen in her honor. While not much more is known of her, a Josephine Anderson in Lynchburg's 1910 census was described as a Negro Virginia native who was thirty-five and single with no children. Her stated occupation was laundress.

Benga did odd jobs for Anderson and sometimes stayed in her

hayloft, where he spent countless hours delighting children with enchanting tales of home, of hunting and singing in a mythical forest teeming with creatures reminiscent of Noah's Ark. After a few years attending school he had taken a job at a tobacco factory.

But by 1916, something had changed. Benga was no longer the eager friend of the neighborhood children. He had lost interest in their excursions to the surrounding woods to hunt or to fish in nearby streams. Many had noticed his darkening disposition, his all-consuming longing to go home. For hours he would sit alone in silence under a tree. Some of his childhood companions would decades later recall a song he'd sing that he had learned at the Virginia Theological Seminary:

> *I believe I'll go home,*
> *Lordy, won't you help me*

It had been ten years since he left the Congo, and his tie to home was fraying. He would know nothing of his village, of the family and friends he left behind. The decade had been marked by his exhibition in a cage and by World War I. During that period the earth seemed to spin off its axis, increasingly consumed by a war that would, over the next four years, claim nine million lives.

Benga would have almost certainly heard about America's preparations for a battle that many African Americans saw as their chance to gain full citizenship and secure jobs in the North. It's less likely, though possible, that he knew about Germany's 1914 invasion of Belgium, which had wrested control of the Congo from Leopold. Now it was Belgium that required international relief efforts, to stave off famine. William Hornaday was among the Americans who campaigned for such efforts. But what would the war mean for Benga's people? What of any siblings, parents, friends, and neighbors left behind? Even Verner had attested to the centrality of family life among the forest dwellers. Benga surely wondered whether his family, his friends, and his companions in St. Louis had survived the genocide of their people.

Did they still think of Ota Benga? Did they recall his face, his name?

The years since his arrival had seemed interminable; in addition to the start of World War I, the period encompassed the tenures of three U.S. presidents; the sinking of the *Titanic*; the death, in 1909, of Leopold; the deaths in 1915 of Booker T. Washington and John Chilembwe. Chilembwe, who had graduated from Virginia Theological Seminary and College, had gone on to fight for freedom in his country. He was publicly hanged for his role in its 1915 uprising.

The decade since Benga's arrival had also brought 640 reported lynchings, a southern horror that was celebrated in the 1915 film *Birth of a Nation*, based on *The Clansman*, Thomas Dixon's bestselling book. President Wilson, a close friend of Dixon's, hailed the book as "history written in lightning" and screened the film at the White House. By 1916 many black southerners had begun their trek North to find jobs in the war industry and escape the surge of southern tyranny that precipitated the founding of the National Association for the Advancement of Colored People and the National Urban League.

William Sheppard, of whom Benga would undoubtedly have known, had left Virginia and was now living in Louisville, where he was the pastor of Grace Church and running a mission for the city's most impoverished. MacArthur, the man who had first protested against Benga's exhibition at the zoo, had retired in 1911 after forty-one years as pastor of Calvary Baptist Church, and was now seventy-three and president of the Baptist World Alliance. From that post he went on to build a Baptist college in St. Petersburg, Russia.

John Condola, the child whom Verner had brought from the Congo and educated in Tuscaloosa, was twenty-four and still living in Memphis, where he was a student at the Howe Institute. He would become a minister and never marry.

Howard Colored Orphan Asylum had fallen on hard times. Five months after Benga left, the state board of charities declared the Weeksville building unfit for habitation, and a month later the property was purchased by the Brooklyn Rapid Transit Company, ending Howard's revered place in Weeksville

After a brief illness James Gordon—who had worked tirelessly to raise funds for the impoverished school—died in 1914 at age fifty-six, leaving behind his wife, Mary, and their daughter. The longtime house matron succeeded him as Howard's superintendent. But that same year Howard's St. James farm, and Gordon's dream of a Tuskegee-style school, went up in smoke. The school burned to the ground, some believed as a result of arson. While the school relocated to a 572-acre farm in King's Park, Long Island, it never regained its footing and would permanently close a few years later.

Verner had not been to the Congo since his trip there for the American Congo Company in 1908. His draft record indicates that during World War I he was based in Panama's Cristobal Canal Zone, working as a censor in the mailroom; was married; and had two children under age twelve. He continued to recount his world's fair expedition with characteristic self-delusion and self-aggrandizement. Sometime following McGee's death in 1912, Verner wrote to his widow to reflect on what he said was his and McGee's desire to awaken global interest in Benga's people. "I was anxious to see the last vestiges of the continental slave trade removed, to have the natives adequately treated for sleeping sickness and other tropical diseases; to give them employment instead of leaving them to the perpetual petty wars over palm-trees and hunting grounds, and to make the region more accessible for humanitarian efforts as might join the movement."[2]

He remained an apologist for Leopold, saying that the government had been handicapped by the enormous expenses administering to such a vast territory without adequate resources.

Meanwhile, in the midst of the raging war, any chance Benga had of returning home was fading.

As Benga longed for home, Roger Casement, whose courageous campaign had helped topple a cruel and corrupt king, was on trial in England for his alleged involvement in an Irish nationalist revolt in Dublin. That summer Casement would be hanged.

The man who had been referred to by so many names—including Mbye Otabenga, Ota Benga, Otto Bingo, Otto Binga, Bengal, Artiba, Autobank, and Ottobang—was in Lynchburg without any known intimate relationships. For all the many kindnesses he had been shown in Lynchburg, he was isolated—an ocean and a river away from the life he knew. In a city of thirty thousand people, he alone sang lustily to the forest and had roamed amid beasts, wild and free.

The music of home was getting fainter; the drumbeats, the rumbling elephants, a distant dream.

In the late afternoon on March 19, 1916, the boys watched as Benga gathered wood to build a fire in the field between Mary's house and the seminary. As the fire rose to a brilliant flame, Benga danced around it while chanting and moaning. He danced faster and faster, twirling and moaning, as the boys watched in solemn silence. They had seen his ritual before, but this time they detected a profound and boundless sorrow. This time their beloved Benga seemed eerily distant, as vacant and frightening as a ghost.

That night, as they slept, Ota Benga entered the battered gray shed behind Mammy Joe's store where a chorus of giggles had pierced the air. Sometime before daybreak he recovered a gun he had apparently hidden in the hayloft and fired a bullet through his broken heart.

And in the harrowing stillness, he was free.

TWENTY-SEVEN

HOMEGOING

A t about nine o'clock the next morning Benga's lifeless body was found in the hayloft in a pool of blood that had streamed from the wound in his heart. The certificate of death exposed the tattered remnants of a ravaged life. Like a gutted carcass, it was woefully incomplete. The deceased had lived in Lynchburg for six years, but the spaces for marital status, date of birth, and names and birthplaces of parents were marked by a dash or "Don't know." Even Otto Bingo, the name on the document, was an invention to somehow mask his African past.

What was certain was that the young gentleman from the Congo had died sometime on March 20, 1916. The cause of death, determined by an autopsy conducted by Dr. J. W. Davis, the coroner, was suicide from a pistol shot to his left breast. There would be no family to grieve for him; no one in Lynchburg even knew his name.

But Benga's death unleashed a flood of sad reflections by those who had noticed the intensity, in recent months, of his enduring desire to go home. Years later some wondered what more could have been done to return him to his homeland.

An article in the *Lynchburg News* claimed that Benga had threatened suicide several weeks earlier.[1] "For a long time the young negro pined for his African relations and grew morose when he realized that such a trip was out of the question because of the lack of resources," the newspaper said.[2]

The shame-evoking episodes Benga had experienced in St. Louis and at the Bronx Zoo would have already predisposed him to suffer from depression, anxiety, and post-traumatic stress. According to one study, "Shame has been demonstrated repreatedly to be a strong risk factor for a diversity of symptoms."[3] "Shame is associated strongly with post-traumatic stress," this study found.[4]

The research also indicated that those most prone to develop post-traumatic stress disorder related to shame had experienced fear, horror, and helplessness during childhood.[5]

Growing up amid the ghastly genocide of his people, Benga was certain to have experienced a profound sense of powerlessness and fear. That anxiety would be exacerbated by his permanent separation from loved ones and his humiliating experiences in St. Louis and at the Bronx Zoo.

Attempting to explain the curious circumstances of his tragic life, the *Lynchburg News* reported that he had recently told an unidentified white friend that he was about thirteen years old and playing with friends in his homeland when he was captured by Englishmen. He claimed that his companions had managed to escape. After a trip around the world, he said, he was given to the curator of the city zoo in New York, and a furor had ensued over his exhibition, which zoo officials denied staging. The newspaper said he had then somehow been brought "by some kindly disposed person" to Lynchburg, where he attended school for a few years and then worked at a tobacco factory and as a day laborer.

Benga may well have relayed such a story; it closely adheres to what actually happened. Since the article does not refer to the numerous newspaper accounts of the Bronx Zoo's exhibit and the subsequent protests, nor divulge the name by which he was previously known, it doesn't appear to stem from what had been reported years earlier. The account, if true, intriguingly suggests that Benga, like Kondola, may have been far younger than Verner had indicated. For Benga, it would mean that he was just fifteen—and not twenty-three—when he was exhibited at the Bronx Zoo, and twenty-five at the end of his life. Moreover, the account of abduction would jibe with Verner's message to McGee that, if necessary, he would resort to unspecified means to bring those not willing to travel with him to St. Louis. Verner had already disclosed that, while hunting people, he had entered villages accompanied by state police and sometimes found a need to sedate Africans, given the "ecstatic frenzies which sometimes occur among the natives." He had also divulged that some families had cried through the night over the prospect of his taking their people, while others had run away.

The newspaper article went on to describe Benga as under five feet tall with short legs and a long torso, and said: "His disposition was good and he responded quickly to kind treatment though he seldom had anything to say excepting to those with whom he had become acquainted."[6]

Beyond our awareness of the corrosive forces that in general facilitated Benga's journey from the Congo, and of Verner's particular disclosures to McGee in the midst of his expedition, the exact circumstances by which Benga was twice brought to the United States cannot be known. However, what's certain is that he had been hunted and captured and was at least once, and possibly twice, brought to the United States under undesirable circumstances. Once finally released from his captor's net he made it known that he wished neither to remain in America nor to reunite with Verner. Faced with the prospect of never returning to his homeland, he took his life.

He had been warmly embraced by the Lynchburg Theological

Seminary community, but none of the people who had supported him by providing housing, schooling, and friendship were quoted in the articles that appeared following his death. As if behind a veil, they gathered to mourn their loss. They ensured that Benga would not have a homeless man's burial in a potter's field. His surrogate family would honor him by making arrangements for a proper funeral and burial. The Colored Baptist Ministers Convention hired the People's Undertaking Company, a black-owned funeral business established in 1914. The ledger for Diuguid Funeral Home shows that while the People's Undertaking Company prepared the body, Diuguid provided embalming services and a black hearse for the funeral.

The funeral was held on March 22, 1916, at 3:30 P.M. at the Diamond Hill Baptist Church, a redbrick Gothic Revival building. The church had already made a storied place for itself in the city's black community. The sanctuary where Benga was remembered had been built to accommodate a growing congregation; its cornerstone was laid in 1886.

Benga's rosewood casket was probably placed on the raised altar in front of the white-walled sanctuary bejeweled with radiant stained-glass windows beneath a vaulted Gothic ceiling.

While no program of the funeral is known to have survived, Bernard Tyrell, the Yale-educated pastor and dean of Virginia Theological Seminary College, would likely have presided over the service. Known as a brilliant scholar and orator, he had taught Greek, philosophy, and theology at Virginia Theological and in 1903 had retired the church's debt. Five years later he oversaw the addition of a second floor and the founding of a Mission and Education Club.

In addition to many of the church congregants, the Spencers, the Allens, faculty members, students, and Virginia Theological Seminary's president—Robert C. Woods—and his staff would be among those filling the church pews.

Benga's body was placed inside the hearse and driven several miles away to the City Cemetery, known today as the "Old City Cemetery." This cemetery where Benga was laid to rest was on twenty-six acres of rolling hills sloping down toward Blackwater Creek, with sweeping vistas of the valley below. Established in 1806, it was the city's only public burial ground and, like the rest of the city, was racially segregated.

"Otto Bingo," age thirty, with C for colored, is listed in the public cemetery superintendent's burial log, indicating that he would be buried in the colored section. It is unclear why Benga's age was given as thirty, if ten years earlier, at the zoo, he was said to have been twenty-three.

In the weeks that followed Benga would once again appear in headlines in many of the nation's newspapers.

Even in death, he was a subject of sensationalized, insensitive, and inaccurate news coverage. Calling him Ota "Benza," the *Washington Post* reported that when Benga no longer had the opportunity to return to Africa "he was surrounded by all the evidences of civilized life" and "the call of the wild came to him." The paper said he was "disgusted with the 'white man's magic,' " and incorrectly reported that he had "sent a bullet through his brain."[7]

In the May issue of the (New York) *Zoological Society Bulletin*, Hornaday, who ten years earlier had brazenly defended Benga's exhibition, and complained of his resistance to it, now characterized him as one who "had a mind of his own, and a decided preference for life in the Park, where he was kindly treated."[8]

Hornaday said "charitably-inclined persons" had "conceived" the idea that the Zoological Society had secured Benga as an exhibit. Benga, he said, "elected to stay."[9]

The denial, of course, could be easily disputed by his own statements to reporters a decade earlier, and by the sign posted outside Benga's cage announcing his daily afternoon exhibit during the month of September. The sign had memorably prompted a *New York Times* reporter to write: "Any suspicion that the exhibition was the result of error was contradicted by yesterday's developments."[10] The denial was also disproved by Hornaday's handwritten article on the exhibition for the *Zoological Society Bulletin*, which he had entitled "Exhibition at the Zoological Gardens."

A decade later, with no sense of compassion or culpability, Hornaday berated Benga for attending school, saying that "the gap between the heart of a savage African jungle and the civilized civilian fields of his desire, was too great to be bridged by Ota Benga." The suicide, according to Hornaday, ended the life of "a savage" who, he said, "vainly tried to leap from savagery to civilization, over the intermediate stage of barbarism."[11]

Two months later Verner, from Panama, was given nearly two full pages, with a third for Benga's portrait, in the July 1916 issue of the *Zoological Society Bulletin* to reflect on Benga's life and death. He compared Benga's suicide to that of Skeletu, "the devoted companion of David Livingstone," who jumped overboard from the ship on which he was traveling with the explorer. Skeletu, Verner reasoned, was "apparently rendered suddenly insane by the marvels of civilization as they grew upon him."[12]

This time Verner said he had discovered Benga when his steamer docked at the confluence of the Kasai and the Sankuru Rivers, where Commandant Loos of the Belgian army told him of a "strange little man" in his station. Loos said Benga had been found by his soldiers in the hands of the Baschilele. "The Baschilele nearly always ate their captives, and therefore Ota Benga was released just in time to save his life," Verner claimed. In this version of events it was the army, not Verner, who saved Benga's life.

Like Hornaday, Verner insisted that Benga had never been exhibited at the zoo. "The Zoological Park simply gave him temporary employment in feeding the anthropoid apes, and a safe and comfortable home for a short time," he said.[13] Verner accurately reported that he had offered Benga a chance to return to Africa on his next expedition, an offer Benga declined. He said he later offered him an opportunity to work with him in Panama on the canal "but he still stood firm." No evidence of this offer has been uncovered, but in any case Benga would never again be caught in Verner's net.

Benga, Verner opined, was "very human; a brave, shrewd, even smart little man, who preferred to match himself against civilization than to the Baschilele."

Meanwhile, on July 16, 1916, the *New York Times*, under the heartless headline "Ota Benga, Pygmy, Tired of America," identified Benga as a "protégé" of the man who had first exhibited and exploited him in St. Louis. In the same article Verner revealed that in 1906 he had offered Benga the choice of returning to America with him, or being returned to the Belgian state post, a known site of forced labor and countless atrocities. "I got back to Ndombe and offered to leave Ota at the Belgian station below, but he would not stay," Verner now claimed. Such a Hobson's choice could explain how Benga ended up returning to America even after his unsettling experience in St. Louis. "Ota said he wanted to go to America, and with some misgivings I permitted him to go," Verner told the *Times*.

Verner, who famously claimed to have purchased Benga with a bolt of cloth and a pound of salt, an account recorded in the *Zoological Society Bulletin* and sent around the world, now said (as mentioned above) that it was the Belgian army that had rescued Benga from the Baschilele. He also claimed that Benga told him he'd rather stay in America then return to Africa a slave. Again, Benga early on expressed a desire to return to Africa. He simply did not wish to go with Verner. But now Verner could claim prescience and magnanimity. He said he never agreed with the decision to send Benga to school, but, "At the same time, I was not willing to combat his chance along that line, especially since his other friends sincerely believed it wise."

The *Times* likewise reported that Benga had been "employed" by the zoological park, adding, "It was this employment that gave rise to the unfounded report that he was being held in the park as one of the exhibits in the monkey cage."[14]

In this rewriting of history, Verner—the man who ruthlessly exploited Benga and his people—was his friend; and Hornaday, who had exhibited him in a cage, was his employer. The writer apparently neglected to check the paper's own archives, where no fewer than two dozen articles exposed the details of Benga's captivity. The *New York Times*, in fact, could have rightly claimed credit for breaking the story that prompted his release, and that for weeks kept his plight in the public eye. Instead, ten years after publishing detailed reports on Benga's exhibition in the Bronx Zoo monkey house, the paper of record dismissed those reports as an urban legend, concluding, "The story, though denied, persisted, and Ota became the center of a discussion in which the public became interested."

It is an account that for nearly a century would reverberate around the world.

EPILOGUE

I n 2012 the Wildlife Conservation Society permanently closed the
Monkey House to the public, but not before I had an opportunity to stroll along its narrow, dimly lit corridor and imagine the
heckling crowds that gathered daily around a cage at the far end that
housed Ota Benga. A century later no public markers of Benga's captivity remain. Benga's bust and image are stored at the American Museum
of Natural History and his life cast made at the St. Louis world's fair
is warehoused at Dartmouth's Hood Museum, but the Bronx Zoo has
not put up a plaque or any other fitting tribute to his memory, nor has
it told his story accurately in institutional chronicles. Worse yet, shame
over the episode has led those charged with recording the history of the
Bronx Zoo to resort to what can only be viewed as subterfuge.

In *Gathering of Animals: An Unconventional History of the New
York Zoological Society*, published in 1974 and still in print, the Zoo-
logical Society's curator of publications emeritus leaves the matter of
Benga's exhibition unclear, open to interpretation, or unknowable.
Ignoring overwhelming evidence in the organization's own archives,
William Bridges wrote:

Was Ota Benga "exhibited"—like some strange, rare animal?
That he was locked behind bars in a bare cage to be stared at

during certain hours seems unlikely; that he did for the first few days enter a cage in the Primate House to play with the chimpanzee that had accompanied him from Africa is certain; also it is certain that a "label of information" about him was hung on the front of the cage while he was in it. At this distance in time. that is about all that can be said for sure, except that it was all done with the best of intentions, for Ota Benga *was* interesting to the New York public that had not been privileged to see Verner's family of Pygmies in St. Louis.[1]

The incredible account goes on to say that after the uproar, Benga was "immediately withdrawn from official exhibition (or employment) and the label was stowed away." There is no evidence to suggest, even vaguely, that Benga was ever employed by the zoo. On the other hand, as the preceding pages show, there are reams of documents revealing that he was intentionally (and unapologetically) placed on display in a cage, at times with an orangutan, in the Primate House. Eyewitness accounts in letters and newspaper articles also indicate that this was done against his wishes.

Bridges's question notwithstanding, all evidence irrefutably shows that Benga was, in fact, "locked behind bars in a bare cage to be stared at during certain hours."

In 1992 a book cowritten by Samuel Verner's grandson and predicated on the notion of a friendship between Verner and Ota Benga was published. According to the introduction, the book "is the story of the friendship between S. P. Verner and Ota Benga, but in the end it is one man's story. Ota's lifeline knits it all together."[2] The book largely draws on Verner's unreliable accounts of his purported adventures with Benga, with little corroboration or investigation. The claim of their friendship has been accepted and recycled in dozens of accounts in newspapers, magazines, and academic journals, and, regrettably, in *Encyclopedia Virginia*, published online by the Virginia Foundation for the Humanities and the Library of Virginia.[3]

More recently the grandson, Phillips Verner Bradford, was quoted in the *New York Post* as insisting that Benga was complicit in his own degradation.

"Benga loved entertaining the crowds, singing, dancing and playing his horn, and he wanted to put on skits," claimed Bradford. He also alleged that zoo attendance was greatest on Mondays when Benga's "loincloth" was laundered "and he appeared naked. Sadly, he didn't fully understand that the people were not laughing with him but were laughing at him."[4]

However, none of this—the alleged friendship, Benga's delight, his nudity—can be supported by evidence. Moreover, it strains credulity to suggest that Ota Benga and Verner were friends. One, with the authority of the state, was able to prey on, demean, and traffic in humans for profit; the other was a vulnerable captive belonging to a conquered people. Whatever Verner's feelings toward Benga, the overarching character of their relationship was exploitation, not friendship.

Also, when given a choice, Benga refused to reunite with Verner. There is no indication that the two ever saw each other again after they parted in Brooklyn on September 30, 1906.

Still, years after Benga's death Verner would continue to insist that they had been friends, and to boast about his African adventures with cannibals. In 1929, while working for an insurance company, Verner recalled "two years of the most arduous and dangerous journeys among cannibal tribes, on rivers infested with giant crocodiles and bordered with forests abounding in gorillas, elephants, leopards and lions." He also claimed to have "laid the foundations of the American enterprises on the Congo."

In 1934, nine years before he died (apparently of a heart attack), he wrote a rambling letter to the *New York Herald Tribune*'s columnist Walter Lippmann about his dream to return to the Congo. "There are still some mighty interesting things to do and find there," he said. "If I can get back to my land in Kasai, I imagine there would be something doing."

Through much of the 1980s Gordon Gibson, a curator and then curator emeritus of African ethnology at the Smithsonian, continued to conduct research on Verner, which he hoped to someday publish. As part of his research he attempted to establish Verner's role in assembling the Starr collection in the American Museum of Natural History. Enid Schildkrout, the associate curator at the American Museum of Natural History, said she could not substantiate Verner's role in the Starr collection. Gibson also inquired about the correspondence between the museum's director Hermon Bumpus and Verner. Said Schildkrout: "I have, of course, some trepidation about publishing these juicy tidbits, but on the other hand I would like to find out what happened to the Pygmy. He does not seem to be still around, though that's not surprising."[5]

In 1988 Verner's role in Starr's Congo expedition collection for the museum was still raising questions. In her correspondence with Gordon Gibson, Schildkrout said the records of the American Museum of Natural History did not indicate that Verner had played any role in Starr's Congo expedition. She added that the collection was "almost totally undocumented." She welcomed any information Gibson found on the relationship between Verner and Starr and noted that Verner's grandson was working on a book, which he hoped to sell as a film. "Given the racial explosiveness of the subject, I will be surprised if it comes to pass—but anything is possible."[6] Since that time the American Museum of Natural History has made Starr's field notes from his Congo expedition available to researchers. The notes clearly document Verner's role collecting for Starr, but as of this writing Verner's contribution has not been credited.

In recent years Benga has inspired artists, poets, filmmakers, and human rights activists the world over. Carrie Allen McCray, the poet whose family befriended Benga in Lynchburg, wrote a book-length meditation on his life: *Ota Benga: Under My Mother's Roof.* She also recorded her brothers' recollections of Benga in a chapter of her memoir of her mother. The wise, diminutive character named Oti in the film *The Curious Case of Benjamin Button* was partially based on Benga, who has also inspired several stage works and a forthcoming documentary film.[7]

In 2005 the artist Fred Wilson took the life casts of Ota Benga and others exhibited in St. Louis out of storage at Dartmouth's Hood Museum of Art for his provocative interventionist installation "So Much Trouble in the World: Believe It or Not!" Dartmouth was one of the institutions that purchased sets of the life casts of the so-called primitive people done on the fairgrounds; these had been commissioned by the American Museum of Natural History. For the installation, Wilson lined up the busts along a wall, with a white cloth draped over their dehumanizing ethnic labels. Benga's label was simply "Pygmy." To reassert his humanity and individuality, Wilson placed Benga's bust on a pedestal four feet eleven inches tall—his height as recorded by the fair's officials. Beneath the bust were the words: "I'm the one who left, and didn't come back." Captured in his expression, as in those of the others, are pain and unbridled dignity.

In 2007 an international conference—"Lynchburg, Ota Benga, and the Empowerment of the Pygmies"—at Sweet Briar College in Virginia brought together scholars and activists to explore the plight of the current-day African forest dwellers. The participants examined the continuing marginalization and exploitation of so-called pygmies in Central Africa. They are among the Democratic Republic of the Congo's poorest and most spurned people, and, like their fellow citizens, are caught in a cycle of civil war and instability.

The growing interest in Benga's life and the enduring fascination of his astonishing saga have inspired a search for his final resting place by scholars and Lynchburg residents. Documents show that Benga was initially interred in Lynchburg's City Cemetery, but oral history suggests that he was later moved to White Rock Cemetery. Chauncey Spencer, who was nine when Benga died, recalled the reburial in the latter cemetery, located at White Rock Hill. Spencer's recollection is supported by the popularity of White Rock as a burial ground among members of the Virginia Theological Seminary community during that period. As of this writing, the exact location of Benga's resting place could not be positively determined.

While a single volume cannot begin to right the grave injustice that so tragically marked Benga's life, it can help untangle the web of egregious fallacies that mark our historical record and dishonor his memory.

ACKNOWLEDGMENTS

nfinite thanks are owed Neeti Madan, my agent and friend, who convinced me that I should tackle a chapter in history distorted by omission, misstatement, and deceit and then championed this book into being. I also thank Dawn Davis for believing in the book's early promise and Tracy Sherrod for her astute editorial guidance. This is a better book because of their enthusiasm, counsel, and care.

I am indebted to New York University for generous research support and to my incomparable colleagues, with a deep bow to Thomas Carew, Perri Klass, David Levering Lewis, James McBride, and Deb Willis. I am profoundly grateful to each of you for your unerring support at critical junctures along the way.

I'm enormously thankful for fellowships awarded by the Leon Levy Biography Center and the Brown Foundation. Both provided residencies in idyllic settings at the CUNY Graduate Center in New York City and the Dora Maar House in Menèrbes, France, respectively. Thanks to Gary Giddins for his exuberant guidance and to Michael Gately and Gwen Strauss for their kind assistance. Many thanks to my fellow fellows in Menèrbes and New York, with an extra nod to Andrew Meier for being a steady sounding board and font of wisdom and cheer. I also drew inspiration from the memory of the late George Clement Bond, a remarkably gifted teacher, anthropologist, mentor, and friend.

I profited from the helpful assistance of a host of librarians in the United States and Belgium, among them Madeleine Thompson at the Wildlife Conservation Society (formerly the New York Zoological Society, which operates the Bronx Zoo); Graham Duncan at the University of South Carolina's South Caroliniana Library; Gregory August Raml at the American Museum of Natural History; Cathy Ball at the Smithtown Library; Tad Bennicoff at the Smithsonian; Adam Minakowski and Sarah Ganderup at the Smithsonian's National Anthropological Archives; and Maarten Couttenier at the Royal Museum for Central Africa in Tervuren, Belgium. I also wish to gratefully acknowledge Brad Harris, the Smithtown historian; the research assistance of Faith Briggs and Sandrine Colard-De Bock, graduates of NYU's graduate program; Juliette Bianco at Dartmouth's Hood Museum; and librarians and curators at the American Museum of Natural History, the New York Society Library, the New-York Historical Society, the Brooklyn Historical Society, the Schomburg Center for Research in Black Culture, Calvary Baptist Church, Columbia University's Butler Library, the Library of Congress, the Presbyterian Historical Society, and the University of Chicago. I am deeply indebted to Saleh Mwanamilongo for ably assisting with the translations of letters written in a Tshiluba dialect, and Dr. Mady Hornig at Columbia University's Mailman School of Public Health for directing me to invaluable research on the causes and effects of post-traumatic stress disorder.

The people of Lynchburg, Virginia, graciously welcomed me into their homes, churches, libraries, and businesses, eager to help me solve the mystery of Benga's life and to honor his memory. Special thanks to Reverend Warren L. Anderson, pastor of Diamond Hill Baptist Church, and his wonderful staff; Ted Delaney, archivist at the Old City Cemetery; Ann Van de Graaf of Africa House; Shaun Spencer-Hester of the Anne Spencer House and Garden Museum; and the late Carrie Allen McCray who stirringly bore witness to Benga's life in Lynchburg in *Ota Benga Under My Mother's Roof* and *Freedom's*

Child: The Life of a Confederate General's Black Daughter, the latter a tribute to her remarkable mother, who befriended Ota Benga.

A huge hug to my family and treasured friends who heartened me during periods of disillusionment and doubt. Thanks for listening and always believing. An ocean of gratitude is especially due Mykel, Marjani, and Michael for generously making room for Ota Benga in our family life.

NOTES

CHAPTER ONE: GARDENS OF WONDER

1. William Bridges, *Gathering of Animals: An Unconventional History of the New York Zoological Society*. New York: Harper and Row, 1974, p. 89.
2. Ibid.
3. Ibid, p. 90.
4. *New York Times*, November 9, 1899, p. 14.
5. R. U. Johnson to William Hornaday, July 31, 1906, General Correspondence, Control No. 1001, Wildlife Conservation Society Archives.
6. Samuel Verner to Madison Grant, Sunday morning, September 2, 1906, New York Zoological Park. General correspondence and subject files, 1895–1939, Wildlife Conservation Society Archives.
7. The inscription was changed to "Monkeys" in the 1950s.
8. "Bushman Shares a Cage with Bronx Park Apes," *New York Times*, September 9, 1906, p. 17.

CHAPTER TWO: THE BRONX ZOO MONKEY HOUSE

1. "Fire in Monkey House: Chimpanzee Helps Put Out Blaze in His Cage," *New York Tribune*, February 8, 1903, p. 6.
2. Andrew P. Morrison, MD, "The Breadth and Boundaries of a Self-Psychological Immersion in Shame: A One-and-a-Half-Person

Perspective." *Psychoanalytic Dialogues: The International Journal of Relational Perspectives*, 4(1): (1994), p. 19.

3. J. P. Gump, "A White Therapist, an African American Patient—Shame in the Dyad," *Psychoanalytic Dialogues: The International Journal of Relational Perspectives*, 10(4): (2000), p. 823.

4. Gilda Graff, "The Name of the Game Is Shame," *Journal of Psychohistory*, 39(2) (Fall 2011), p. 134. Citing H. B. Lewis, *Shame and Guilt in Neurosis*. New York: International Universities Press, 1971.

5. Morrison, "The Breadth and Boundaries of a Self-Psychological Immersion in Shame." See also Olof Semb et al., "Distress After a Single Violent Crime: How Shame Proneness and Event-Related Shame Work Together as Risk Factors for Post-Victimization Symptoms," *Psychological Reports*, 109(1) (2011).

6. "Bushman Shares a Cage with Bronx Park Apes," *New York Times*, September 9, 1906, p. 17.

7. Heidi Ardizzone, in *An Illuminated Life* (New York: Norton, 2007), notes that throughout the nineteenth century Princeton drew many of its students and faculty members from the South, and many brought their servants and (before the Civil War) slaves with them. Moreover, she says, Princeton was the only Ivy League institution that did not admit black students by the turn of the twentieth century. See also Marcia G. Gummptt, "The Admission and Assimilation of Minority Students at Harvard, Yale, and Princeton, 1900–1970," *History of Education Quarterly*, 19 (Autumn 1979), pp. 285–304; Dan Klein, "The Young Man Who Pushed Princeton Toward Racial Integration," *Journal of Blacks in Higher Education*, Spring 1996, p. 85.

8. Cited in Editors, "Woodrow Wilson and the Negro Question at Princeton University," *Journal of Blacks in Higher Education*, Autumn 1997, p. 120.

9. William K. Gregory, "Biographical Memoir of Henry Fairfield Osborn," *National Academy of Sciences of the United States of America Biographical Memoirs*, 29 (1937), Third Memoir, pp. 53–99.

10. "Zoological Park Opened: Ex-Gov. Morton Presides at the Public Ceremonies," *New York Times*, November 9, 1899, p. 14.

11. "Bushman Shares a Cage with Bronx Park Apes," *New York Times*, September 9, 1906, p. 17.

12. See Clifton Crais and Pamela Scully, *Sara Baartman and the Hottentot Venus: A Ghost Story and a Biography*. Princeton, NJ: Princeton University Press, 2009. Similarly, a stuffed African man was exhibited at the Darden Museum in Banyoles, Spain, some seventy miles from Barcelona, until 2000, when years of protest resulted in the body's finally being returned to Botswana for burial.

13. Pascal Biachard, Nicolas Bancel, et al., *Human Zoos: Science and Spectacle in the Age of Empire*. Liverpool: Liverpool University Press, 2009. See also Gilles Boetsch and Nanette Jacomjin Snoep, *Human Zoos: The Invention of the Savage*. Actes Sud, Arles, 2012.

14. Biachard et al.

15. "Negro Ministers Act to Free the Pygmy," *New York Times*, September 11, 1906, p. 2.

CHAPTER THREE: CRIMES OF THE CONGO

1. "An African Pigmy," *Zoological Society Bulletin*, 23 (October 1906). Published by New York Zoological Society. Wildlife Conservation Society Archives, pp. 301–2.

2. Ibid.

3. Ibid.

4. Samuel P. Verner, "An Untold Chapter of My Adventures While Hunting Pygmies in Africa," *St. Louis Post-Dispatch*, September 4, 1904, p. 3; Samuel Verner, "Adventures of an Explorer in Africa: How the Batwa Pygmies Were Brought to the St. Louis World's Fair," *Harper's Weekly*, 48 (October 22, 1904), pp. 1618–20.

5. "The People of the Kasai Basin," *Royal Geographical Society Journal*, 1910, p. 50.

6. Ngokwey Ndolamb to Gordon Gibson, 1980. Gordon Gibson Papers, Smithsonian, National Anthropological Archives.

7. "A New Race of African Discovered and Brought to America: Among Them Are Cannibals," *Columbus Dispatch*, September 11, 1904.

8. Samuel P. Verner, "Canning the Crocodile," unpublished manuscript. Samuel Phillips Verner Papers, University of South Carolina, South Caroliniana Library (hereafter cited as SPV Papers).

9. Williams was the author of *The History of the Negro Race in America*

from 1619 to 1880: Negroes as Slaves, Soldiers and as Citizens. New York: Putnam, 1883. It's also worth noting that in 1874 he was the first African American to graduate from Newton Theological Institution. In 1885 he was appointed minister resident and consul general to Haiti, but he never served.

10. George W. Williams, *Open Letter to His Serene Majesty Leopold II, King of the Belgians and Sovereign of the Independent State of Congo.* Ann Arbor, MI: ProQuest Information and Learning, 2005. Internet resource.

11. Ibid.

12. Stanley's *The Congo and the Founding of Its Free State* (Harper, 1885) chronicles his journey through the Congo and depicts his relations with the "savages" as friendly.

13. "Negro Ministers Act to Free the Pygmy," *New York Times,* September 11, 1906, p. 2.

CHAPTER FOUR: HORNADAY'S FOLLY

1. William Temple Hornaday, *Free Rum on the Congo.* Chicago: Woman's Temperance Publication Association, 1887, p. 5.

2. Ibid.

3. Ibid, p. 8.

4. Ibid, p. 18.

5. "Man and Monkey Show Disapproved by Clergy," *New York Times,* September 10, 1901, p. 1.

6. Figures provided by the Wildlife Conservation Society, citing the 1906 annual report. A digitized copy can be found at http://archive.org/stream /annualreportnewy111906newy#page/52/ mode/2up.

7. Ibid.

8. Ibid.

9. "Man and Monkey Show Disapproved by Clergy."

10. Edward Colgate served as a deacon for more than a decade. On his death in 1891 his siblings established the Edward Colgate Memorial Fund.

11. Robert Stuart MacArthur Papers, Calvary Baptist Church (hereafter cited as MacArthur Papers). The church records note more than twenty books and dozens of articles published by MacArthur.

12. Robert MacArthur and Frank R. Morse, *History of Calvary Baptist Church*. New York: E. Scott Printer and Publisher, 1890, p. 37.

13. MacArthur Papers.

14. William Hornaday, *Two Years in the Jungle: The Experience of a Hunter and Naturalist in India, Ceylon, the Malay Peninsula, and Borneo*. New York: Scribner, 1885.

15. Stefan Bechtel, *Mr. Hornaday's War*. Boston: Beacon, 2012, p. 51.

16. William Bridges, *Gathering of Animals: An Unconventional History of the New York Zoological Society*. New York: Harper and Row, 1974, p. 26.

CHAPTER FIVE: BENGA'S BRIGADE

1. David W. Dunlap, *From Abyssinian to Zion: A Guide to Manhattan's Houses of Worship*. New York: Columbia University Press, 2004, p. 152.

2. Mount Olivet, like many other black establishments on Fifty-Third Street, relocated to Harlem in 1925.

3. Frank Lincoln Mather, ed., *Who's Who of the Colored Race: A General Biographical Dictionary of Men and Women of African Descent*. Chicago, 1915, p. 115. (Possibly self-published.)

4. "Hot Talk in Church After Dixon Spoke," *New York Times*, January 29, 1906.

5. Carleton Mabee, "Charity in Travail: Two Orphan Asylums for Blacks," *New York History*, 55 (1) (January 1974), p. 71.

6. William S. Pelletreau, *Historic Homes and Institutions and Genealogical and Family History of New York*, Vol. 4. New York: Lewis, 1907, p. 59.

7. "Negro Ministers Act to Free the Pygmy," *New York Times*, September 11, 1906, p. 2.

8. Ibid.

9. Ibid.

10. Ibid.

11. "The Mayor Won't Help to Free Caged Pygmy," *New York Times*, September 12, 1906, p. 9. Also see "Negro Ministers Act to Free the Pygmy," *New York Times,* September 11, 1906, p. 2; and "Negro Clergy Protest," *New York Daily Tribune*, September 11, 1906, p. 6.

12. "Negro Ministers Act to Free the Pygmy."

13. Ibid.

14. Ibid.

15. "Topics of the Times: Send Him Back to the Woods," *New York Times*, p. 6, col. 4.

16. Ibid.

17. Ibid.

18. Lee Baker, "Savage Inequality: Anthropology in the Erosion of the Fifteenth Amendment," *Transforming Anthropology* 5(1) (1994), pp. 28–33.

19. Ibid.

20. Henry Fairfield Osborn to William Hornaday, Director's Incoming Correspondence, handwritten letter dated "Tuesday," Wildlife Conservation Society Archives.

CHAPTER SIX: FIGHTING CITY HALL

1. "The Mayor Won't Help to Free Caged Pygmy," *New York Times*, September 12, 1906, p. 9.

2. "Bushman Champions Angry," *New York Tribune*, September 12, 1906, p. 3.

3. Madison Grant, "The Vanishing Moose and Their Extermination in the Adirondacks," *Century Magazine*, January 1, 1894. (Also issued as a pamphlet.)

4. Jonathan Peter Spiro, *Defending the Master Race: Conservation, Eugenics, and the Legacy of Madison Grant.* Burlington, VT: University Press of New England, 2009, pp. 15–66.

5. Madison Grant, *The Passing of the Great Race.* New York: Scribner, 1916, pp. 15–16.

6. Madison Grant and Henry Fairfield Osborn, *The Passing of the Great Race, Or, The Racial Basis of European History*, 4th Rev. Ed., *With a Documentary Supplement, with Prefaces by Henry Fairfield Osborn.* New York: Scribner, 1922, p. 77.

7. According to Grant's biographer Jonathan Spiro, a long letter Roosevelt had written to Grant from Sagamore Hill detailing his reaction to the book disappeared from the archives.

8. Timothy W. Ryback, "A Disquieting Book from Hitler's Library," *International Herald Tribune*, December 8, 2011, p. 10. Ryback is the

author of *Hitler's Private Library: The Books That Shaped His Life*. New York: Vintage, 2010. He called Grant's *Passing of the Great Race* Hitler's "most valued book on America."

9. "The Mayor Won't Help to Free Caged Pygmy."

10. "Hot Talk About the South," *New York Sun*, February 2, 1906, p. 3; "Negrophiles Hold Enthusiastic Meeting," *Los Angeles Herald*, February 5, 1906, p. 1.

11. John Henry Elmer Milholland, *The Negro and the Nation: An Address to the National Negro Business League in Convention Assembled at New York, August 16, 17, 18, 1905*. New York: Moore Print, 1906, p. 6.

12. Letter from the *Sketch* to William Hornaday, September 15, 1906, in Director's General Correspondence, Wildlife Conservation Society Archives.

13. William Hornaday to Franklin Fishler, September 12, 1906, Director's Letter Book, February 24 to September 13, 1906, Wildlife Conservation Society Archives.

14. M. S. Gabriel, "Ota Benga Having a Fine Time," *New York Times*, September 13, 1906, p. 6.

15. Ibid.

16. Ibid.

17. Henry Fairfield Osborn to William Hornaday, Director's Incoming Correspondence, September 18, 1906, Wildlife Conservation Society Archives.

CHAPTER SEVEN: BENGA SPEAKS

1. William Hornaday to Henry Fairfield Osborn, Director's Outgoing Correspondence, September 13, 1906, Wildlife Conservation Society Archives.

2. Ibid.

3. Ibid.

4. Olof Semb et al., "Distress After a Single Violent Crime: How Shame Proneness and Event-Related Shame Work Together as Risk Factors for Post-Victimization Symptoms," *Psychological Reports*, 109(1) (2011), p. 6.

5. William Hornaday to Samuel Verner, Director's Outgoing Corre-

spondence, handwritten, undated, and addressed to 116 West 79th Street, Wildlife Conservation Society Archives.

6. Samuel Verner to William Hornaday, September 14, 1906, Director's Correspondence, Wildlife Conservation Society Archives.

7. William Hornaday to John S. Verner, phoned station September 15, 1906, at 9:30 A.M., Director's Outgoing Correspondence, Wildlife Conservation Society Archives.

8. Daniel Garrison Brinton, a professor of linguistics and archaeology at the University of Pennsylvania, who had served as president of the American Association for the Advancement of Science, so described African blacks in *The Basis of Social Relations: A Study in Ethnic Psychology*, published posthumously in 1902 by G. P. Putnam's Sons in New York and London as part of the Webster Collection of Social Anthropology. Brinton is immortalized in a portrait by Thomas Eakins that hangs in the Smithsonian American Art Museum in Washington, D.C.

9. *American Anthropologist*, 7 (1905), p. 182. Also see Gordon Gibson, "Samuel Phillips Verner in the Kasai." Unpublished.

10. Samuel Verner, "Pygmies and Chimpanzee," unpublished article, SPV Papers. Also in Gordon Gibson Papers, Smithsonian, Bureau of American Ethnology, National Anthropological Archives.

11. Samuel Verner to J. Jackson and Sons, July 17, 1906. Reply from Cunard Steam Ship Company, dated July 10, 1906, SPV Papers.

12. Samuel Verner to Hermon Bumpus, undated, Director's Correspondence, American Museum of Natural History Archives.

13. Ibid.

14. Mark Sullivan to Samuel Verner, November 22, 1906, SPV Papers.

15. "African Pygmy's Fate Is Still Undecided," *New York Times*, September 18, 1906, p. 9.

16. Jonathan Peter Spiro, *Defending the Master Race: Conservation, Eugenics, and the Legacy of Madison Grant*. Lebanon, NH: University Press of New England, 2009, p. 44.

17. William Hornaday to Samuel Verner, Director's Outgoing Correspondence, September 17, 1906, Wildlife Conservation Society Archives.

18. Ibid.

19. Ibid.
20. "African Pygmy's Fate Is Still Undecided."

CHAPTER EIGHT: BACKLASH

1. "African Pygmy's Fate Is Still Undecided," *New York Times*, September 18, 1906, p. 9.
2. "Zoo Has a Pygmy Too Many," *New York Sun*, September 17, 1906, p. 7.
3. Ibid.
4. "The Black Pigmy in the Monkey Cage: An Exhibition in Bad Taste," *New York Journal*, September 17, 1906.
5. Ibid.
6. William Hornaday to Samuel Verner, September 17, 1906, Wildlife Conservation Society Archives.
7. "Zoo Has a Pygmy Too Many."
8. Many thanks to Saleh Mwanamilongo Nasibu, for making arrangements to translate Verner's note.
9. "African Pygmy's Fate Is Still Undecided."
10. Ibid.
11. Ibid.
12. Ibid.
13. Ibid.
14. "Civilization," *North American*, September 17, 1906.
15. Josephine Vandes, letter dated September 19, 1906, to Hornaday, Director's Incoming Correspondence, New York Zoological Society.
16. Hornaday to Verner, September 29, 1906, in Director's Outgoing Correspondence, Wildlife Conservation Society Archives.
17. M. E. Buhler, "Ota Benga," *New York Times*, September 19, 1906, p. 8.
18. "Topics of the Times: Need Not Wait for Consent," *New York Times*, September 20, 1906.
19. Ibid.
20. Ibid.
21. Telephone wire, Hornaday to Verner, September 21, 1906, Director's Outgoing Correspondence, Wildlife Conservation Society Archives.

CHAPTER NINE: NATURE'S FURY

1. Samuel Verner to Hornaday, September 19, 1906, Wildlife Conservation Society Archives.
2. Ibid.
3. Ibid.
4. Thanks to Saleh Mwanamilongo Nasibu, who arranged for the translation.
5. Franz Boas, "Commencement Address for Atlanta University," in *A Franz Boas Reader*, ed. G. Stocking. Chicago: University of Chicago Press, 1974 (1906), p. 311.
6. *Atlanta Journal*, January 10, 1906, cited in Laughlin McDonald, *A Voting Rights Odyssey: Black Enfranchisement in Georgia*. Cambridge: Cambridge University Press, 2003, p. 40.
7. *New York Age*, October 25, 1906, p. 1.
8. Hornaday to Editor of *Sketch*, September 27, 1906, Director's Outgoing Correspondence, Wildlife Conservation Society Archives.
9. Ibid.
10. "Benga," *New York Times*, September 23, 1906, p. 8.
11. Ibid.
12. *New York Tribune*, September 23, 1906, p. 22.
13. *Indianapolis Sun*, September 24, 1906.
14. "What Is Ota Benga?" *New York Times*, September 24, 1906, p. 7.
15. "Still Stirred About Benga," *New York Times*, September 23, 1906, p. 9.
16. Ibid.
17. "Lives in Monkey Cage," *Minneapolis Journal*, September 26, 1906. See *Chronicling America: Historic American Newspapers*. Washington, D.C.: National Endowment for the Humanities and Library of Congress.
18. Ibid.

CHAPTER TEN: DELIVERANCE

1. "Ota Benga Attacks Keeper," *New York Times*, September 25, 1906, p. 1.
2. Ibid.
3. "Pigmy Officially Viewed: How Ota Benga Impressed One of the Controller's Examiners," *New York Times*, September 27, 1906, p. 9.

4. Ibid.

5. Letter to the editor, "Ota Benga and the Public Curiosities," *New York Times*, September 25, 1906.

6. "A Northern Outrage," *Lafayette Advertiser*, October 10, 1906.

7. New York Academy of Sciences to Hornaday, September 27, 1906, Director's General Correspondence, Wildlife Conservation Society Archives.

8. Based on figures provided by the Wildlife Conservation Society, citing the New York Zoological Society's Annual Report, http://archive.org/stream/annualreportnewy111906newy#page/52/ mode/2up.

9. "Colored Orphan Home Gets the Pigmy," *New York Times*, September 29, 1906, p. 7.

10. "The Mayor Won't Help to Free Caged Pygmy," *New York Times*, September 12, 1906, p. 9.

11. "Colored Orphan Home Gets the Pigmy."

CHAPTER ELEVEN: SAMUEL PHILLIPS VERNER

1. "Shotgun Rule Defended by U.S. Senator Tillman," *New York Press*, February 27, 1900, p. 1.

2. Annie Stillman to Verner's mother, written in 1895 after Verner left Tuscaloosa, SPV Papers. Cited in John R. Crawford, "The Instructive Missionary Career of Samuel Phillips Verner," *Presbyterian Journal*, 1972.

3. *Missionary*, September 1895, p. 398, SPV Papers.

4. Verner outlined his early beliefs before setting out to the Congo in *Pioneering in Central Africa* (Richmond, VA: Presbyterian Committee, 1903), which chronicles his voyage to Africa; see pp. 3–4.

5. Charles E. Robinson, "An African Returned to Africa," *Evangelist*, 70 (February 23, 1899), p. 6.

6. Ibid.

7. Verner, letter to his mother, December 9, 1895, SPV Papers.

8. Samuel P. Verner, "To Africa via Westminster Abbey," in *Pioneering in Central Africa*, p. 3.

9. Verner to Executive Committee of the Board of World Missions, from Matadi, May 1, 1896, SPV Papers.

10. Verner, *Pioneering in Central Africa*, Preface, p. v.
11. Verner to Executive Committee, May 1, 1896, SPV Papers.
12. *Missionary*, March 1897, pp. 114–16.
13. Verner, *Pioneering in Central Africa*, p. 5.

CHAPTER TWELVE: LUEBO MISSION

1. Samuel P. Verner, *Pioneering in Central Africa*. Richmond, VA: Presbyterian Committee, 1903, p. 95.
2. Samuel P. Verner, "Sketch of Mr. Verner's African Experience," unpublished manuscript written in late 1906 or early 1907, SPV Papers.
3. Charles E. Robinson, "An African Returned to Africa," *Evangelist*, 70 (February 23, 1899), p. 6.
4. Verner to S. P. Langley, March 11, 1896, Smithsonian, National Anthropological Archives.
5. Samuel P. Verner, "Woman in Africa," *Missionary*, August 1899, pp. 374–78, SPV Papers.
6. Verner to mother from Luebo, November 14, 1896, SPV Papers.
7. Samuel P. Verner, "The African Pygmies," *Atlantic Monthly*, August 1902, p. 185.
8. Ibid., p. 193.
9. Ibid., p. 194. Verner and the explorer Henry Morton Stanley referred to the forest dwellers as "Batwa," but others, including anthropologists Frederick Starr and Ludwig Wolf, used the spelling "Batua." Stanley notes, in his book *In Darkest Africa*, Vol. 2 (New York: Scribner, 1890, p. 42), that, depending on the region, they are also alternatively referred to as Batwa, Watwa, Bushmen, Akka, Monbuttu, Balia, and Wambutti.
10. Reverend R. C. Rees, Executive Chariman of Foreign Missions of the Presbyterian Church of the United States, to Samuel Verner, September 14, 1897, SPV Papers.
11. Ibid.
12. John S. Verner to Samuel Verner, October 22, 1897, SPV Papers.
13. Reverend D. Asa Blackburn to Verner, on Church of the Strangers letterhead, October 21, 1897, SPV Papers.

14. Verner, *Pioneering in Central Africa*, pp. 345–46.

15. E. D. Morel, *King Leopold's Rule in Africa*. Westport, CT: Negro Universities, 1970, p. 236.

16. Ibid.

17. Robert B. Edgerton, *The Troubled Heart of Africa: A History of the Congo*. New York: St. Martin's, 2002, p. 136.

18. Samuel P. Verner, "The Yellow People of Central Africa," *American Anthropologist*, 5(3) (September 1903), p. 540.

19 Gordon Gibson, unpublished manuscript, National Anthropological Archives.

20. Reverend S. H. Chester to Verner, June 16, 1899, SPV Papers.

21. Ibid.

22. Stanley Shaloff, *Reform in Leopold's Congo*. Richmond, VA: John Knox, 1970, p. 100.

23. According to Verner's biography written for the Verner Papers at South Caroliniana Library, Dr. John C. Crawford, professor of history at Montreat College in North Carolina, met Verner's children during his trip to Luebo in the 1950s. According to Crawford, who was retracing Verner's steps in the Congo, Verner's daughter married a village chief and had many children between 1915 and 1930.

CHAPTER THIRTEEN: KONDOLA, KASSONGO,
AND VERNER'S AFRICAN TREASURES

1. Samuel P. Verner, *Pioneering in Central Africa*. Richmond, VA: Presbyterian Committee, 1903, p. 399.

2. Verner, unpublished manuscript, SPV Papers.

3. C. K. Davis to Honorable Ballamy Storer, June 24, 1899, SPV Papers.

4. Samuel P. Verner, "An Educational Experiment with Cannibals," *World's Work*, 4 (May–October 1902), pp. 2289–95.

5. Ibid.

6. Ibid.

7. Gordon D. Gibson, "Samuel Phillips Verner in the Kasai," Smithsonian Institution, unpublished, Gordon D. Gibson Papers, Smithsonian, Bureau of Ethnology, National Anthropological Archives.

8. Ibid.

9. "Congo Boys in Town: They Ride in a Hansom Cab and Start for Alabama," *Washington Post*, March 10, 1899, p. 4.

10. Ibid.

11. Verner, "An Educational Experiment with Cannibals."

12. Ibid., p. 2290.

13. Verner, *Pioneering in Central Africa*, p. 122.

14. Ibid., p. 129.

15. Family records indicate that they were married in December 1899, but the year given in the 1900 census was 1900.

16. According to Gordon Gibson, a former Smithsonian curator, no catalog has never been located: "Rather, there are some scanty notes on certain items filed among the papers of the curator, Walter Hough." Gordon Gibson, unpublished manuscript on Verner, pp. 23–24, Gordon Gibson Papers, National Anthropological Archives.

17. W. M. Drennen to Honorable John Hay, September 25, 1902, SPV Papers. An assistant secretary replied on October 25, saying that the letter had been forwarded to Brussels to be transmitted to the minister for foreign affairs.

CHAPTER FOURTEEN: THE HUNT

1. Verner to McGee, September 26, 1904, SPV Papers.

2. Verner to McGee, October 9, 1903, William J. McGee Papers, Library of Congress (hereafter cited as McGee Papers).

3. McGee to Verner, October 22, 1903, SPV Papers.

4. McGee to Verner, October 30, 1904, McGee Papers and SPV Papers.

5. McGee to Sirs, October 22, 1903, SPV Papers.

6. Julia Kellersberger, *A Life for the Congo: The Story of Althea Brown Edmiston*. New York: Fleming H. Revell, 1947.

7. Verner to McGee, December 24, 1903, SPV Papers.

8. Ibid.

9. Brook Frindle to S. P. Verner, December 24, 1903, SPV Papers.

10. Verner to McGee, December 11, 1903, SPV Papers.

11. Solomon Berliner to Verner, December 12, 1903, SPV Papers.

12. Verner to McGee, January 6, 1903, SPV and McGee Papers.

13. Ibid.

14. Ibid.

15. Military Equipment Company to Verner, January 5 and 6, 1903, SPV Papers.

16. Verner to His Excellency the Governor-General, February 1, 1904, SPV Papers.

17. Verner to McGee, February 18, 1904, SPV Papers.

18. Ibid.

19. Ibid.

20. McGee to Verner, April 1, 1904, SPV Papers.

21. Verner to Monsieur le Gouvernneur Général de l'État Indépendent du Congo, February 26, 1904, SPV Papers.

22. Verner to McGee. March 20, 1904, SPV Papers.

CHAPTER FIFTEEN: VERNER'S PREY

1 Verner to McGee, March 20, 1904, SPV Papers.

2. Samuel P. Verner, "The Adventures of an Explorer in Africa: How the Batwa Pygmies Were Brought to the St. Louis Fair," *Harper's Weekly*, 48 (October 22, 1904), p. 1618.

3. *Columbus* (South Carolina) *Dispatch*, September 11, 1904.

4. Samuel Verner, "How We Tamed the Baschilele," unpublished essay, SPV Papers.

5. Arthur Conan Doyle, *The Crime of the Congo*, "Consul Roger Casement's Report." New York: Doubleday, 1909, p. 65.

6. McGee to Verner, January 11, 1904, SPV Papers.

7. Verner to McGee, March 20, 1904, SPV Papers.

8. Verner, "The Situation of the African Expedition," April 30, 1904, SPV Papers.

9. Ibid.

10. Verner to McGee, March 21, 1904, SPV Papers.

11. McGee to Verner, April 1, 1904, SPV Papers.

12. Ibid.

13. Verner to McGee, December 11, 1903, SPV Papers.

14. McGee to Verner, April 1, 1904, SPV Papers.

15. "Exposition Envoy Pygmies' Victim? Fair Officials Have Not Heard

for Two Months from Explorer Sent to African Wilds," *St. Louis Post-Dispatch*, April 18, 1904.

16. Verner, "The Adventures of an Explorer in Africa," p. 1619. First quotation in the paragraph below is from p. 1620.

17. "World's Fair Bulletin," Louisiana Purchase Exposition, The 1904 St. Louis World's Fair Collection. University of Missouri Digital Library. February 1904, p. 4.

18. *Boston Journal*, July 2, 1904; August 12, 1904, p. 2.

19. Stanley Shaloff, *Reform in Leopold's Congo*. Richmond, VA: John Knox, 1970, p. 99.

20. McGee to Verner, July 4, 1904, McGee Papers.

21. Ibid.

22. Ibid.

CHAPTER SIXTEEN: THE ST. LOUIS WORLD'S FAIR

1. "The World's Progress," *Baltimore American*, May 1, 1904, p. 4.

2. Hrdlicka to Livingston Farrand, May 27, 1904, American Museum of Natural History (hereafter cited as AMNH), in Dartmouth Hood Museum Archives.

3. "African Pygmies for the World's Fair," *St. Louis Post-Dispatch*, June 26, 1904, p. 5.

4. Ibid.

5. David Rowland Francis, *The Universal Exposition of 1904*, Vol. 1. St. Louis, MO: Louisiana Purchase Exposition, 1913, p. 522.

6. Ibid., p. 527.

7. Samuel Verner, "An Untold Chapter of My Adventures While Hunting Pygmies in Africa," *St. Louis Post-Dispatch*, September 4, 1904, p. 3.

8. *Columbus* (South Carolina) *Dispatch*, September 14, 1904, p. 1.

9. "The Racial Exhibit at the St. Louis Fair," *Scientific American*, 91 (December 10, 1904), p. 414.

10. Francis, *The Universal Exposition of 1904*, p. 526.

11. Ancestry.com. Tennessee Naturalization Records, 1907–1991 (database online). Provo, UT: Ancestry.com Operations, 2013.

12. According to his naturalization papers, dated September 26, 1923. Ibid.

13. "Pygmies Demand a Monkey Diet," *St. Louis Post-Dispatch*, July 2, 1904.

14. *St. Louis Post-Dispatch,* July 17, 1904.

15. "Barbarians Meet in Athletic Games," *St. Louis Post-Dispatch*, August 6, 1904.

16. Francis, *The Universal Exposition of 1904*, p. 527.

17. Negative 299134, St. Louis Expo, Dartmouth Hood Museum of Art Archives.

18. Franz Boas to McGee, March 5, 1904, Dartmouth Hood Museum of Art Archives.

19. Livingston Farrand to Caspar Mayer, August 20, 1904, Dartmouth Hood Museum of Art Archives.

20. McGee to Doctor Jenkes, August 22, 1904, Dartmouth Hood Museum of Art Archives.

21. Mayer to Boas, October 7, 1904, Dartmouth Hood Museum of Art Archives. This letter indicates that life casts were purchased for the American Museum of Natural History, which commissioned them; but in 2014 AMNH officials insisted that the life casts of Benga and others were not in its possession.

22. Alfred Haddon, Preface, in Caroline Furness Jayne, *String Figures and How to Make Them: A Study of Cat's Cradle in Many Lands.* New York: Scribner, 1906 (reprint, Dove), p. xi.

23. Ibid.

24. Jayne, *String Figures and How to Make Them*, p. 176.

25. Frederick Starr, "Ethnographic Notes from the Congo Free State: An African Miscellany," *Proceedings of the Davenport Academy of Sciences*, 40 (May 1909), diagram 45, p. 121.

26. Francis, *The Universal Exposition of 1904*, p. 527.

27. Verner, unpublished autobiography, pp. 5–6, SPV Papers.

CHAPTER SEVENTEEN: CONGO FIELD NOTES

1. Verner to McGee, March 18, 1905, SPV Papers and McGee Papers.

2. Ibid.

3. Ibid.

4. "To Study the Pygmies," *Kansas City Star*, October 27, 1905, p. 18.

5. Frederick Starr, *The Truth About the Congo: The Chicago Tribune Articles.* Chicago: Forbes, 1907, p. 3.

6. Ibid., p. 8.

7. Frederick Starr, "Ethnographic Field Notes from the Congo Free State," *Proceedings of the Davenport Academy of Natural Sciences*, 40 (May 1909), pp. 96–222.

8. Sidney Langford Hinde, *The Fall of the Congo Arabs.* New York: Negro Universities, 1969, pp. 82–85.

9. Colin M. Turnbull, *The Forest People.* New York: Simon and Schuster, 1962, p. 12.

10. Ibid., p. 13.

11. Starr, "Ethnographic Notes from the Congo Free State," pp. 120–21.

12. Ibid., p. 115.

13. Ibid.

14. Ibid.

15. Ibid., pp. 116–17.

16. Ibid., p. 116.

17. Starr, Field Notes, Notebook 3, pages 161–62, December 24, 1905, AMNH.

18. Ibid., Notebook 5, p. 225.

19. Ibid. p. 240.

20. Frederick Starr, *Congo Natives: An Ethnographic Album.* Chicago: Lakeside, 1912, p. 20. (Three hundred twenty signed and numbered copies were published.)

21. Frederick Starr, Preface, *In Indian Mexico.* Chicago: Forbes, 1908, www.gutenberg.org/files/16188-h.htm.

22. Starr to his mother, February 3, 1906, Frederick Starr Papers, Special Collections Research Center, University of Chicago Library (hereafter cited as Frederick Starr Papers).

23. Starr to his mother, February 6, 1906, Frederick Starr Papers.

24. Ibid.

25. Starr to his mother, January 30, 1906, Frederick Starr Papers.

26. Ibid.

27. Starr to his mother, February 3, 1906, Frederick Starr Papers.

28. Starr to his mother, February 20, 1906, Frederick Starr Papers.

29. Ibid.

30. Ibid.

31. Starr to his mother, February 28, 1906. Frederick Starr Papers.

32. Starr to his mother, February 20, 1906, Frederick Starr Papers.

33. Starr to his mother, March 9, 1906. Frederick Starr Papers.

34. Ibid.

35. This is according to Starr, in the introduction to *Congo Natives*. However, while the images have been found, no documents of the exhibition have been located.

36. As of fall 2014, however, neither the university nor AMNH could locate the photos.

CHAPTER EIGHTEEN: LEOPOLD'S LOBBY

1. Frederick Starr, *The Truth About the Congo: The Chicago Tribune Articles*. Chicago: Forbes, 1907. Quotations here are from pp. 2, 5–6, 13, 14, 15, 27, 31, 33, 41, 43, 90, and 92.

2. Prince Albert de Ligne to Starr, February 14, 1907, Frederick Starr Papers.

3. Prince Albert de Ligne to Starr, March 8, 1907, Frederick Starr Papers.

4. See "King Leopold's Feat: Empire of the Congo Unparalleled in All History," *Washington Post,* July 3, 1904, p. E8; and "King Leopold as a Captain of Industry," *Washington Post*, September 10, 1904, p. 4.

5. "The Congo Free State: Consul General Whitely Denies Rev. Johnson's Statement," *Washington Evening Star*, August 27, 1906.

6. Ibid.

7. Morrison to Morel, November 1, 1904, M.P. Cited in Stanley Shaloff, *Reform in Leopold's Congo*. Richmond, VA: John Knox, 1970, p. 99.

8. Ibid.

9. Casement to Farnell, February 18, 1904, F.O. 10/808. Cited in Shaloff, *Reform in Leopold's Congo*, p. 99.

10. Samuel P. Verner, "Farewell to Ndombe," in *Pioneering in Central Africa*. Richmond, VA: Presbyterian Committee, 1903, p. 397.

11. Ludovic Moncheur to Verner, December 2, 1904, SPV Papers.

12. Ibid.

13. Ibid.

14. Samuel Verner File, Gordon Gibson Papers, National Anthropological Archives.
15. Samuel P. Verner, "Belgian Rule in the Congo," *World's Work*, 13 (1907), p. 8572. (Published by Doubleday Page.)
16. Ibid.
17. Ibid., p. 8573.
18. Samuel P. Verner, "The White Man's Zone in Africa," *World's Work*, 13 (1907), p. 8233.
19. Ibid.
20. Ibid., p. 8235.
21. Ibid., p. 8234.

CHAPTER NINETEEN: BENGA'S CHOICE

1. Harriet Verner to John McGee, November 2, 1905, SPV Papers.
2. David Francis to Harriet Verner, October 7, 1905, SPV Papers.
3. Verner to Harriet Verner, January 24, 1905, SPV Papers.
4. McGee to Verner, August 10, 1906, SPV Papers.
5. Arthur Conan Doyle, *The Crime of the Congo*. London: Hutchinson, 1909, p. 252.
6. Ibid., p. 104.
7. According to the biographical overview of Verner in the SPV Papers, he had at least two children—a son and a daughter—by an African woman who resided at the Southern Presbyterian Missionary House for orphans at Luebo. Their births are believed to have occurred sometime between 1895 and 1899. He may also have stayed with this woman during his third trip in 1905 to 1906.

CHAPTER TWENTY: A MUSEUM MOST UNNATURAL

1. Verner to Bumpus, October 13, 1904, SPV Papers.
2. Hermon Bumpus to Clark Wissler, August 77, 1906, General Archives, Box 87, Folder 240, Papers, AMNH.
3. Ibid.
4. "Too Warm for Eskimos: Unaccustomed to a Temperate Climate,

They Are Suffering with a Hitherto Unknown Complaint," *New York Times*, October 11, 1897, p. 12.

5. Ibid.

6. *San Francisco Examiner* (Magazine Supplement), May 9, 1909, p. 33.

7. "Give Me My Father's Body," *World Magazine Supplement*, January 6, 1907, p. 3.

8. "Taming a Little Savage," *New York World*, January 27, 1899, p. 9.

9. "Give Me My Father's Body." See also "Minik, the Esquimau Body," *New York World*, January 6, 1907, p. 3.

10. "The Esquimau's Body," *New York Daily Tribune*, February 19, 1898, p. 10.

11. Kenn Harper, *Give Me My Father's Body: The Life of Minik, the New York Eskimo.* New York: Simon and Schuster, 2000, p. 145.

12. Verner to Bumpus, received August 6, 1906, AMNH, No. 176.

13. Ibid.

14. Ibid.

15. I am enormously grateful to Saleh Mwanamilongo Nasibu, a reporter for the Associated Press in Kinshasa, Democratic Republic of the Congo, for his kind assistance in securing translations of this and other letters Verner wrote to Ota Benga during his time in New York.

16. Verner to Bumpus, August 6, 1906, Bumpus Papers, Box 176, AMNH.

17. Ibid.

18. Hermon Bumpus to Clark Wissler, August 10, 1906, General Archives, Box 176, AMNH.

19. Bumpus to Verner, August 10, 1906, Director's Correspondence, AMNH.

20. McGee to Miss Fruchte, August 31, 1906, SPV Papers.

21. McGee to Paul Morton, President, Equitable Life Assurance Society, January 17, 1907, SPV Papers.

22. Bumpus to Verner, August 14, 1906, AMNH Archives.

23. Bumpus to Verner, August 16, 1906, AMNH Archives.

CHAPTER TWENTY-ONE: FONDLESS FAREWELL

1. Verner to Bumpus, August 27, 1906, AMNH Archives.

2. "The Congo Free State," *Washington* (D.C.) *Evening Star*, April 27, 1906,

p. 19. *Chronicling America: Historic American Newspapers.* Washington, D.C.: National Endowment for the Humanities and Library of Congress.

3. Verner, "Pygmy and Chimpanzees," unpublished article, SPV Papers.
4. Verner, unpublished article, SPV Papers, Microfilm Reel I, Item 69.
5. Verner to Bumpus, September 16, 1906, AMNH Archives.
6. Bumpus's secretary to Verner, September 18, 1906, AMNH Archives.
7. Verner to Bumpus, September 17, 1906, AMNH Archives.
8. Bumpus to Verner, October 6, 1906, AMNH Archives.

CHAPTER TWENTY-TWO: WEEKSVILLE REFUGE

1. "The Troubles in Weeksville," *Brooklyn Eagle*, March 10, 1869, p. 3.
2. *Christian Recorder*, July 25, 1863. Founded in 1848, the *Christian Recorder* was a national weekly published by the Philadelphia-based African Methodist Episcopal Church.
3. Article II, p. 4, in the society's charter.
4. "A White Teacher Not Wanted in Colored School No. 2," *Brooklyn Eagle*, February 3, 1869, p. 2.
5. "Little Colored Orphans: Their Pleasant Brooklyn Asylum and How They Live," *New York Times*, July 22, 1894, p. 16.
6. Ibid.
7. Annual Report, October 1906–1907, Howard Colored Orphans Asylum, Superintendent's Report, p. 19.
8. Ibid., p. 20.
9. Ibid.
10. Ibid., p. 22.
11. "Colored Orphan Home Gets the Pigmy," *New York Times*, September 29, 1906, p. 7.
12. Ibid.
13. Ibid.
14. Ibid.
15. "Ota Benga an 'Orphan' Clamoring for a Wife," *Brooklyn Daily Eagle*, September 29, 1906, p. 2. See also *New York Tribune*, October 7, 1906; "Pigmy Wants a Wife: Is in Love with His Nurse," *Afro-American*, October 6, 1906, p. 1.

16. "Colored Orphan Home Gets the Pigmy."

17. "Hope for Ota: If Little, He's No Fool," *New York Times,* September 30, 1906, p. 9.

18. "Church News," *New York Age,* October 11, 1906, p. 7.

19. "Hope for Ota."

20. Gunja SenGupta, *From Slavery to Poverty: The Racial Origins of Welfare in New York, 1840–1918.* New York: New York University Press, 2009, p. 221. Following quotations are from pp. 221, 222, and 235.

21. "Benga at the Hippodrome; The African Pigmy Well Pleased with the Performance," *New York Times,* October 3, 1906, p. 9.

22. Olof Semb et al., "Distress After a Single Violent Crime: How Shame Proneness and Event-Related Shame Work Together as Risk Factors for Post-Victimization Symptoms," *Psychological Reports,* 109(1) (2011), p. 13.

23. "Mr. Verner Asks New York Not to Spoil His Friend, the Bushman," *New York Tribune,* Letters to the Editor, October 6, 1906, p. 7.

24. Ibid.

25. Hamilton Holt to Verner, October 16, 1906, SPV Papers.

26. Samuel P. Verner, "Thomas F. Ryan as a Benefactor of a Carolina Boy: How the Great Financier Made the Dream of an African Explorer Come True," unpublished article, SPV Papers.

27. Ibid.

28. Adam Hochschild, *King Leopold's Ghost.* Boston: Houghton Mifflin, 1998, pp. 248–49.

29. A. T. Wilkinson to Dr. J. H. Gordon, April 10, 1907, SPV Papers.

30. "Pygmy Missionary: Ota Benga Refuses to Go Back," *Washington Post,* March 10, 1907, p. E8.

31. "Ota Benga Will Remain Here; Won't Return to Congo Until He's a Missionary," *New York Sun,* March 4, 1907, p. 9.

32. Ibid.

33. "Pygmy Missionary."

34. Annual Report, October 1907–October 1908, Howard Colored Orphan Asylum, p. 21.

CHAPTER TWENTY-THREE: ST. JAMES

1. Dated August 1, 1908, and reprinted in Annual Report, year ending 1908, Howard Colored Orphans Asylum.

2. Annual Report, October 1907–1908, Howard Colored Orphan Asylum, p. 22.

3. Ibid., p. 15.

4. Ibid., p. 21.

5. Ibid.

6. Ibid., p. 23.

7. Bradley Harris, *Black Roots in Smithtown: A Short History of the Black Community*. Smithtown, NY: Office of the Town Historian, 1986.

8. Annual Report, year ending October 1909, Howard Colored Orphans Asylum, p. 12.

9. Ibid.

10. Annual Report, October 1908–October 1909, Howard Colored Orphan Asylum, p. 11.

11. Ibid., p. 8.

12. Annual Report, October 1908–October 1909, Howard Colored Orphans Asylum, Superintendent Report, p. 11.

13. Ibid., p. 12.

14. This estimate is based on the cost of a third-class ticket on the Cunard line that year.

15. *History of Suffolk County*. New York: W. W. Munsell, 1882.

16. Harris, *Black Roots in Smithtown*, p. 26.

17. Arthur Conan Doyle, *The Crime of the Congo*. New York: Doubleday, Page, 1909, p. 107.

18. Ibid.

19. SPV Papers.

20. Pagan Kennedy, *Black Livingstone: A True Tale of Adventure in the Nineteenth-Century Congo*. New York: Viking, 2002, p. 185.

21. Reverend J. H. Gordon to Verner, December 28, 1909, SPV Papers.

22. Ibid.

CHAPTER TWENTY-FOUR: SOUTHERN COMFORT

1. James M. Elson, *Lynchburg, Virginia: The First Two Hundred Years, 1786–1986.* Lynchburg: Warwick House, 2004, p. 33.

2. Benjamin Guy Childs, *The Negroes of Lynchburg, Virginia*, Charlottesville, VA: Surber-Arundale, 1923, Publication of the University of Virginia Phelps-Stokes Fellowship Papers, No. 5, p. 13.

3. Elson, *Lynchburg, Virginia*, p. 42.

4. Childs, *The Negroes of Lynchburg*, p. 17.

5. Ralph Reavis, *Virginia Seminary: A Journey of Black Independence.* Bedford, VA: Print Shop, 1989, p. 45.

6. Ibid.

7. Ibid., p. 81.

8. "Normal School: Oratorical Flourishes from the Speakers," *Daily Times*, June 15, 1889. Cited in Reavis, *Virginia Seminary*, p. 64.

9. Leroy Fitts, *A History of Black Baptists.* Nashville, TN: Broadman, 1985, p. 80.

10. Reverend L. G. Jordan, corresponding secretary of the Foreign Mission Board of the National Baptist Convention; and Reverend William W. Brown, pastor of the High Street Baptist Church, introduced Chilembwe to Hayes and sponsored his education. Ibid., p. 137.

11. Sandy D. Martin, *Black Baptists and African Missions: The Origin of a Movement, 1880–1915.* Macon, GA: Mercer University Press, 1998, p. 76.

12. Special Collections and University Archives, University of Massachusetts Amherst Libraries, Ms. 312. Also see James L. Conyers Jr., *Charles H. Wesley: The Intellectual Tradition of a Black Historian*, Routledge, 1997, p. 89.

13. Thomas Jesse Jones, ed., *Negro Education: A Study of the Private and Higher Schools for Colored People in the United States*, Vol. 1. New York: Arno and New York Times, 1969. (Originally published 1917.)

14. Jeni Sandberg, "Mrs. George M. Jones and Her Monumental Reality," *Lynch's Ferry*, Spring/Summer 1994, pp. 36–39.

15. Elson, "Cameo: Anne Spencer, the Harlem Renaissance in the Hill City," in *Lynchburg, Virginia*, p. 310.

CHAPTER TWENTY-FIVE: HOME

1. Carrie Allen McCray, *Freedom's Child: The Life of a Confederate General's Black Daughter.* Chapel Hill, NC: Algonquin Books, 1998, p. 112.
2. Their marriage license is dated September 20, 1911.
3. The American Baptist Home Missionary Society later merged with the formerly coeducational Wayland Seminary and Richmond Theological Seminary, which in 1899 became Virginia Union University.
4. McCray, *Freedom's Child*, p. 66.
5. Benjamin Guy Childs, *The Negroes of Lynchburg. Virginia.* Charlottesville, VA: Surber-Arundale, 1923, p. 8.
6. Ibid.
7. McCray, *Freedom's Child*, p. 115.
8. Anne Karan, "Tale of African as 'Specimen' Recounted," Associated Press, November 21, 1992.
9. Olof Semb et al., "Distress After a Single Violent Crime: How Shame Proneness and Event-Related Shame Work Together as Risk Factors for Post-Victimization Symptoms," *Psychological Reports*, 109(1) (2011), p. 19.

CHAPTER TWENTY-SIX: FREE

1. Carrie Allen McCray, *Freedom's Child: The Life of a Confederate General's Black Daughter.* Chapel Hill, NC: Algonquin Books, 1998, p. 116.
2. Verner to Anita McGee, date unclear, 1912, SPV Papers.

CHAPTER TWENTY-SEVEN: HOMEGOING

1. "African a Suicide," *Lynchburg News*, March 21, 1916.
2. Ibid.
3. Olof Semb et al., "Distress After a Single Violent Crime; How Shame Proneness and Event-Related Shame Work Together as Risk Factors for Post-Victimization Symptoms," *Psychological Reports*, 109(1) (2011), p. 6.
4. Ibid.
5. Ibid., pp. 3–23.
6. "African a Suicide."

7. "African Pygmy a Suicide: Longing for Life of Jungle Leads to Death of Ota Benza," *Washington Post*, May 14, 1916, p. 2.

8. "Suicide of Ota Benga, the African Pygmy," *Zoological Society Bulletin*, 19(3) (May 1916), p. 1356.

9. Ibid.

10. "Man and Monkey Show Disapproved by Clergy," *New York Times*, September 10, 1906, p. 1.

11. Ibid.

12. *Zoological Society Bulletin*, 19(4) (July 1916), p. 1377.

13. Ibid., p. 1379.

14. "Ota Benga, Pygmy, Tired of America," *New York Times*. July 16, 1916, p. 12.

EPILOGUE

1. William Bridges, *Gathering of Animals*. New York: Harper and Row, p. 225.

2. Phillips Verner Bradford and Harvey Blume, *Ota Benga: The Pygmy in the Zoo*. New York: St. Martin's, 1992.

3. See www.encyclopediavirgina.org/Benga_Ota_ca_1883–1916.

4. Jerry Oppenheimer, "Treated Like an Animal," *New York Post*, November 18, 2012, http://nypost.com/2012/11/18/treated-like-an-animal.

5. Enid Schildkrout to Gordon Gibson, March 13, 1980, Gordon Gibson Papers, National Anthropological Archives, Smithsonian.

6. Schildkrout to Gordon Gibson, June 29, 1988, Gordon Gibson Papers, National Anthropological Archives, Smithsonian.

7. Ann Hornaday, "A Critical Connection to the Curious Case of Ota Benga," *Washington Post*, January 3, 2009. Eric Roth, the screenwriter, told *News and Advance* that the character Oti was partly based on Ota Benga, who, like Oti, was a stranger in a strange land. See Casey Gillis, "Curious Connection," *News and Advance*, December 24, 2008.

BIBLIOGRAPHY

Ahlstrom, Sydney E. *A Religious History of the American People.* New Haven, CT: Yale University Press, 1972.

Allwood, John. *The Great Exhibitions.* London: Studio Vista, 1977.

Anderson, James D. *The Education of Blacks in the South, 1860–1935.* Chapel Hill: University of North Carolina Press, 1998.

Anderson, Jervis. *This Was Harlem: A Cultural Portrait 1900–1950.* New York: Farrar, Straus and Giroux, 1981.

Aptheker, Herbert. *The Correspondence of W. E. B. Du Bois*, Vol. 1, *Selection, 1877–1934.* Amherst: University of Massachusetts Press, 1973.

Ardizzone, Heidi. *An Illuminated Life: Belle da Costa Greene's Journey from Prejudice to Privilege.* New York: Norton, 2007.

Arnold, B. W. "Concerning the Negroes of the City of Lynchburg, Virginia," *Southern History Association Publications*, 10 (1906), pp. 19–30.

Bacote, Samuel William. "Franz Boas Within the Struggle for Racial Equality," *Critique of Anthropology*, 14(2) (1994), pp. 199–217.

Baker, Lee. *From Savage to Negro: Anthropology and the Construction of Race, 1896–1954.* Berkeley: University of California Press, 1998.

———. "Ota Benga: Story of a Tragic Travesty," *Teaching Anthropology Newsletter*, 5 (1993), pp. 21–22.

———. "Savage Inequality: Anthropology in the Erosion of the Fifteenth Amendment," *Transforming Anthropology*, 5(1) (1994), pp. 28–33.

Bannister, Robert C. *Social Darwinism: Science and Myth in Anglo American Social Thought.* Philadelphia: Temple University Press, 1979.

Barnard, John. *From Evangelicalism to Progressivism at Oberlin College, 1866–1917.* Columbus: Ohio State University Press, 1969.

Barnum, P. T. *Barnum's Own Story: The Autobiography of P. T. Barnum.* Gloucester, MA: Peter Smith, 1972.

Bean, Robert B. "The Negro Brain," *Century Magazine,* 72 (1906), pp. 778–84.

Bechtel, Stefan. *Mr. Hornaday's War.* Boston: Beacon, 2012.

Benedetto, Robert (ed.). *Presbyterian Reformers in Central Africa: A Documentary Account of the American Presbyterian Congo Mission and the Human Rights Struggle in the Congo, 1890–1918.* Boston: Brill Academic, 1997.

Bennett, Mark. *Louisiana Purchase Exhibition.* St. Louis, MO: Universal Exposition, 1905.

Bennett, Mark, and Frank P. Stockbridge. *History of the Louisiana Purchase Exposition.* St. Louis, MO: Universal Exposition, 1905.

Biggleston, W. E. "Oberlin College and the Negro Student, 1865–1940," *Journal of Negro History,* 56 (July 1971), pp. 199–209.

Birmingham, Stephen. *Certain People: America's Black Elite.* Boston: Little, Brown, 1977.

Blackford, Charles M. *Campaign and Battle of Lynchburg, Virginia.* Lynchburg: Warwick House, 1994.

Blackwell, James E., and Morris Janowitz (eds.). *Black Sociologists: Historical and Contemporary Perspectives.* Chicago: University of Chicago Press, 1974.

Blauner, Robert. *Racial Oppression in America.* New York: Harper and Row, 1972.

Bogdan, Robert. *Freak Show—Presenting Human Oddities for Amusement and Profit.* Chicago: University of Chicago Press, 1988.

Boris, Joseph E. (ed.). *Who's Who in Colored America: A Biographical Dictionary of Notable Living Persons of African Descent in America.* New York: Who's Who in Colored America, 1927.

Bosley, Paul R., Sr. "Stop 68: Nostalgic Recollections and Reminiscences of the 'Good Old Days,' " *Lake County, Ohio, Historical Society Quarterly,* 16(1) (February 1974), pp. 296–300.

Bracey, John H., August Meier, and Elliott Rudwick (eds.). *The Black Sociologists: The First Half Century.* Belmont, CA: Wadsworth, 1971.

Bradford, Phillips Verner, and Harvey Blume. *Ota Benga: The Pygmy in the Zoo*. New York: St. Martin's, 1992.

Bridges, William. *Gathering of Animals: An Unconventional History of the New York Zoological Society*. New York: Harper and Row, 1974.

Brisbane, Robert H. *The Black Vanguard: Origins of the Negro Social Revolution 1900–1960*. Valley Forge, PA: Judson, 1970.

Broderick, Francis L. "The Fight Against Booker T. Washington," in Hugh Hawkins (ed.), *Booker T. Washington and His Critics*. Lexington, MA: Heath, 1959, pp. 67–80.

Broderick, Francis L., and August Meier (eds.). *Negro Protest Thought in the Twentieth Century*. Indianapolis, IN: Bobbs-Merrill, 1965.

Broderick, Mosette. *Triumvirate: McKim, Mead and White*. New York: Knopf, 2010.

Brodie, Fawn M. *Thomas Jefferson: An Intimate History*. New York: Norton, 1974.

Brush, John W. *Who's Who in Church History*. Boston: Whittemore Associates, 1962.

Buel, J. W. (ed.). *Louisiana and the Fair: An Exposition of the World, Its People and Their Achievements*. St. Louis, MO: World's Progress, 1904.

Bullock, Henry Allen. *A History of Negro Education in the South: From 1619 to the Present*. Cambridge, MA: Harvard University Press, 1967.

Buni, Andrew. *The Negro in Virginia Politics*. Charlottesville: University Press of Virginia, 1967.

Burrows, Guy. *The Land of the Pigmies*. New York: Thomas Crowell, 1898.

Cable, George Washington. "The Dance in Place Congo," in Bernard Katz (ed.), *The Social Implications of Early Negro Music in The United States*. New York: Arno and New York Times, 1969, pp. 31–47.

———. "The Story of Bras-Coupé" in Arlin Turner (ed.), *Creoles and Cajuns: Stories of Old Louisiana by George Washington Cable* Garden City, NY: Doubleday, 1959.

Casement, Roger. *Roger Casement's Diaries: 1910—The Black and the White*, ed. Roger Sawyer. London: Pimlico, c. 1997.

Cash, Wilbur J. *The Mind of the South*. New York: Knopf, 1941.

Cavalli-Sforza, Luigi. *African Pygmies*. Orlando, FL: Academic, 1986.

Childs, Benjamin Guy. *The Negroes of Lynchburg, Virginia.* Charlottesville, VA: Surber-Arundale, 1923.

Clark, B. F. Telephone interview, October 30, 1997.

Clark, Jewell Spencer. Interview with the author, September 8, 1997.

Clegg, Legrand H., II. "The Mystery of the Arctic Twa: A Letter to the Editor" in Ivan Van Sertima, *African Presence in Early Europe.* New Brunswick, NJ: Transaction, 1985.

Conrad, Joseph. "Geography and Some Explorers," in *Last Essays,* with an introduction by Richard Curle. Garden City, NY: Doubleday, Page, 1926.

————. *Heart of Darkness.* Boston: Bedford Books of St. Martin's, c. 1996.

————. "Outpost of Progress," in *Two Tales of the Congo.* London: Folio Society, c. 1952.

Cook, Adrian. *The Armies of the Streets: The New York City Draft Riots of 1863.* Lexington: University Press of Kentucky, 1974.

Court Street Baptist Church. "A Historical Sketch of the Court Street Baptist Church of Lynchburg, Virginia, Sixth and Court Streets." Mimeographed, 1960.

Crais, Clifton C., and Pamela Sculley. *Sara, Baartman, and the Hottentot Venus: A Ghost Story and a Biography.* Princeton, NJ: Princeton University Press, 2009.

Crawford, Jack. *"Pioneer African Missionary: Samuel Phillips Verner,"* Journal of Presbyterian History, 60 (Spring 1982), pp. 42–57.

————. "Samuel Phillips Verner: Presbyterian Missionary in the Congo, 1895–1899: Racial Attitudes of the Lone White in an All-Black Mission." Unpublished, n.d.

Crenson, Matthew A. *Building the Invisible Orphanage: A Prehistory of the American Welfare System.* Cambridge, MA: Harvard University Press, 1998.

Dabney, Virginius. *Virginia: The New Dominion.* Garden City, NY: Doubleday, 1971.

Dollard, John. *Caste and Class in a Southern Town,* 2nd ed. Garden City, NY: Doubleday Anchor, 1949. (Originally published 1937.)

Doyle, Arthur Conan. *The Crime of the Congo.* New York: Doubleday, 1909.

Drinnon, Richard. *Facing West: The Metaphysics of Indian-Hating and Empire Building.* Minneapolis: University of Minnesota Press, 1980.

Du Bois, W. E. B. *The World and Africa.* New York: International, 1965.

Duffy, Kevin. *Children of the Forest.* New York: Dodd, Mead, 1984.

Elson, James M. *Lynchburg, Virginia: The First Two Hundred Years.* Lynchburg: Warwick House, 2004.

Emerson, Barbara. *Leopold II of the Belgians, King of Colonialism.* New York: St. Martin's, 1979.

Fiedler, Leslie. *Freaks.* New York: Simon and Schuster, 1978.

Findling, John. *Historical Dictionary of World's Fairs.* New York: Greenwood, 1990.

Fitts, Leroy. *A History of Black Baptists.* Nashville, TN: Broadman, 1985.

Fleming, G. James, and Christian E. Burckel (eds.). *Who's Who in Colored America 1950.* Yonkers, NY: Christian E. Burckel and Associates, 1950.

Francis, David Rowland. *The Universal Exposition of 1904.* St. Louis, MO: Louisiana Purchase Exposition, 1913.

Franklin, John Hope. *George Washington Williams: A Biography.* Chicago: University of Chicago Press, 1985.

Frischkorn, Rebecca T., and Reuben M. Rainey. *Half My World: The Garden of Anne Spencer—A History and Guide.* Lynchburg, VA: Warwick House, 2003.

Gann, L. H., and Duignan, Peter. *The Rules of Belgian Africa 1884–1914.* Princeton, NJ: Princeton University Press, 1979.

Gatewood, Willard B. *Aristocrats of Color: The Black Elite, 1880–1920.* Bloomington: Indiana University Press, 1990.

Gavins, Raymond. *The Perils and Prospects of Southern Black Leadership: Gordon Blaine Hancock, 1884–1970.* Durham, NC: Duke University Press, 1977.

Gould, Stephen Jay. *Ever Since Darwin.* New York: Norton, 1979.

———. "The Hottentot Venus," in *The Flamingo's Smile.* New York: Norton, 1983.

———. *The Mismeasure of Man.* New York: Norton, 1981.

Grant, Madison. *The Passing of the Great Race.* New York: Scribner, 1916.

Greene, Lee J. *Time's Unfading Garden: Anne Spencer's Life and Poetry.* Baton Rouge: Louisiana State University Press, 1977.

Greenhalgh, Paul. *Ephemeral Vistas: The Expositions Universelles, Great Exhibitions and World's Fairs, 1851–1939.* Manchester, U.K.: Manchester University Press, 1988.

Hair, William Ivy. *Carnival of Fury: Robert Charles and the New Orleans Race Riot of 1900.* Baton Rouge: Louisiana State University Press, 1976.

Haller, John S. *Outcasts from Evolution: Scientific Attitudes of Racial Inferiority, 1859–1900.* New York: McGraw-Hill, 1975.

Hamilton, R. *Class and Politics in the United States.* New York: Wiley, 1972.

Harlan, Louis R. *Booker T. Washington: The Making of a Black Leader, 1856–1901.* New York: Oxford University Press, 1972.

———. *Booker T. Washington: The Wizard of Tuskegee 1901–1915.* New York: Oxford University Press, 1983.

———. *Separate and Unequal: Public School Compaigns and Racism in the Southern Seaboard States 1901–1915.* New York: Atheneum, 1968.

Harris, Bradley. "Black Roots in Smithtown: A Short History of the Black Community." Smithtown, NY: Office of Town Historian, 1986.

Harris, Joan Elizabeth. "The Progressive Era in Smithtown, New York: A Study of Five Charitable Institutions." Unpublished, n.d.

Harris, M. A. *A Negro History Tour of Manhattan.* New York: Greenwood, 1968.

Harris, Neil. *Humbug: The Art of P. T. Barnum.* Boston/Toronto: Little, Brown, 1973.

Hellman, Geoffrey. *Bankers, Bones, and Beetles: The First Century of the American Museum of Natural History.* Garden City, NY: Natural History Press, 1969.

Hochschild, Adam. *King Leopold's Ghost.* New York: Houghlin Mifflin, 1998.

Holmes, Dwight Oliver Wendell. *The Evolution of the Negro College.* New York: Arno and New York Times, 1969.

Hornaday, William Temple. *Free Pum on the Congo.* Chicago: Woman's Temperance, 1887.

Hyland, Paul. *The Black Heart: A Voyage into Central Africa.* New York: Holt, c. 1988.

Inglis, Brian. *Roger Casement*. New York: Harcourt Brace Jovanovich, 1974.

Jayne, Caroline Furness. *String Figures and How to Make Them: A Study of Cat's Cradle in Many Lands*. New York, Scribner, 1906.

Johnson, James Weldon. *Black Manhattan*. New York: Da Capo, 1930.

Jones, Thomas Jesse (ed.). *Negro Education: A Study of the Private and Higher Schools for Colored People in the United States*, Vol. 1. New York: Arno and New York Times, 1969. (Originally published 1917.)

Keith, Arthur. *The Belgian Congo and the Berlin Act*. New York: Negro Universities Press, 1979.

Kellersberger, Julia. *A Life for the Congo: The Story of Althea Brown Edmiston*. New York: Fleming H. Revell, 1947.

Kennedy, Pagan. *Black Livingstone: A True Tale of Adventure in the Nineteenth-Century Congo*. New York: Viking, 2002.

Ladd, Everett C., Jr. *Negro Political Leadership in the South*. Ithaca, NY: Cornell University Press, 1966.

Lewis, David Levering. *The Race to Fashoda*. New York: Weidenfeld and Nicolson, 1987.

Lindquist, Sven. *Exterminate All the Brutes*. New York: New Press, 1996.

Logan, Rayford W. *Howard University: The First Hundred Years 1867–1967*. New York: New York University Press, 1969.

Logan, Rayford W., and Michael R. Winston. *Dictionary of American Negro Biography*. New York: Norton, 1982.

Long, Richard A., and Eugenia W. Collier (eds.). *Afro-American Writing: An Anthology of Prose and Poetry*, Vol. 2. New York: New York University Press, 1972.

Love, Donald M. *Henry Churchill King of Oberlin*. New Haven, CT: Yale University Press, 1956.

Luckhurst, Kenneth W. *The Story of Exhibitions*. London: Studio, 1951.

Lyman, Stanford M. "Race Relations as Social Process: Sociology's Resistance to a Civil Rights Orientation," in Herbert Hill and James E. Jones (eds.), *Racism in America*. Madison: University of Wisconsin Press, 1993, p. 394.

Mabee, Carleton. "Charity in Travail: Two Orphan Asylums for Blacks." *New York History*, 55 (January 1974), pp. 55–77.

MacColl, Rene. *Roger Casement: A New Judgment*. New York: Norton, c. 1957.

Martin, Sandy D. *Black Baptists and African Missions*, Macon, GA: Mercer University Press, 1998.

Matthiessen, Peter. *African Silences*. New York: Random House, 1991.

McCray, Carrie Allen. *Freedom's Child*. Chapel Hill, NC: Algonquin Books, 1998.

———. *Ota Benga Under My Mother's Roof*. Columbia: University of South Carolina Press, 2012.

Meier, August. *A White Scholar and the Black Community, 1945–1965*. Amherst: University of Massachusetts Press, 1992.

Morel, E. D. *Red Rubber*. New York: Negro Universities Press, 1969.

Morton, Richard Lee. *Negro in Virginia Politics*. Charlottesville: University of Virginia Press, 1919.

Myrdal, Gunnar. *An American Dilemma*, Vol. 2, *The Negro Social Structure*. New York: McGraw-Hill, 1964.

Noyes, Alfred. *The Accusing Ghost of Roger Casement*. New York: Citadel, c. 1957.

Oberlin College. *Alumni Register: Graduates and Former Students, Teaching and Administrative Staff, 1833–1960*, ed. Louis D. Hartson. Oberlin, OH: Oberlin College Press, 1960.

———. *Catalogue of Graduates, 1833–1948*, ed. John E. Wirkler. Oberlin, OH: Oberlin College Press, 1948.

Preston, Douglas J. *Dinosaurs in the Attic: An Excursion into the American Museum of Natural History*. New York: St. Martin's, 1986.

Reavis, Ralph. *Virginia Seminary: A Journey of Black Independence*. Bedford, VA: Print Shop, 1989.

Reid, Benjamin Lawrence. *The Lives of Roger Casement*. New Haven, CT: Yale University Press, c. 1976.

Rydell, Robert. *All the World's a Fair: Visions of Empire of American International Expositions, 1876–1916*. Chicago: University of Chicago Press, 1984.

Sawyer, Roger. *Casement, the Flawed Hero*. London and Boston: Routledge and K. Paul, c. 1984.

Saxon, A. H. *P. T. Barnum: The Legend and the Man*. New York: Columbia University Press, 1989.

SenGupta, Gunja. *From Slavery to Poverty: The Racial Origins of Wel-*

fare in New York, 1840–1918. New York: New York University Press, 2009.

Shaloff, Stanley. *Reform in Leopold's Congo.* Richmond, VA: John Knox, 1970.

Shapiro, Herbert. "The Populists and the Negro: A Reconsideration," in August Meier and Elliott Rudwick (eds.), *The Making of Black America: Essays in Negro Life and History,* Vol. 2. New York: Atheneum, 1969. (Originally published 1939.)

Sheppard, William Henry. "An African's Work for Africa." *Missionary Review of the World,* 19 (October 1906), pp. 770–74.

———. "Light in Darkest Africa." *Southern Workman,* April 1905, pp. 218–27.

———. *Pioneers in Congo.* Louisville, KY: Pentecostal, 1902.

———. *Presbyterian Pioneers in Congo.* Richmond, VA: Presbyterian Committee of Publication, c. 1917.

Singleton-Gates, Peter, and Maurice Girodias. *The Black Diaries: An Account of Roger Casement's Life and Times with a Collection of His Diaries and Public Writings.* Paris: Olympia Press, c. 1959.

Spiro, Jonathan Peter. *Defending the Master Race: Conservation, Eugenics, and the Legacy of Madison Grant.* Burlington, VT: University Press of New England, 2009.

Stanley, Henry Morton. *The Congo and the Founding of the Free State: A Story of Work and Exploration.* New York: Harper, 1885.

———. *In Darkest Africa,* Vols. 1 and 2. New York: Scribner, 1890.

Taylor, Arnold H. *Travail and Triumph: Black Life and Culture in the South Since the Civil War.* Westport, CT: Greenwood, 1976.

Torgonick, Marianna. *Gone Promotive: Savage Intellects, Modern Lives.* Chicago: University of Chicago Press, 1890.

Tull, James E. *Shapers of Baptist Thought.* Valley Forge, PA: Judson, 1972.

Turnbull, Colin. *The Forest People.* New York: Simon and Schuster, 1962.

Twain, Mark. *King Leopold's Soliloquy.* Boston: P. R. Warren, 1905.

Verner, Samuel Phillips. "Adventures of an Explorer in Africa." *Harper's Weekly,* July 1, 1899.

———. "African Pygmies." *Atlantic Monthly,* August 1902, pp. 184–95.

———. "African Pygmies." *Scientific American,* Supplement, 59 (1905).

————. "The African Pygmies." *Popular Science*, September 1906, pp. 471–73.

————. "American Invasion of the Congo." *Harper's Weekly*, November 2, 1907, p. 644.

————. "Belgian Rule on the Congo." *World's Work*, November 1906–April 1907, pp. 8568–75.

————. "The Development of Africa." *Forum,* 32 (1902).

————. "An Educational Experiment with Cannibals." *World's Work*, May–October 1902, pp. 2289–95.

————. *Pioneering in Central Africa*. Richmond, VA: Presbyterian Committee of Publication, 1903.

————. "Pygmies, and a Step Lower." *Spectator* (London), 82 (1899).

————. "Railroads of Africa Fifty Years Hence." *World's Work*, November 1906–April 1907, pp. 8727–37.

————. Samuel Phillips Verner Papers. South Caroliniana Library, Columbia, SC. Includes numerous unpublished manuscripts, among them Autobiography, "Condola Gets an Education," "Empire Building in Central Africa," "How We Tamed the Baschilele," "Sketch of Mr. Verner's African Experience," "Thomas F. Ryan: A Benefactor of a Carolina Boy," and "The Travels of Ntoka."

————. "The Story of Ota Benga, the Pygmy." *Zoological Society Bulletin*, July 19, 1916, pp. 137–139.

————. "A Trip Through Africa." *World's Work*, May–October 1908, pp. 68–73.

————. "The White Man's Zone in Africa." *World's Work*, November 1906–April 1907, pp. 8727–37.

————. "White Race in the Tropics." *World's Work*, May–October 1908, pp. 10715–20.

————. "The Yellow Men of Central Africa." *American Anthropologist*, October–December 1903, pp. 539–44.

Wack, Henry Wellington. *The Story of the Congo Free State*. New York and London: Putnam, 1905.

Wall, Cheryl A. *Women of the Harlem Renaissance*. Bloomington: Indiana University Press, 1995.

Weatherford, W. D. *Negro Life in the South*. New York: Young Men's Christian Press, 1910.

Wilkerson, Doxey A. "The Negro School Movement in Virginia: From 'Equalization' to 'Integration,' " in August Meier and Elliott Rudwick (eds.), *The Making of Black America: Essays in Negro Life and History,* Vol. 2. New York: Atheneum, 1969, pp. 250–73. (Originally published 1939.)

Williams, Ethel L. *Biographical Directory of Negro Ministers.* New York: Scarecrow, 1965.

Williams, Rebecca Yancey. *Carry Me Back.* New York: Dutton, 1940.

Woodson, Carter G. *The History of the Negro Church,* 2nd ed. Washington, DC: Associated Publishers, 1921.

——— (ed.). *Negro Orators and Their Orations.* New York: Russel and Russel, 1925.

Works Progress Administration (WPA). *Atlanta: A City of the Modern South.* New York: Smith and Durrell, 1942.

———. *Directory of Negro Baptist Churches in the United States.* Chicago: Illinois Historical Records Survey, Division of Community Service Program, WPA, 1942.

———. *The Negro in Virginia.* New York: Arno and New York Times, 1969.

Young, Henry J. *Major Black Religious Leaders, 1755–1940.* Nashville, TN: Abingdon, 1977.

INDEX

Note: All references to Leopold indicate Leopold II, King of Belgium.

ABOUT THE AUTHOR

PAMELA NEWKIRK is a professor of journalism at New York University, where she directs undergraduate studies at the Arthur Carter Journalism Institute. She is the author of *Within the Veil: Black Journalists, White Media,* which won the National Press Club Award for Media Criticism; and is editor of *Letters from Black America.* Newkirk holds journalism degrees from New York and Columbia Universities, and a doctorate in Comparative and International Education from Columbia University. Her articles on race, media, and African American art and culture have been widely published, including in the *New York Times,* the *Washington Post, Artnews,* the *Columbia Journalism Review,* and *The Nation.* She makes her home in her native New York, where she lives with her husband.